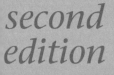

second edition

Still Learning to Read

teaching students in grades 3–6

Stenhouse Publishers
Portland, Maine

Franki Sibberson

Karen Szymusiak

Foreword by Colby Sharp

Stenhouse Publishers
www.stenhouse.com

Credits
Figure 8.1: From *Mick Harte Was Here* by Barbara Park, copyright © 1995 by Barbara Park. Used by permission of Alfred A. Knopf, an imprint of Random House Children's Books, a division of Random House, Inc.
Page 183 and Figure 10.4: From *Once Upon a Fairy Tale: Four Favorite Stories Retold by the Stars,* copyright © 2001, reprinted with permission of The Starbright Foundation.
Figure 10.2: Text copyright © 2001 by Rebecca Kai Dotlick from *When Riddles Come Rumbling* by Rebecca Kai Dotlich. Published by Wordsong, Boyds Mills Press, Inc. Reprinted by permission.

Library of Congress Cataloging-in-Publication Data
Names: Sibberson, Franki. | Szymusiak, Karen.
Title: Still learning to read : teaching students in grades 3–6 / Franki Sibberson and Karen Szymusiak.
Description: Second edition. | Portland, Maine : Stenhouse Publishers, 2016. | Includes bibliographical references and index.
Identifiers: LCCN 2016008289 (print) | LCCN 2016009111 (ebook) | ISBN 9781625310262 (pbk. : alk. paper) | ISBN 9781625311252 (ebook)
Subjects: LCSH: Reading (Elementary)
Classification: LCC LB1573 .S5475 2016 (print) | LCC LB1573 (ebook) | DDC 372.4—dc23
LC record available at http://lccn.loc.gov/2016008289

Cover design, interior design, and typesetting by Martha Drury

Manufactured in the United States of America

PRINTED ON 30% PCW
RECYCLED PAPER

22 21 20 19 18 17 16   9 8 7 6 5 4 3 2 1

Contents

Videos

Foreword
By Colby Sharp

When I decided to become a teacher, I had this vision in my head of what my fourth- or fifth-grade classroom would look like. I envisioned a room filled with kids reading amazing books. Kids would be sprawled about reading novel after novel, engaging in rich and powerful discussions. Each day I would read aloud from a book like *Hatchet* or *Tales of a Fourth Grade Nothing.* Kids would hang on my every word, and they would race off to grab the next book in the series.

Receiving my student teaching placement was shocking. When I opened the envelope and read the words *first grade*, I wept. Teaching tiny people how to read, write, and think sounded terrifying. And yet, my student teaching adventure turned out to be amazing. I quickly fell in love with those little buggers, and I learned so much about teaching reading that semester in Mrs. Warren's first-grade classroom.

Following my student teaching, I was hired in the same building as a long-term sub in a third-grade classroom. My excitement to teach kids who already knew how to read was hard to contain. I figured that by third grade, all of the kids would have figured out the things that the first graders in my student teaching struggled with. We'd be able to spend our time having wonderful literary conversations around the novels my students would surely be reading.

Things didn't work out quite the way I expected. My students did not have the skills as readers that I anticipated, and I spent most of the year trying to survive and not mess them up too much. What I needed more than anything my first year in a classroom was the book *Still Learning to Read. Still Learning to Read* would have given me permission to slow down the first six weeks of school to get to know my readers. I would have had a resource to help me design my classroom in a way in which my readers would have everything they needed, and I would have been able to think about my schedule in a way that would have allowed my students extended reading time while I worked with small groups and one-on-one. *Still Learning to Read* would have helped me think about how I group my students, and it would have helped me read aloud to them more effectively.

Unfortunately, I didn't read *Still Learning to Read* until my seventh year of teaching. By then I was friends with Franki, and I had already learned so much from her by reading her blog, interacting with her on social media, and watching her speak at conferences. The entire time I was reading *Still Learning to Read* I thought about those kids that first year, and how much more they would have gotten from their year with me if I had read *Still Learning to Read* when I was their teacher.

I am so excited that, thirteen years after *Still Learning to Read* was published, Franki and Karen are releasing an updated version. Reading this new and improved book had the same effect on me that reading the original version did: I found myself eager to go to school the next day to try out some of the ideas. If you walked into my classroom today, you'd see one of my students reading Eddie Pittman's *Red Planet*, a brand-new graphic novel that half my class is dying to read, with a bookmark inside it containing a list of the names of students who want to read the book next.

Rereading Franki and Karen's book not only makes me want to rush into my classroom to try something new right away, it also helps me to think deeply about my classroom design. This isn't something that I will be able to change tomorrow, but it is something that I'll be looking long and hard at during the summer months. *Still Learning to Read* has me totally rethinking how I organize the nonfiction portion of my classroom library.

The new edition of *Still Learning to Read* holds true to the values we found in the first edition: choice and authenticity are still the foundation that this book stands on. The new edition includes new book lists and new digital pieces sprinkled throughout. If you read the first edition, you'll notice other additions as you read this version. Franki and Karen have created a book that all elementary teachers need to have access to. I know that this will be a book that I continue to look to for guidance as I teach the readers in my classroom.

Acknowledgments

I've always depended on the conversations of others to bring my own thinking to light.

—Dorothy Watson

Conversations have been the foundation of our own thinking and writing. The talk that surrounds our teaching and learning clarifies, strengthens, and extends our commitment to help our students become thoughtful readers. The conversations we have with children give us insight into the process of learning to read and connect us to our own reading experiences. Within our learning communities, conversations count.

We thank the staff, students, and communities of Dublin City Schools. Our colleagues in Dublin City Schools have been important to our work every step of the way. We are fortunate to be part of a school district that puts children first and knows the importance of teacher learning.

We have been fortunate throughout our teaching lives to work with and learn from amazing people. We are grateful for all our professional learning communities, including the National Council of Teachers of English, Choice Literacy, The Literacy Connection, Ohio Council of Teachers of English, our Sunday Books and Breakfast Group, and the people we learn with every day on blogs, Twitter, Facebook, and Voxer.

We are grateful to the authors of all the superbly written books and texts our students have to read. Their beautiful words and pictures provide our classrooms with many windows for learning. In each and every book or text, our children find their own independence and a lifetime of reading.

We appreciate our editor, Maureen Barbieri, and all the talented and amazing staff members at Stenhouse who understand what we believe about learning and teaching. The Stenhouse community has supported us along the way as we've documented our learning journey.

And of course, we could not have written this book without the support of our families.

We have learned the most from the children with whom we work on a daily basis. We have both been lucky to spend many of our years learning alongside children in elementary schools. We are grateful for all that we've learned from them.

Teaching Reading in the Upper Elementary Classroom

I've known how to read for almost four years now.
Courtney

Early in the school year, we asked fourth graders to think about their growth as readers and to write about their reading lives. We smiled as we read Courtney's words, but they started us thinking. Courtney wrote, "I've known how to read for almost four years now." Courtney was proud of how far she had come as a reader. In those four years, she had moved from being a nonreader to being a very good reader of many texts. However, we know that four years is only the beginning of her life as a reader. Courtney's comment reminds us that students in the upper elementary grades have not been reading for very long. We can't possibly expect them to have learned all that they need to know about understanding complex texts during the first few years of their reading life. Over time, she will learn much more about herself as a reader, her preferences, her strategies for making sense of the text, and the tools she will use along the way. We need to consider the many ways we can help students continue to establish themselves as skilled, independent, lifelong readers.

Teachers in the upper elementary grades face realistic fears about teaching reading. First of all, many of us received relatively little training in how to teach reading. We might not feel as capable and confident as primary teachers in this area. Much of the public still believes that in grades K–2 we teach children how to read and in grades 3–6 our students read to learn. The implication is that at the upper elementary levels, we don't need to spend time teaching children how to read. People assume that because students in these grades already know how to read, they should be focused on learning content.

Laura Robb (2002), in an article for *Scholastic Instructor*, questions our past practices and encourages us to rethink the teaching of reading in the upper elementary grades. "For years," she writes, "many elementary and middle school teachers have shaped their teaching practices around the deeply rooted myth of 'Learning to Read and Reading to Learn' . . . Although the myth and the practices associated with it do not by any means tell the entire reading story, they have influenced reading instruction in many classrooms for years. The problem? The myth and its practices aren't working. What many researchers have now shown is that for all children, learning to read and reading to learn should be happening simultaneously and continuously, from preschool through middle school—and perhaps beyond" (23).

We believed this in 2002, and we believe it even more now. The educational landscape has changed since we wrote the first edition of *Still Learning to Read*. Common Core State Standards were adopted in many states, and the standards seemed to change what was expected for all of our readers. Testing and other mandates have become a bigger part of our world, and some states have even implemented retention laws requiring students to read at level by third grade or be retained.

Teachers and students are being asked to meet new requirements and facing more pressures than ever. Digital tools have become a staple in our reading workshops. Students are using digital tools to determine what they read and to respond to reading in a variety of digital formats. Nonfiction reading has become more prevalent in our teaching and learning, and there has been a big push for close reading in the elementary grades. Classroom libraries are expanded to include a broad selection of nonfiction reading materials as well as digital texts. Teachers are intentional about helping students use close reading strategies to become more competent as readers.

Another big change has been the way the world defines what it means to be literate. As technology has entered our world, the definition of literacy has expanded. In 2013, the National Council of Teachers of English published their definition of "21st Century Literacies":

> *Literacy has always been a collection of cultural and communicative practices shared among members of particular groups. As society and technology change, so does literacy. Because technology has increased the intensity and complexity of literate environments, the 21st century demands that a literate person possess a wide range of abilities and competencies, many literacies. These literacies are multiple, dynamic, and malleable. As in the past, they are inextricably linked with particular histories, life possibilities, and social trajectories of individuals and groups. Active, successful participants in this 21st century global society must be able to*

- *Develop proficiency and fluency with the tools of technology;*
- *Build intentional cross-cultural connections and relationships with others so to pose and solve problems collaboratively and strengthen independent thought;*
- *Design and share information for global communities to meet a variety of purposes;*
- *Manage, analyze, and synthesize multiple streams of simultaneous information;*
- *Create, critique, analyze, and evaluate multimedia texts;*
- *Attend to the ethical responsibilities required by these complex environments.*

As we face these recent changes to our educational landscape, we need to remember how important it is to hold on to what we know is best for our students. Strong, thoughtful instruction with children in mind will always encourage the most lasting results. We know that our older readers still have much to learn about reading. It makes sense that students in grades 3–6 need more instruction. The texts, both traditional and digital, that they are reading are becoming much more complex and sophisticated. They are learning to use new tools and strategies to make sense of what they read and become more thoughtful, competent readers. As readers, they will be asked to think through complex themes, analyze characters, and respond at higher levels. And we want more for them than just becoming skilled readers.

Students in grades 3–6 begin to build identities as readers and develop into lifelong readers. For these students to grow as readers, they need more instruction. We can't assume that the skills our students learned in grades K–2 will carry them through their lives as readers. They are ready for new skills and more independence. We agree with Donalyn Miller when she says, "You see, my students are not just strong, capable readers, they love books and reading. Building lifelong readers has to start here. Anyone who calls herself or himself a reader can tell you that it starts with encountering great books, heartfelt recommendations, and a community of readers who share this passion. I am convinced that if we show students how to embrace reading as a lifelong pursuit and not just a collection of skills for school performance, we will be doing what I believe we have been charged to do: create readers" (2009, 4).

As teachers of readers in the upper elementary grades, we have learned that students can really benefit from our teaching skills and strategies they can use as they read independently. We also realize that students do not progress at the same rate; therefore, we have students who are still at the early and transitional stages of reading in our upper elementary classrooms. Rather than continuing to rely on adults to model and guide them through the reading process, as they have done in earlier grades, they are now ready to move to more complex texts, learn new strategies, make intentional decisions about their reading, problem solve, develop reading preferences, and become more independent.

Meeting New Challenges in Reading

The children who enter our classrooms have had support and instruction that built a foundation for their early reading experiences. They are accustomed to reading books that clearly build success for the reader from the first page on. Here, for example, is the start of *Junie B. Jones and the Stupid Smelly Bus*, a book for early readers, by Barbara Park.

> *My name is June B. Jones. The B stands for Beatrice. Except I don't like Beatrice. I just like B. and that's all.*
>> *I'm almost six years old.*
>> *Almost six is when you get to go to kindergarten. Kindergarten is where you go to meet new friends and not watch T.V.*
>> *My kindergarten is the afternoon kind.*
>> *Today was my first day of school. I'd been to my room before, though. Last week, Mother took me there to meet my teacher.* (1992, 1)

It's easy for early readers to understand what they read because the framework for the story is clearly presented on the first page or two. But they meet new challenges in reading as they enter the upper elementary grades. The stories they read unfold more slowly, and readers need persistence and have to be comfortable with some ambiguity until the pieces of the story fit together. New complexities arise in nonfiction as well, as students begin to understand the formats and features of the texts they read.

Several years ago, we worked with a small group of sixth-grade students. They were having trouble choosing books and sustaining their reading over time. They were quitting many of the books they started. We watched them, and we realized that they usually chose books based on the cover illustration and the title. They didn't seem to know how else to preview a book for selection. So we led them through a preview of *Flying Solo* by Ralph Fletcher. This book is always a favorite with students in the upper elementary grades: it's about what sixth graders do on a day when the substitute teacher doesn't show up!

We asked the children to look at the title and illustration on the cover. Then we had them look at the blurb on the back of the book, the review excerpts they found there, and the first page of the story. They looked at each of these features one at a time and talked with us about what they learned from each. The students then began to piece together what they knew about the story before they began to read the book. After drawing their attention to each feature, we asked the children whether this looked like a book that would be interesting to them. After taking a look at the cover, all of the children initially decided they were eager to read the book. They remained eager to read the book after reading the blurb about the story. They were even more eager to read the book after having read the reviews. At this point, we expected that these students would be fighting over the few copies of *Flying Solo* that we had in the classroom.

But then the students read the first page with us. We were shocked. The entire group of children changed their minds and no longer seemed interested in reading *Flying Solo*. The whole group immediately shut down and was ready to abandon the book.

What had happened? We knew that the text wasn't too difficult and that the children had a good idea of what would happen in the story from the previewing we had done. We talked for a while about what had changed their minds. After considerable discussion, we realized that the children had expected the substitute to be a no-show on the very first page of the story. When that didn't happen, they lost confidence, knowing that they would have to get past the "setup" to get to the "real story." It wasn't until page 26 when the students in *Flying Solo* realized they would be without a teacher for the day. These sixth graders didn't have the skills and stamina necessary to work through those first pages of a new story on their own. Although the actual text level wasn't too hard for them, the nature of the first few chapters made the book difficult.

For these readers, twenty-six pages was a *lot* of reading—far too much to "get through" before the story became exciting to them. They wanted to read the book, but they didn't have the skills to read to page 26 on their own, to build a story and get to know characters slowly over time. A few students asked if they could just start reading on page 26. Other students begged us to read the first twenty-five pages aloud to them. Because some of the students had not had many successful experiences with reading, they didn't have enough trust in books to know that what they read on the first twenty-five pages would be critical throughout the story. These children were reading the Junie B. Jones books just a few years earlier. Books like the ones in the Junie B. Jones series set up the entire story on the first page. Students who are accustomed to reading books that set up the story on the first page or have had a teacher introduce every book for them are confused and frustrated when the first page of a book does not do that. They need instruction to learn to read stories that unfold slowly and provide the background for the rest of the book.

When we think about our own reading, we recall that sometimes stories start out differently from what we'd expected; yet these are often some of the best books we've read. As is the case with *Flying Solo*, we need to get to know the characters and become familiar with other aspects of the story first. We know that the decisions the author has made about the beginning of the story are deliberate. At the beginning of a book, readers begin to piece together information that will help them understand the rest of the story. As experienced readers, we know that there will be parts of a book that don't move as quickly as others. But we know how to get engaged in a book we have chosen and how to be persistent. We have also learned that sometimes parts that seem unimportant or slow moving can be critical to the story. We love the beginning of books. We love to figure out how the pieces will fit together and where the author is going with the story. From the start, we come up with questions, predictions, and inferences, and we become fascinated as the story unfolds. Our students don't necessarily have the experience to know how to do these things. We need to support them in their reading until they can sustain interest and understanding on their own.

There are several things we could have done to support the sixth-grade readers in our earlier example. At first, we thought that maybe *Flying Solo* wasn't the right choice for them, but because they were truly interested in the book, we came to realize that they just needed a bit of support. Their suggestions to skip the first twenty-five pages or that we read the first twenty-five pages to them helped us see that their enthusiasm for the book was still strong. We knew that if we could help these students get to page 26, they would probably be committed to reading the rest of the book. We also knew that experiencing a powerful book that unfolds slowly could help them grow as readers and help them become more independent. Instead of having them choose another book, we had to find a way to support these students through those first pages *and* give them skills that would help them with similar books that they would read in the future. We didn't want to help them read just this book. After all, imagine how many great books our students would miss if they expected to be hooked on the first page of every one.

The first step in helping our students get through the beginning pages of many stories is to help them realize that all readers face this challenge. We sometimes ask students to interview adult family members and friends about books that took them several pages to get into. Then we have the children share what they have learned. Knowing that adult readers go through the same challenges in their reading often helps our students understand the importance of overcoming them.

We also have students find books that they have read in the past—picture books and novels, books read independently, and books that were read aloud to them. We ask them to skim the books to see if they can remember when and where they became "hooked" on an individual book. Was it on the first page? Was it

---

Class Chart Brainstormed by Fourth Graders

When do you know you are hooked on a book?

- Time goes really fast.
- Can't stop reading.
- Can't put the book down.
- Relaxed—you have a good feeling.
- You are doing a lot of thinking without knowing it.
- You *have* to know what happens next.
- You can see and feel everything that's going on—like you're there.
- You want to buy the book.
- It gets exciting.
- You are trying to figure something out.
- You want to read it again.
- You keep asking yourself questions.

How do you read differently when you are not hooked? (Can be at the beginning of the book or in the middle of the book.)

- Hope for exciting times/hope that it gets better.
- Work hard to pay attention so you don't think of anything else.
- More predicting—makes me want to keep reading.
- Motivate yourself.
- Read it like it's a hard book (because it is not interesting).
- Remind yourself that a good part is probably coming.
- Trust other people who have read it.

later? Then we ask the group what they could do to get through the beginning part of the new book.

During a similar discussion in a fourth-grade class, Chris reminded us that readers can become unhooked at different times in the book. He and his classmates remembered several places where a book they were reading moved a bit more slowly once they were already hooked. We talked as a class about how and why we'd keep reading when we aren't hooked, and wrote down our ideas. We then posted our list in the room as a reference for future reading.

As adults, we can trust that a book will be worth the energy it takes to read through confusing or less engaging sections because of our past experiences with books. We were talking with Cris Tovani about a book we are planning to read, *The Poisonwood Bible*, by Barbara Kingsolver. The book had been recommended highly by friends whose opinions we trust. We heard that it is a great book "if you can get through the first seventy-five pages." We have all read books that started slowly but hooked us once we got to a certain point in the story. We know there is this magical moment when readers become so engaged that they no longer think of abandoning the book. We found that happened as we read *The Poisonwood Bible*.

For children who have only recently started to read novels or who are encountering a challenging nonfiction genre for the first time, this need for perseverance is difficult to explain. We need to think about ways to teach our students how to get through slow or confusing parts of a book. When we talk to adults about books like *The Poisonwood Bible*, many will say things like, "I am going to read that one when I have a long stretch of time for reading, so I can get into it." As adult readers, we know that with a book like *The Poisonwood Bible*, we won't ever get through those first seventy-five pages if we set aside only ten to fifteen minutes to read each day. We might be able to get through a Danielle Steele book with fifteen minutes each day, but books like *The Poisonwood Bible* require a different approach.

> ### Books That Offer Quick Engagement
>
> When we know that certain students have difficulty with books that do not hook them on the first page or two, we need to have books available for them that do get them involved quickly until they have developed strategies for reading books that develop more slowly. We don't want our developing readers to be challenged with every book. They need to know that they can still pick up and enjoy a book that is not so difficult to begin. Here are some of our favorites that seem to get readers hooked from the very start:
>
> *The One and Only Ivan* by Katherine Applegate
> *The Terrible Two* by Mac Barnett and Jory John
> *The Watsons Go to Birmingham—1963* by Christopher Paul Curtis
> *Fig Pudding* by Ralph Fletcher
> *Joey Pigza Swallowed the Key* by Jack Gantos
> *Capture the Flag* by Kate Messner
> *The Fantastic Secret of Owen Jester* by Barbara O'Connor
> *Wonder* by R. J. Palacio
> *Mick Harte Was Here* by Barbara Park
> *A Series of Unfortunate Events* series by Lemony Snicket
> *Wringer* by Jerry Spinelli

Supporting Older Readers

When we first started working with older readers, we were tempted to support them in the same ways we supported younger students years ago when we both taught first grade. As primary teachers we selected the children's books, introduced them to the books before reading, and guided them throughout the reading of the text. We knew the importance of matching kids with books, introducing each book, and guiding them at the early stages of learning how to read. Because we provided constant support, our students didn't always learn how to help themselves. They continued to be dependent on us well past the early stages of reading.

We worry when we see scripted book introductions that are so detailed, they take all the thinking out of reading. Although an introduction provides a scaffold for the book students are currently reading, it doesn't give them what they need to start a book on their own. And we worry when teachers assess to see if students use the scripted introduction in their understanding of the book. By providing too much information before children read a book, we deprive them of opportunities to discover text elements as they unfold and to develop the skills they will need to read independently. With too much assistance, students come to think that good readers never get stuck and never get confused. They never know the joy of putting the pieces of a story together. Instead, they expect someone else (author or teacher) to do it for them. They begin to think that if they do get stuck or confused, it is up to a teacher or an adult to help them. We need to teach students the skills to use when they start a new book, get stuck, or don't have sufficient background knowledge. Although upper-elementary-grade students can read the words, they may not be able to understand the texts they are reading.

In her book *I Read It, but I Don't Get It*, Cris Tovani (2000) cautions us about our students who are "word callers." She writes, "Word callers have mastered decoding and, as a bonus, also choose to read. However, they don't understand that reading involves thinking. They go through the motions of reading but assume all they have to do is pronounce words. When they don't understand or remember what they have read, they quit. Word callers are fairly good students but often don't do well with tasks that require them to use the words they read to think on their own. These readers feel powerless because the only strategy they have for gaining meaning is sounding out words" (15).

As we began to work with older readers, we realized that children are ready to develop more sophisticated strategies on their own, but they need continuous instruction and support to become successful. We know that instead of sending children to the blue basket to find a book at their level, we can help them think about their own reading, learn about authors, understand their own strengths and challenges, and interact within a larger community of readers. Instead of introducing a new book to a child ourselves, we can teach him or her to preview the book, read reviews, and talk to friends before starting it.

Text Complexity and Close Reading

Rigor is not an attribute of a text but rather a characteristic of our behavior with that text.

—Kylene Beers and Bob Probst

Several years ago, we both read *Tuesdays with Morrie* by Mitch Albom. Although the book is short and the words are simple, it was a very intense read with layers of meaning. If a readability analysis had been done on this book, we imagine it would have been rated "too easy" for the millions of Americans who read it. But *Tuesdays with Morrie* is not an easy book. The characters are complex and the message is profound. It is not a book we chose to read in one sitting because it took us to deeper levels of thought and response.

No matter which grades we have taught, we have found that children feel pressured to read longer, fatter books with smaller type that are more challenging. Their perspective is that longer is harder, and harder is better. Often, parents have this perspective as well. When students talk about their goals in reading, they often imply that they believe that reading thick books quickly is the sign of a successful reader. We know this is not true. As a result, we focus on helping upper elementary students (and their parents) recognize that reading deeply and understanding the complexities of a text are the real signs of a successful reader.

We look for texts that support older readers in their understanding and help them recognize that the length and size of a book does not determine its complexity. There are many books we share with students that seem easy at first glance but require deep thinking. If we always push students toward books that are longer and harder, they can never take the time to be thoughtful about their book choices. They will be too busy "getting through" the books.

We talk about *Tuesdays with Morrie* with our students to make this point through our own experience as readers. We tell them that it is one of the most challenging books we have ever read, and yet the text looks *really easy*. We show them the words, the number of pages, and the size of the book. Yet this is not a "quick book," one that we could read in a day. We tell them that what made the book right for us was not the size of the words or its thickness, but the thinking we did as we were reading. Then we often introduce several books in the classroom library that are short but require deep thinking. We invite our students to read them during independent reading time or we share them together in a read-aloud. A lesson like this often validates books that are not lengthy and reminds kids that reading is about thinking.

Students learn that deep reading involves more than just sticking with a book. It means reading the text with the same enthusiasm during the hard parts as during the easy parts. We want our students to spend much of their reading time on books that are comfortable for them, but, to grow as readers, they need to stretch a bit. We also deliberately choose short texts with the potential for deep, thoughtful reading and conversation. Books such as *Through My Eyes* by Ruby Bridges allow our students to understand the events depicted in the book but also help them understand what life might have been like for Ruby and her family. There are layers upon layers of

Some of Our Favorite Short Books with Layers of Meaning

El Deafo by Cece Bell
Love That Dog by Sharon Creech
Because of Winn-Dixie by Kate DiCamillo
The Tiger Rising by Kate DiCamillo
Diamond Willow by Helen Frost
Pictures of Hollis Woods by Patricia Reilly Giff
My Heart Is Laughing by Rose Lagercrantz
A Dog Called Homeless by Sarah Lean
Baby by Patricia MacLachlan
Waiting for Magic by Patricia MacLachlan
White Fur Flying by Patricia MacLachlan
The Turtle of Oman by Naomi Shihab Nye
How to Steal a Dog by Barbara O'Connor
Like Carrot Juice on a Cupcake by Julie Sternberg
Mississippi Bridge by Mildred Taylor
Becoming Joe DiMaggio by Maria Testa
Hound Dog True by Linda Urban

insight to uncover in the text; uncovering them gives students a much deeper understanding.

The Common Core State Standards shares a model of text complexity that includes qualitative dimensions, quantitative dimensions, and reader and task considerations. This definition takes into consideration that there is far more to understanding a text than level alone. We agree with Beers and Probst, who say, "This concept of text complexity, moving as it does beyond the measurable elements to include attention to qualitative issues and to the connection between reader and text, transfers a great deal of responsibility to the teacher and the media specialist and implies a great respect for their judgment" (2013, 59).

Because we believe that we, as teachers, have a great deal of responsibility to understand the complexities in the texts we have in our classrooms, we have taken a close look at what readers at the upper elementary grades need to do to be successful. We have found that breaking down skills that students need is critical. We've learned that students in grades 3–6 can often read more complex texts when they are able to

- read across an entire, longer story;
- struggle through meaning in both fiction and nonfiction that is not directly stated;
- infer an author's message based on evidence in the text;
- use skills to build a story line as longer introductions become more common
- infer events in a plot;
- understand beyond what is written on the page;
- keep track of multiple, complex characters;
- keep track of change in setting throughout the story;
- keep track of dialogue;
- identify characters' internal and external conflict;
- follow a character's changes over time;
- begin to see metaphor and symbolism in text;
- understand the big message and theme of a book;
- understand settings that are unfamiliar and settings that are more important;
- read about topics/issues that are uninteresting to the reader;
- synthesize information in a way that is not merely pulling facts;
- understand complex vocabulary and text features;
- put several pieces of information in a text together to build meaning;

- understand unique text structures such as flashbacks, elapsed time, different chapters' focus on different characters' perspectives, and so on; and
- understand new genres and formats.

Skills, Strategies, and Behaviors for Upper Elementary Readers

Our teaching is driven by the challenges that our upper elementary readers will encounter as they relate to the standards students are required to meet. We need to teach students that a new genre with unusual conventions is worth the energy it takes them to read, reread, and read again until they gain understanding. There are all kinds of ways to help students build these interests and skills. As Lucy Calkins writes, "In the teaching of reading, there are a handful of goals we need to work toward with decisiveness and firm clarity, so that we can accomplish them and move on to other goals" (2000, 339). When we identify the handful of skills that are important for understanding increasingly complex texts, we can better think about the implications for instruction.

The following is a list of skills, strategies, and behaviors that we spend much of our time teaching to students in grades 3–6 as they encounter a wide variety of fiction and nonfiction:

- Sustaining interest and understanding throughout a challenging text
- Choosing text that matches individual needs
- Keeping track of characters
- Using skills and strategies to get through the hardest sections of a text
- Having the skills to get through text that is not interesting
- Understanding complex meaning and subtexts
- Trusting that texts that aren't immediately engaging might have value
- Reading a variety of texts with a repertoire of tools for working through different text conventions, formats, and features
- Changing thinking while reading to revise predictions and clarify understanding
- Having conversations in a community of readers with an increasing level of sophistication about different types of texts and reading experiences
- Reflecting on thinking and monitoring strategies and behaviors
- Knowing yourself as a reader
- Using strategies flexibly for different kinds of text

Readers in the upper elementary grades often struggle, for example, with book choice. How many times have they wandered in front of the bookcases and baskets of books looking for the next book to read? Do they know how the classroom library is set up, and do they know how to use it to their advantage? Can they transfer those skills to school libraries, public libraries, bookstores, and online bookstores? Do they know how to use digital tools to select reading material? Do they have conversations with other readers about the books they are reading? On whom do they rely for good book recommendations? Do they know other readers in the classroom well enough to make those recommendations? There are many classroom decisions we can make that will support our students' book choices, but we can make good decisions only when we know these readers well through conversations and observations.

Older readers need to develop certain behaviors, such as sustaining comprehension through a long text. We might have some insight from an assessment instrument that certain of our students are struggling in this area. But until we talk with them about their reading and watch over their shoulder as they read, we might not know where and how comprehension breaks down for them. We need the information we gather in observations and conversations to bring clarity and purpose to our planning and instruction. Teaching is a balance of knowing what our students need to learn (the standards), looking at each child as an individual learner, and finding the resources to support the learning.

We want our teaching to take older elementary readers to higher levels of literacy. To do this, we consider everything we do to be sure that we are teaching a more sophisticated perspective of reading and that we are passing the responsibility for understanding what they read on to our students. We plan how best to use space and time to foster a community of readers who have meaningful conversations about reading. We consider instructional experiences for our students that will help them understand that reading is thinking. We make sure that conversations in our reading workshop lead our students to deeper understanding. And we keep in mind that, like Courtney, our students are still learning to read.

Part 1
Making the Most of Time and Space

Chapter 2

Being Intentional About Classroom Library Design

When Karen was growing up, going to the library near her home was her weekly escape. She was one of four children in her family, so she treasured the rare occasion when she could set out on her own. She would walk out her front door and begin her journey with a sense of adventure. When she arrived at the library, the smell of the books met her as she walked in the door, and the feel of the all-important library card in her back pocket was her ticket to a world of wonder. Anything she would ever want was there. Karen was a novice artist who loved to sketch, so art books on drawing techniques fascinated her. For a time, she and her friends were hooked on Nancy Drew, and she checked out every new book in the series that appeared on the shelves. For hours she would sit and read the inside flaps of dust jackets for stories that somehow connected to her emerging self. And sometimes she would just wander from shelf to shelf, browsing for a book that would somehow reach out and choose her. Karen came to know every corner of the library because for at least one day a week, it was her adventure.

Karen learned to choose books from the library that were right for her at the time. She considered her interests, experiences, and purpose for reading. At first she may have taken out books that were too difficult or that, for lack of interest, sat unread on her stack until it was time for another visit to the library. But over time she became skilled at choosing books from the library that defined her as a reader.

Karen had every experience she needed to become a lifelong reader. She had time to read. She had access to books. And, she was able to choose the books she read. She had friends who read and talked about books. Because of these things, Karen saw herself as a reader, and her identity as a reader grew as she did. All of the readers in our classrooms deserve similar experiences.

Today our students have access to many things to read. Not only do we have literature-rich classroom libraries, school libraries, and public libraries, but children have access to digital tools that provide them with a variety of reading material as well as new ways to choose. These tools are reshaping the way students choose what they read and are giving them access to a larger variety of things to read.

We know that the more children read, the better readers they become. Stephen Krashen (2004) reminds us that the single factor most strongly associated with reading achievement—more than socioeconomic status or any instructional approach—is independent reading. Giving every child time to read every day is critical.

We also believe that every child deserves to choose what he or she reads. Building an identity as a lifelong reader is critical for our students, and knowing tastes as readers is one way to begin to build that reader identity. We want our students to be engaged in their reading, and we know that when they can articulate the books that engage them, name favorite authors, and share books with others, they begin to have a stronger sense of who they are as readers. And, if our students begin to make meaningful and thoughtful choices about what they read, they are more committed readers. Donalyn Miller makes this point clear: "Providing students with the opportunity to choose their own books to read empowers and encourages them. It strengthens their self-confidence, rewards their interests, and promotes a positive attitude toward reading by valuing the reader and giving him or her a level of control. Readers without power to make their own choices are unmotivated" (2009, 23).

Supporting Our Students in Making Good Choices About Their Reading

We know that for students to make good choices in the things they read, they need support. One of our most important roles as teachers is to make sure that the right texts are in students' hands—texts that match their interests, their skills, and their stamina. But that doesn't mean we put limits on our students' reading. There are texts we choose to teach a specific skill or behavior, but beyond that, children benefit from making choices that inspire them as readers and people and build their reader identity. When we consider our own reading patterns as adults, we realize that "just right" isn't about readability alone. We choose "just-right" texts that serve a purpose we have for reading, are interesting, that match the mood we are in at the time, or that make us think in new ways. As we talk about reading with our students, we know we don't always want to be the ones who take responsibility for putting "just-right" texts in their hands. If we want our students to build agency and identity as readers, we want them to take ownership of their reading. We want our students to learn the strategies and tools for matching themselves with the texts that are right for them. We believe strongly in student choice and have learned that the purpose-fulness with which we design our classroom libraries can be the most important tool we have to support our students in becoming independent in their choices.

Curating a Classroom Library That Supports All Students

Because we believe that every student deserves big chunks of time for inde-pendent reading and that all children deserve to choose the books they read, an extensive classroom library is critical. We agree with what Donalyn Miller says about classroom libraries: "Offering students an engaging, diverse class-room library requires more than buying books and putting them on book-shelves. Managing a classroom library requires curation—selecting the best, most current materials for both curriculum needs and students' interests" (2013, 80).

We've learned that our libraries give our students strong messages about what is valued in our classrooms. If students walk into our classrooms and see primarily fiction texts or very few picture books, that gives them a message about what "counts" as reading. If our students enter our classrooms and the highlighted books are fat, chunky novels, our library gives the message that length and difficulty are valued here. Because we believe so strongly in choice for all students, we must create a library that values every reader in our class-room. As Donalyn Miller said at the 2015 Scholastic Reading Summit in Cincinnati, Ohio, "When we diminish a child's reading choice, we diminish the child who made that choice." Making sure that every reader is valued is the most important goal of our classroom library.

Organizing the classroom library thoughtfully is the best way we've found to support choice reading in the classroom. The careful and purpose-ful setup of the library can teach students much about what it is to be a reader. We know that if we group books by author and begin conversations about why people often read several books by the same author, our students will eventually begin to discover authors they love and look forward to read-ing new books by that author. In our classroom, you will often see baskets of books by a particular author so students can quickly locate them if they choose. When we organize our books by topic, students will be better equipped to choose a book about an idea that interests them. We organize our classroom libraries to encourage readers to make their own choices about what they read.

Authenticity in Book Choice

Several years ago when we began to realize how critical our classroom library organization was to our teaching, we became interested in the ways in which our favorite bookstores and libraries are organized. The goal of bookstores and libraries is to get the right books in the hands of their readers. Books need to be displayed in ways that support patrons in finding the right books. We thought of our own reading and the ways in which we choose books when we walk into a bookstore or library. When we asked friends how they choose books in their favorite bookstores and libraries, we realized that readers have very different ways of selecting books. Some go straight to the best-seller table when they enter a bookstore. Some find their favorite author or genre and then choose. Some select books by topic. Often readers look for books that friends have recommended. Some look for the staff recommendations. Good bookstores and libraries are set up to support all of these different readers.

We spent time doing some research on the displays in local bookstores. We visited Cover to Cover, our favorite children's bookstore, as well as a large store that is part of a popular chain of bookstores. We talked to the owners about the ways in which they set up books to market them to the right readers. After visiting several bookstores, we found that they often display books in the following ways:

- Books are organized by genre.
- Many titles are displayed face out.
- Rotating displays appear in each section.
- Staff picks and best-seller lists are featured.
- Many titles by the same author are organized within a genre.
- New books are displayed in the same area, often in a prominent location.
- Popular books are easy to reach.
- Books that face out are displayed between several titles arranged with the spine out.
- Some titles may be found in two or three different places in the bookstore (new-book section, by author, by genre).

We continue to consider authentic ways in which readers choose books so that we can keep our classrooms authentic. We know that we not only visit bookstores and libraries, but also read book reviews and join social networks, such as Goodreads, that allow us to follow other readers whose tastes are similar to our own. We watch book trailers and get recommendations from other readers through face-to-face conversations, by reading blogs, by connecting with other readers on Twitter, and more. We no longer rely exclusively on visits to a local bookstore, because much of our book "shopping" is online through bookstore and library websites. It is always fascinating to see which books pop up on our computer screens when we visit these sites. For example, the last time Karen signed on to an online bookstore, she was greeted with a list of recommended books chosen specifically for her. These online stores base such recommendations on books we and other readers have browsed or purchased. They seem to know us as readers almost better than we know ourselves.

And if we are serious about authentic reading experiences for our children, we cannot limit our students' reading to books or to a certain kind of book. We must be sure that in our classrooms *every* kind of reading counts. That means our shelves must be filled with picture books, magazines, graphic novels, and hybrid novels. And we must make sure that blogs, websites, videos, audiobooks, and e-books are available for our students' reading and that these become a virtual piece of our classroom library.

Intentional Design of the Classroom Library

What we've learned from our own behaviors as we make our reading choices is that although there is no one formula for setting up the classroom library, there are techniques we can use that might help the readers in our classrooms find the texts that matter to them and support them as they become more independent. We constantly have to consider the categories in which our books are organized to make sure that they support students' book choice and engagement. We should be curators of our libraries, not just collectors.

Early in our teaching careers, we started to organize part of our classroom library books into baskets with similar topics, titles, or authors. We were pleased with the inviting look that resulted, but we realized that not all of the baskets were serving a purpose. We also tried to organize the books based on reading level for a very short time. But we realized quickly the harm that this did. As we said in *Beyond Leveled Books*, "When students' reading diet is exclusively a leveled one, their purpose for reading disappears. They read for us. They become eager to reach the next level instead of being eager to learn more from what they are reading. In our haste to put skills instruction back into reading programs, we may have forgotten what we know about teaching children to read. We have abandoned the important lessons we learned about real reading, real books, and real children" (2008, 70).

Although children were better able to find books they could read with this organization of leveled baskets, we realized that a system based solely on reading level was inauthentic and wasn't really helping our students become independent in their book choices. It was actually doing a great deal of harm to the strong reader identities we were committed to helping each child build. Picking out books only from a certain leveled basket was not teaching them how to decide whether a book was "just right," and it was not helping them build tastes and preferences as readers. The small benefits that were gained were heavily outweighed by the harm this organization did to children.

When we think about the classroom library as a tool for learning, we must first decide what we want to teach our children about book choice before we organize it. We know, for example, that if we have baskets of books that are organized by author, our children will start to discuss authors, recommend books by various authors, and discover favorite authors. If our library is designed thoughtfully, it will serve many purposes in supporting children on the road to lifelong reading.

A well-designed classroom library provides

- a variety of texts for every reader;
- opportunities for students to build stamina and engagement when they have books that are right for them;
- series, authors, and topics that help readers begin to define tastes and preferences;
- books to move to when students are ready for something new to read;
- books to help all readers meet individual goals;
- new releases that allow students to anticipate books as readers;
- accessible books that allow students to think ahead as readers; and
- an organization that students understand and are able to use independently.

Why We Use Baskets in the Classroom Library

We have found that organizing books in baskets is not only a good way to display books but is also a scaffold that builds agency in our readers. We have learned that when students read series books or books by a favorite author, they begin to have expectations as a reader. They know they are coming to the next book in the basket with some understanding based on previous reading. They also become readers who can articulate their tastes and preferences as readers because the setup of the library scaffolds that language.

When we started to display some of our books in baskets, our main goal was for the books to attract students. With the books facing out in the baskets, they were easy for students to browse. We were also pleased to find that when children put books away, they usually put them in the correct place! Although having a well-organized classroom library is a nice perk, it was never the reason we made the choices about book arrangement that we did.

We have used baskets to organize library materials in a variety of ways over the years to support the readers in our classroom. Here are a few of them.

Favorite Authors

Often the basket label includes the name of the author as well as a picture and some information about the author so children can begin to think about authors who would interest them. When books are categorized by author, children often learn that if they like one book by an author, they might like another one by the same author. Although not all the books in the library are organized by author and placed in baskets, children often start to realize how important authors are in their book choice. They begin to pay attention to authors' names and ask about other books by authors who are not represented in classroom baskets.

A student browses books organized by series and author.

In one third-grade class, Beth and Kristin were talking informally about Alfred Slote, an author they had recently discovered in the school library. Because a portion of the classroom library was dedicated to author baskets, the girls had learned how to find authors they love and how to talk about books in new ways. Students often introduce us to authors they discover in their own reading despite there not being baskets for those authors in the classroom.

We make sure to highlight authors who write in a variety of genres or who write various types of books. For example, Jon Scieszka and Ralph Fletcher are two of our favorites because both authors write a variety of books. Again, grouping books by author takes the focus off the reading level and places it on other reasons for choosing a book. It also invites readers to try a genre they would not normally try. Students who loved *The True Story of the Three Little Pigs!* will realize that Jon Scieszka also writes the Time Warp Trio series. Someone who loved *Fig Pudding* may decide to try one of Ralph Fletcher's poetry books. In the same way, we also try to find authors who write books of varying difficulty.

We put all of Kate Messner's middle grades novels in a basket with her Marty McGuire series, her Ranger in Time series, and her picture books. We place the James Howe books, including the Pinky and Rex series

Labeling Baskets

We are often asked how we teach our students to put books away in the correct baskets. We have avoided putting stickers on books because we want the children to understand why the books are where they are. Instead, we often have picture prompts on our labels. For author baskets, we have found photographs of the authors to put next to the author's name on each basket. This gives children a visual clue and helps them become more familiar with the author. For series books, we may put a picture of the main character on the label. We have found that by labeling the baskets in this way, children understand the organization and learn that the library is organized in ways that support them as readers.

Some Author Baskets

Katherine Applegate	Grace Lin
Andrew Clements	Cynthia Lord
Sharon Creech	Patricia MacLachlan
Christopher Paul Curtis	Barbara O'Connor
Kate DiCamillo	James Preller
Sharon Draper	Rick Riordin
Ralph Fletcher	Pam Munoz Ryan
Lisa Graff	John Scieszka
Jess Keating	Jacqueline Woodson

Some Favorite Series for Students in Grades 3–6

Origami Yoda Files by Tom Angleberger
Poppy by Avi
The Sisters Grimm by Michael Buckley
The Spiderwick Chronicles by Tony DiTerlizzi and
    Holly Black
Books of Ember by Jeanne DuPrau
Swindle by Gordon Korman
The Princess Tales by Gail Carson Levine
The Chronicles of Narnia by C. S. Lewis
Pacy Lin by Grace Lin
Whatever After by Sarah Mlynowski
Capture the Flag by Kate Messner
Shiloh by Phyllis Reynolds Naylor
Maximum Ride by James Patterson
Kingdom Keepers by Ridley Pearson
Percy Jackson by Rick Riordin
Olympians by Rick Riordin
Time Warp Trio by Jon Scieszka
The Imaginary Veterinary by Suzanne Selfors
A Series of Unfortunate Events by Lemony Snicket
The Quirks by Erin Soderberg
I Survived by Lauren Tarshis

Series Books for Transitional Readers in Grades 3–6

Roscoe Riley by Katherine Applegate
Violet Mackerel by Anna Branford
Heidi Heckelbeck by Wanda Coven
Mercy Watson by Kate DiCamillo
Dyamonde Daniel by Nikki Grimes
Zapato Power by Jacqueline Jules
Arnie the Doughnut by Laurie Keller
Magic Bone by Nancy Krulik
Shelter Pet Squad by Cynthia Lord
Stink by Megan McDonald
Marty McGuire by Kate Messner
Ranger in Time by Kate Messner
Scary Tales by James Preller
Like Carrot Juice by Julie Sternberg
Keena Ford by Melissa Thomson
Lulu by Judith Viorst

and *Bunnicula*, in the same basket. These authors appeal to many readers, but their books are written at different levels of difficulty. By putting all of an author's books in the same basket, we can validate the author choices children make without focusing on the level of the text.

Favorite Series

We usually put all of the books in a series in one basket. Series books provide great support for students as they move through the upper elementary grades. In an interview with Scholastic, author R. L. Stine says, "It excites me when kids write and say, 'I've read thirty or forty of your books.' It means that they have developed a reading habit. And they will go on to read all kinds of books." We also make sure to place all the Cam Jansen series books in one basket with the Young Cam Jansen series, an easier version, to support a variety of reading abilities.

Many of our books are organized in baskets by series.

Once children are hooked on a series, they can use baskets to help them choose what to read next.

Some Favorite Character Baskets

Character	Author
Amber Brown	Paula Danziger
Big Nate	Lincoln Pierce
Clementine	Sara Pennypacker
Dyamonde Daniel	Nikki Grimes
Elray Jakes	Sally Warner
Fudge	Judy Blume
George Brown	Nancy Krulik
Harry Potter	J. K. Rowling
Joey Pigza	Jack Gantos
Judy Moody	Megan McDonald
Percy Jackson	Rick Riordin
Poppy	Avi

Baskets help scaffold student book choice.

Favorite Characters

It is fun to read several books about the same character. Like the series basket, the Favorite Characters basket encourages students to read more about the same characters. As Richard Allington notes, "After a couple of books, the central character becomes familiar, predictable. It is easier to predict how DW will respond after having read several Arthur books, which means that you have read a lot about DW and her brother" (2000, 64). Many of the Favorite Characters titles could also fit in the series book category, but the main character is more important than in other series. For example, if a student likes the character of Anastasia in the Anastasia series by Lois Lowry, he or she may want to read more about her, so we might include *Anastasia Krupnik, Anastasia at Your Service*, and *Anastasia on Her Own*.

Topic Sets

We also have baskets that include a variety of books on a specific topic that is usually interesting to upper elementary students. Each basket includes books in a wide variety of genres related to the topic. For example, the Dinosaur basket might include poetry books about dinosaurs, picture books about dinosaurs, and nonfiction books and articles related to dinosaurs.

If You Liked_____, You Might Like . . .

Several "If you liked . . ." baskets can be in use at any one time. Such baskets are often suggested by popular

A Sports Basket

These books, which represent many genres, may be placed in a single basket labeled "Sports."

Title	Author	Genre
Sports Pages	Arnold Adoff	Poetry
Home Run	Robert Burleigh	Picture book
Center Court Sting	Matt Christopher	Fiction (novel)
Hoop Genius	John Coy	Nonfiction
Magic on Ice	Patty Cranston	Nonfiction
Macmillan Book of Baseball Stories	Terry Eagan, Stan Friedman, and Mike Levine	Short Stories
The Young Soccer Player	Gary Lineker	Nonfiction
Baseball Saved Us	Ken Mochizuki	Historical fiction
We Are the Ship	Kadie Nelson	Nonfiction
Dirt on Their Skirts	Doreen Rappaport and Lyndall Callan	Nonfiction picture book

In addition, various laminated sports articles from *Sports Illustrated for Kids,* local newspapers, and issues of *Time for Kids* can go in the sports basket.

books in the classroom—books that several children seem to enjoy. The idea is to help children choose a book when they are in the mood for something similar to one they've previously read. The books can be related by topic, genre, or author. For example, the basket labeled with "If you liked *Harry Potter and the Sorcerer's Stone*, you might also like . . ." would include fantasy stories such as *Mrs. Frisby and the Rats of NIMH* by Robert C. O'Brien and *A Wrinkle in Time* by Madeleine L'Engle. For students who enjoyed the picture book biography *Satchel Paige* by Lesa Cline-Ransome and James Ransome, other books about baseball might be placed in the basket (such as *Home Run* by Robert Burleigh), or the basket might include more biographies such as *Touching the Sky: The Flying Adventures of Wilbur and Orville Wright* by Louise Borden and *Pioneer Girl: The Story of Laura Ingalls Wilder* by William Anderson.

Award-Winning Books

We want our students to know about annual awards that are given to various books for their quality. We have a basket of award-winning books available to students throughout the year. Most of the books in this basket have won the Newbery Award. Others have been awarded the National Book Award for Children. Coretta Scott King Award winners (given to a distinguished African American author or illustrator) and Christopher Award winners (books that affirm the highest value of the human spirit) may also be included in this basket.

Read with a Friend

The "Read with a Friend" basket or shelf holds at least two copies of various books that students may want to read together. This is where children go if they would like to read and discuss a book with a friend. It features a variety of authors, genres, and topics. Pairs of students can browse through this collection when they are in the mood to read a book that a friend is also reading. It lets our students know how important we think it is to read and talk with friends about reading, and it encourages informal book chat.

Some Recent Award Winners and Honor Books That Our Students Love

Balloons Over Broadway by Melissa Sweet (Orbis Pictus Award)

Brown Girl Dreaming by Jacqueline Woodson (Newbery Honor, Coretta Scott King Award)

Flora and Ulysses by Kate DiCamillo (Newbery Medal)

Inside Out and Back Again by Thanhha Lai (Newbery Honor)

Little Roja Riding Hood by Susan Middleton Elya (Pura Belpre Honor)

One Crazy Summer by Rita Williams-Garcia (Newbery Honor)

Rain Reign by Ann M. Martin (Schneider Award, Charlotte Huck Award)

Rules by Cynthia Lord (Newbery Honor)

Savvy by Ingrid Law (Newbery Honor)

Viva Frida by Yuyi Morales (Caldecott Honor, Pura Belpre Award)

Where the Mountain Meets the Moon by Grace Lin (Newbery Honor)

Julie and Kelly choose books from the "Read with a Friend" shelf to read together.

Nonfiction Books in the Classroom Library

It was only a few years ago that Franki realized she was not as committed to nonfiction reading as she was to fiction. As a class, her students were creating a Symbaloo of favorite authors. A Symbaloo is a web tool that allows you to collect and bookmark websites in a certain category. Because you can create a visual for each bookmark, it is perfect for elementary students. Franki wanted a place where students could access many of their favorite authors' sites. She created the Symbaloo page with a class of fourth graders. As they were creating it, Franki started categorizing the authors so that fiction authors were on one side of the page and nonfiction authors were on the other, so that children would be able to easily find the authors they loved.

As Franki's students finished listing their favorite authors, it became clear that the fiction side of the Symbaloo was filling up but that they were having difficulty coming up with even a few nonfiction authors they loved. As Franki reflected on this process after the school day, she realized that not only did her students struggle to come up with nonfiction authors they loved, but that they could not even think of the names of many nonfiction authors.

Franki continued to reflect on this activity. She realized that there were many differences in the ways she had been approaching fiction and nonfiction reading in her classroom. In fiction reading, her students knew their favorite authors, characters, series, and formats. Franki's class kept up with new publications in fiction and always knew when a favorite author was releasing a new book. But when Franki looked over the nonfiction section of the library, she realized why. The nonfiction section gave a different message to her students. The baskets of books in the nonfiction section were organized solely by topic. This gave her students the message that we read nonfiction only to learn about a topic. The organization of the library didn't value authors or series or format in nonfiction the way it did in fiction.

So, Franki made a point to rethink the organization of the nonfiction section of the library. As curator of the classroom library, she knew that there must be great nonfiction authors and nonfiction series books that she could showcase. If Franki wanted her readers to value nonfiction in the same ways they valued fiction, she needed to find new ways to help them choose nonfiction books to read. She redesigned the nonfiction section of the classroom library in ways that valued authors and series and celebrated the release of new nonfiction texts.

If Franki wanted her students to have favorite nonfiction authors, she knew she would need to know more favorite authors herself. That would mean some commitment on her part to reading more high-quality nonfiction for children. Franki realized early on that she knew the names of a few nonfiction authors. However, aside from Steve Jenkins and Seymour Simon, she couldn't name many more of her favorite nonfiction authors.

Much of the nonfiction section is organized by author and series.

Students choose nonfiction books based on topic, series, or author.

Franki learned that the reason she didn't know many nonfiction authors was that many authors of nonfiction are not illustrators. Unlike Steve Jenkins or Seymour Simon, whose books can be identified because of the visuals, many nonfiction authors have a variety of illustrators or photographers for their work. She learned to pay attention to the names of authors and to teach her students to do the same.

Franki was pleasantly surprised to find that she did have sets of nonfiction books by the same author. Although she had to add new books to the nonfiction section of the classroom library, most of her work was in reorganizing the titles to invite more authentic reading. Currently, the nonfiction section of Franki's library is organized by topic, author, series, and sometimes sub-genre (biographies). This realization has changed the way her students read nonfiction.

(Other nonfiction book recommendations and additional nonfiction book lists can be found in Chapter 9.)

Graphic Novels, Hybrid Novels, Picture Books, and Poetry

Graphic Novels Series

Babymouse by Jennifer Holm and Matthew Holm
Comics Squad by Matthew Holm and Jennifer Holm
G-Man by Chris Giarrusso
Guinea Pig, Pet Shop Private Eye by Colleen AF Venable
Jellaby by Kean Soo
Lunch Lady by Jarrett Krosoczka
Magic Trixie by Jill Thompson
Phoebe and the Unicorn by Dana Simpson
Ricky Ricotta by Dav Pilkey and Dan Satnat
Squish by Jennifer Holm and Matthew Holm
The Binky Adventures by Ashley Spires
The Chronicles of Claudette by Jorge Aguirre
Zita the Spacegirl by Ben Hatke

In the past decade, graphic novels and hybrid novels have become popular. They're not only popular but are a format that offers a great deal to readers in the ways

We also have a "Graphic Novels" shelf that includes baskets organized by series or author.

Picture Books We've Recently Added to the Classroom Library

Although we have classic picture books in our libraries such as *Twilight Comes Twice* by Ralph Fletcher and *The Other Side* by Jacqueline Woodson, we make sure to update the picture books in our library regularly. Below are some picture books we've recently added to the classroom library.

To the Sea by Cale Atkinson
Sam and Dave Dig a Hole by Mac Barnett
Baseball Is . . . by Louise Borden
Mr. Tiger Goes Wild by Peter Brown
Last Stop on Market Street by Matt De La Peña
I Want My Hat Back by Jon Klassen
Marilyn's Monster by Michelle Knudsen
Finding Winnie by Lindsay Mattick
Mango, Abuela, and Me by Meg Medina
Over and Under the Snow by Kate Messner
Water Is Water by Miranda Paul
The Adventures of Beekle by Dan Santat
The Bear Ate Your Sandwich by Julia Sarcone-Roach
Growing Up Pedro by Matt Tavares
Forest Has a Song by Amy VanDerwater
This Is the Rope by Jacqueline Woodson

Hybrid Novel Series Baskets

Eve Tandoi, on her blog, defines hybrid novels as "novels in which graphic devices like photographs, drawings and experimental typography are integrated into the written text" (http://cambridgechildrenslit.blogspot.com/2012/12/what-do-you-mean-youre-studying-hybrid_11.html). An influx of hybrid novels has been published in the last several years, and they seem to attract our readers in grades 3–6. There are many series of hybrid novels that are perfect for this age.

Diary of a Wimpy Kid by Jeff Kinney
Dork Diaries by Rachel Renee Russell
Dragonbreath by Ursula Vernon
Ellie McDoodle by Ruth McNally Barshaw
Hamster Princess by Ursula Vernon
Lumberjanes by Noelle Stevenson
Ottoline by Chris Riddell
Popularity Papers by Amy Ignatow
Spaceheadz by Jon Scieszka
The Creature from My Closet by Obert Skye
The Invention of Hugo Cabret by Brian Selznick
The Marvels by Brian Selznick
The Treehouse Books by Andy Griffiths
Wonderstruck by Brian Selznick

Stand-Alone Graphic Novels

Drama by Raina Telgemeier
El Deafo by Cece Bell
Into the Volcano by Don Wood
Page by Paige by Laura Lee Gulledge
Roller Girl by Victoria Jamieson
Sidekicks by Dan Santat
Sisters by Raina Telgemeier
Smile by Raina Telgemeier
Sunny Side Up by Jennifer Holm and Matthew Holm
The Bambino: The Story of Babe Ruth's Legendary 1927 Season by Nel Yomtov and Tim Foley
To Dance: A Ballerina's Graphic Novel by Siena Cherson Siegel and Mark Siegel

Poetry and Novels in Verse

Our good friend and colleague Mary Lee Hahn keeps us up to date on the best and most recent poetry out there. These are her latest recommendations of books for our classrooms.

On the Wind by David Elliott
Cowboy Up! Ride the Navajo Rodeo by Nancy Bo Flood
Sweep the Sun by Helen Frost
Firefly July by Paul Janeczko
The Death of the Hat: A Brief History of Poetry in 50 Objects by Paul Janeczko
National Geographic Book of Nature Poetry by J. Patrick Lewis
Flutter and Hum: Animal Poems/Aleteo y Zumbido: Poemas de Animales by Julie Paschkis
Santa Clauses: Short Poems from the North Pole by Bob Raczka
The Popcorn Astronauts and Other Biteable Rhymes by Deborah Ruddell
Winter Bees and Other Poems of the Cold by Joyce Sidman
Follow Follow: A Book of Reverso Poetry by Marilyn Singer
The Pet Project: Cute and Cuddly Vicious Verse by Lisa Wheeler
Pug and Other Animal Poems by Valerie Worth
Grumbles from the Forest: Fairy Tale Voices with a Twist by Jane Yolen and Rebecca Kai Dotlich

Novels in Verse

Crossover by Kwame Alexander
Silver People: Voices from the Panama Canal by Margarita Engle
The Red Pencil by Andrea Pinkney
Blue Birds by Caroline Starr Rose
Red Butterfly by A. L. Sonnichsen
Brown Girl Dreaming by Jacqueline Woodson

that text and visuals go together to create a message. Similarly, the picture books and poetry in our classrooms cannot be pushed to the side or corner if we want students to spend time reading them. It is important to us that all reading is valued equally in the classroom, and our classroom libraries must give that message. We have graphic novel series, favorite authors of hybrid texts, and more. Sometimes we house all graphic novels in one section of the library. At other times they are embedded in other baskets. It depends on the purpose we are trying to serve.

An Extension of the Class Library in the Class Meeting Area

Our class meeting area is in the front of the room near the Smartboard and easel on the opposite side of the main classroom library. Recently we added a small bookshelf under the Smartboard to house rotating book baskets.

We use the meeting area of the classroom to highlight books that students may want to revisit. We change the baskets in this area often.

We wanted books that we used for read-aloud and in mini-lessons to be easily accessible. We also wanted students to know that that area of the room housed books that we had recently shared, books that were new to the classroom, and books that had been introduced in the past few weeks. Some baskets that are often found in this area include the following.

New Books

New books have their own basket in our classroom. Although there is always a "New Books" basket, the books in the basket change throughout the year. This basket holds books that we get through book orders, books that we buy at conferences and bookstores, or books that our students have been waiting for because they are familiar with the author or series. Just as bookstores highlight new books, so do our classroom libraries. If we have read a review of a book we are all eagerly awaiting, we'll display the review somewhere near the basket.

Books We Have Read Together

We also have a basket for books and articles the class has read together. This basket grows fuller as the year goes on. It encourages readers to revisit and reread favorite books throughout the year.

Read-Aloud Connections

The books in our basket of read-aloud books also change throughout the year. As we finish reading a book aloud to the class, we change the contents of the basket. We include the book that was just read aloud, but we try to extend student interest in two ways. We add additional books in the series as well as unrelated titles by the same author. For example, after reading Avi's *Poppy* aloud, we put the other books in the series (*Poppy and Rye, Ragweed,* and *Ereth's Birthday*), as well as

Kelly takes a new book basket to a comfortable place in the room to browse.

other books by Avi, such as *The Secret School*, into the basket. Students who want to read more about the characters they've just been introduced to could choose the other books in the Poppy series for independent reading. Students who liked the author but were in the mood for a different kind of story might choose another title by Avi.

Mentor Texts

We often have baskets that we use as mentor texts in writing, so the books we share in mini-lessons while working on narrative writing are fabulous narratives that we know readers will want to revisit. We may have permanent baskets or we may have temporary baskets that house things such as "Nonfiction with Powerful Leads." The connection to reading and writing is one that we want to be evident in our libraries.

Classroom Website as an Extension of the Classroom Library

Baskets are not the only tools we use when organizing reading materials. Many of the materials available for our students to read are not placed in baskets. One area of growing interest is online and digital reading. We are always

Our classroom library includes digital resources.

Online Resources That We Often Include on Our Classroom Site

Dogo News	www.dogonews.com
Giggle Poetry	www.gigglepoetry.com
Kidsreads	kidsreads.com
NEWSELA	https://newsela.com
Sports Illustrated for Kids	sikids.com
Toon Book Reader	www.professorgarfield.org/ toon_book_reader
Wonderopolis	wonderopolis.org
Zooborns	www.zooborns.com

looking for sites and resources that would be good choices for our students' independent reading time. We want our students to have a variety of opportunities for online reading and have expanded our definition of text to include many forms of media. We try to find sites that are accessible and interesting for our students to read. We use a classroom website as a kind of hub for these resources, a place where students can go to find these sites in one location. We certainly do not use these sites to limit our students' reading but instead to let them know that digital reading is valued and these are some choices.

Keeping the Classroom Library Purposeful Across the Year

At the start of the year, we leave some baskets unlabeled and empty. We will fill them when we get to know our students better. If Gail Carson Levine turns out to be a popular author and we hadn't originally created a basket of Levine books, we can do so. In addition, several baskets hold rotating titles, such as the "New Books" basket. A teacher we met in El Paso, Texas, had a great suggestion for the rotating baskets. She told us that teachers in her school use Velcro to attach the labels to these baskets so that they can be changed easily and quickly as classroom needs and interests change. We know that we will add and remove baskets as we learn more about our readers and as our readers change throughout the year.

Throughout the year, we watch how children choose and talk about books. We constantly ask ourselves if the library design and organization is working. When we see that one area of the library is not working, we try to find ways to make it more engaging and purposeful, or we reorganize the section based on our observations. When we taught third grade, we had a basket of books by Laura Ingalls Wilder that went untouched for a couple of months. After a few book talks with the students, we realized that this class was probably not going to develop an interest in these books. But they were hooked on the Judy Moody books, which did not have their own basket. So we shelved the Laura Ingalls Wilder books with their spines out on a shelf (with students able to view titles only) and highlighted the Judy Moody books in a basket for easier access.

Using the School and Public Libraries

Each year, we worry about baskets that hold only a few titles. For example, when we have only two books by a certain author, we wonder whether it is worth an entire basket. But then we remind ourselves that our arrangement of books is really intended to teach children to make good choices and learn about being readers, so having many books in each basket is not critical. It doesn't matter whether we have two books or fifteen books in the Matt Christopher author basket. What is important is that we have set up a way for children to realize that if they liked one book by Matt Christopher, they might want to read another.

School and public libraries can extend and support the reading our children do in the classroom. When Joey was hooked on books by Louis Sachar, he quickly read through the four that we had in our classroom basket. But there were several more books by this author in our school library and in our public library. The important thing that Joey learned in class was that he liked Louis Sachar and wanted to read more books written by him. He also knew when he visited the library how to look for a book that would be right for him. We can help our students make that connection to resources outside the classroom by helping them use what they have learned about themselves as readers in the classroom.

Some teachers have multiple copies of lists of books in popular series or by a popular author, which they make available to students. Students who are hooked on a series or author can pick up a list and take it with them when they go to the school or public library so they can more easily find the books that are not available in the classroom.

Spine-Out Books

Our libraries are not completely organized into baskets. We use a variety of shelves, files, and other containers to organize the remainder of the library. Some of our books are arranged on shelves with their spines out. If all of our

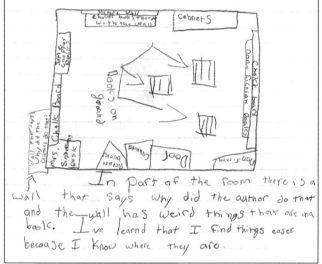

In part of the room there is a wall that says why did the author do that and the wall has weird things that are in a book. I've learnd that I find things easer because I know where they are.

books are organized into baskets by topic, author, genre, or series, students will miss the fun of browsing. We want our students to enjoy the classroom library *and* to learn about ways to choose a book. We all are delighted when we come across a book that we've never heard of—one that looks great—and we end up loving it! Although most readers don't select books that way, we want children to be able to browse books in ways that allow such discovery.

Organizing the classroom library is always the most difficult and time-consuming part of preparing our classroom, and the organizing continues throughout the year. But it can make all the difference in the reading lives of our students. We want our students to consider the classroom library as an adventure in their lives as readers. The classroom library sets the boundaries and promotes endless possibilities for the reading community in our classroom, as Leah's musings on her classroom library suggest (see Figure 2.1).

Figure 2.1
Leah's thoughts on the classroom from her reader's notebook

Grades 3 and 4 Room Tour

http://sten.pub/sltr1

This video features a tour of Franki's classroom.

Chapter 3

Preparing for Thoughtful Instruction Before Our Students Enter the Classroom

If I were to ask you to close your eyes and envision the perfect classroom scene, what would you see? What would you hear and smell and feel? Think big! If everything were going just the way you'd like it to, what would be happening? What would your kids be doing? How about you?

—Debbie Miller

Every fall, we return to school with plans for setting up our classrooms. In our heads, we've pictured what we might do with all the furniture, how our library could be organized, and where our meeting space will be. Every year we want to design the best space to support a classroom environment that promotes collaborative conversations about literacy. We think about what we can do before the students come to school that will showcase what we value and what is possible. When students enter the classroom, we want them to realize that the learning space is designed for them to be active and engaged readers.

Karen remembers the year she worked for weeks to create the perfect classroom arrangement. Books were arranged to be accessible throughout the classroom, student desks were clustered in tables, a comfortable reading space took up one corner of the classroom, a meeting space was in the center of the room, a table was set up as the science and math center, and a welcome mat was placed just inside the classroom door. A bulletin board space was planned so that each child had a space to post pictures, articles of interest, his or her own writing, and personal artifacts. Every inch of the classroom was designed to be inviting and engaging for incoming students.

The week school was to begin, Karen walked into her classroom to find four brand-new computers and a computer table sitting in the middle of the room. She had to quickly rethink her classroom arrangement and still maintain the climate and purpose of her thoughtfully planned environment. The digital tools would have a huge effect on the learning environment, and she needed to think carefully about making them accessible and inviting to her students.

Since that time, our classrooms have changed with the inclusion of many more devices. Smartboards, document cameras, projectors, iPads, and laptops have become important tools in our literacy workshops. The challenge is to design a classroom space that is grounded in our beliefs about literacy regardless of the obstacles. Each year we rethink the classroom design based on the tools, instructional materials, furniture, classroom library, and students we are going to have. We work to create a learning space that is engaging and thoughtfully designed for building community and engaged learning. The classroom design sends a clear message to our students that literacy and learning will be authentic and collaborative. It portrays a vision of the community and culture we expect and invites students to be part of the learning adventure.

Organizing materials, designing bulletin boards, and creating a floor plan for the room at the beginning of the year are always joyful yet challenging tasks. Although we are committed to literacy instruction, we are also committed to the other areas of the curriculum. We know that we need to make the classroom library accessible and inviting for our students, but we also want the math and science materials to be accessible and appealing. When setting up the classroom, we think about priorities. Where won't we compromise? What are the nonnegotiables that we want to implement? What do we consider the most important routines? What are the implications for scheduling and classroom design?

Making the Most of Our Space

> *Whether this year's kindergarten student will merely survive or positively thrive in the decades to come depends in large measure on the experiences she has in school. Those experiences will be shaped by adults, by peers, and ultimately by places, by the physical environments where she does her learning. United in the conviction that environment is our children's third teacher, we can begin anew a vital mission: designing today's schools for tomorrow's world.*
>
> —The Third Teacher

Because we believe that the classroom environment is a child's third teacher, we put a lot of time and energy into getting our classroom ready for children before they arrive. We have found that the more we learn about children and learning, the more our classroom changes. We believe strongly that students need spaces for a variety of learning experiences and that the classroom

The room has a variety of comfortable places for independent reading.

should be flexible enough for them to work in a space that fits their purpose. So we work to create a space that invites many kinds of learning and conversations. We have to have spaces that support the independence in a reading workshop.

No matter how large our classroom is, it seems there is never enough space to do exactly what we envision. We have learned that to stay focused on what is important as we plan classroom setup, we need to set priorities first.

For example, years ago we would walk into our classroom and immediately set up the student desks first. Then we worked around them to find enough space for the rest of the areas we needed. We have since realized that if we start with the learning spaces that are most important to us, we'll always find space for the desks. We no longer worry about students being able to see the screen or front board from every spot in the room, because we know that most of our whole-class lessons will happen with the children in the meeting area rather than at their seats. We no longer need every child to have an assigned seat or a seat at a table, because we know that isn't the best kind of seat for all learning. The way we set up the classroom gives our students a clear message about the culture of the classroom, the kind of work they will do, and the expectations we have for them. When we plan our rooms each year, we keep these beliefs in mind:

- We believe in choice in reading materials. We want books to be readily accessible, and we make sure the classroom library is organized in a way that makes sense for the children.
- We believe that to create a community of learners, a meeting space is critical. The space needs to be large enough for the entire class, and it often includes learning tools such as an easel, a screen, a document camera, and individual tools, including clipboards and dry erase boards.
- We believe that all learning tools such as books, math manipulatives, writing tools, digital devices, and science materials need prominent space and need to be easily accessible to students.
- We believe that students should choose work space based on their current purpose, so we try to create comfortable spaces around the room for groups of various sizes to meet, work on projects, talk, build, and read quietly.
- We believe that the classroom is for the children and should be focused on learning, so we no longer have a teacher desk or specific work area that is "teacher only."
- We believe students learn best when they have ownership over their learning, so we give them as many choices as possible throughout the day about where they can learn.
- We believe that displays and wall space are more than decorations and should be authentic tools to support learning.
- We believe that we need to evaluate every area of our classroom to ask ourselves whether it supports authentic learning or is there because it's "what we've always done."
- We believe that *all* of our readers, regardless of their ability, should have access to the same level of learning experiences, so we do not limit choice and ownership for any student. Because of this, we need to create environments that have accessible learning spaces and tools for all children.
- We believe that any learning space needs to change as the needs of our students change. As a result, we reconsider our classroom's design over time and make changes as needed.

These are the beliefs we hold on to that help us make decisions as we design schedules and space in our classrooms. These are beliefs that we won't sacrifice. By thinking first about our beliefs, we can set up classrooms so that they support all readers.

Reading Cart on Wheels—Where Do We Meet with Students?

Because we believe that a variety of seating options is critical, we don't usually have a "small-group" or conferring table. Instead we have various options throughout the room. Depending on the goal of the small group or conference, and the tools we might need, we change the spaces where these things occur. For example, if we need to meet with a group of students and chart information on the easel, we meet near the easel. If the group focus is on conversation, we might meet on stools or a floor area. If the group's goals are more focused on skill work, we might meet at a small table. When possible, for individual conferences, we go to the spot where the child is working. To support this flexibility, Franki created a cart on wheels to house items used in small groups and conferring. The cart is in a corner of the room and can be moved when needed. On the cart are learning tools such as sticky notes, highlighter tape, and dry erase markers. One shelf also stores a clipboard with notes and plans, as well as books to be used in the week's groups and conferences.

Franki's portable cart holds various tools and supplies for small groups and conferences.

Using Wall Space to Support Learning

Once our classroom design is complete, we begin to think about the wall space. Our aim is to get students using the walls in a way that promotes thinking. We know that wall displays will generate discussions that will last throughout the school year. As Debbie Miller reminds us in *Teaching with Intention*, "Why is making thinking public and permanent in our classrooms a smart thing for us to do? It lets students know that thinking matters. When children are immersed in classroom cultures where thinking is well documented, it reminds students of the results of past endeavors and invites and encourages new ones" (2008, 61).

We know that we want the walls to be filled with student thinking once the school year begins, but we also know that the environment we create before children walk into the classroom gives subtle messages to our new students about what is valued in the classroom. The classroom library, the seating choices, and the wall space all give our students messages about the ways in which learning and literacy are defined before the school year even begins.

Because of this, we find wall space to be the most difficult aspect of room design early in the school year. We know that much of the meaningful wall displays will come once the students arrive. In the days and weeks to come, children will create charts, projects, and displays. We want our students to learn early on that everything in the classroom is a tool for learning, so we want everything accessible to them. We don't clutter the walls just to fill them up. Rather we want our students to learn to use the tools on the walls throughout the day to build independence. Because this is our goal, we have learned to be careful about not putting things on the wall just to "fill space."

We are comfortable starting the year with semi-bare walls, knowing that we will fill them together with our students. We also begin some displays by putting just the titles up, knowing that we'll build them with students once they arrive. Below are some ideas that we've used to create wall displays that invite the kind of conversations we want our students to begin to have as part of a new community of learners. We may use one or two of these for a very short time at the beginning of the school year to help kids see the power of displays as tools for learning.

Some Permanent Wall Displays in the Classroom

We find that having permanent boards where we log books we've read as a classroom community is important. Not only does it help us, as a community, remember where we've been, but it scaffolds conversations for students. So we always save space for a few permanent displays around literacy. We keep a visual log of the read-alouds we share as a class. This log is usually near the meeting areas so students can refer to it as needed in discussions. We find that the visual tool allows kids to naturally connect ideas and themes in books.

We keep a permanent list of books we read aloud and books we read for #classroombookaday so that we can all easily refer to the books we've shared.

A large meeting area allows for whole-class lessons and conversations. The class sits in a circle during read-aloud to support discussion.

Some years, we've participated in the Twitter #classroombookaday community created by Jillian Heise and inspired by Donalyn Miller's #bookaday challenge. We shared a picture book at the end of each day and tweeted about it. Keeping a log of those books is powerful because we refer to the books and revisit them for literacy learning throughout the year.

Because we want our students to think critically in all areas of the curriculum, we try to balance the way in which we use our wall space. Some displays that we have used in the past include the following.

Book Characters

We sometimes have books and book characters displayed prominently around the room. We collect posters from conferences and bookstores that we can cut up and use early in the year. If we know we will be using picture books often and want to get kids thinking about picture-book characters, we may post images of as many as fifty to a hundred characters from books in a spot in the room. Next to the characters, a sign reads, "How many of these characters do you know?" Or we may display favorite series-book characters above the series-book wall. These boards get students thinking about characters they like, and conversations naturally begin around characters they know.

Some Ways We Use Wall Space as Invitations into Books and Conversations

To begin conversations about book choice, we've used one wall space for series-book posters. One year, we chose eight to ten series that we thought would be popular with beginning fourth graders. We made a poster for each that was headed "You might like this series if you . . ." During the first several weeks of school, students began talking about those series they enjoyed the most.

One day, we asked students to put their name on two sticky notes and place them on the two series posters that were most familiar to them—two series on the wall that they could tell other readers about. Then the children whose names were on each series collaborated and filled out the poster telling about the books. For example, for the Horrible Harry poster, the students wrote the following:

You might like the Horrible Harry series if you . . .
like surprises
like to read about troublemakers
like funny books
like characters who do weird things
like to read stories about school
like to read about characters that are all different

Next to each completed poster, photographs of the students who filled in the chart were hung, with a note that said, "If you want to know more about this series, ask these readers." The wall served several purposes. First of all, it helped the students think about things they could count on in series books. The posters helped students realize that different readers like different books. It also served as a great message to kids about the importance of recommending books to each other—kids asking kids about other books they'd read.

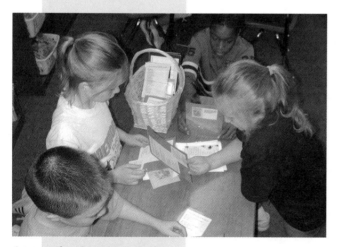

A group of students sits on the floor around the coffee table to read poetry.

Poetry

Poetry is often the least-used book collection early in the year. To get kids more interested in poetry, we often enlarge a fun poem, such as "My Dog Ate My Homework" by Sara Holbrook. In her book *Wham! It's a Poetry Jam*, Sara gives kids ways to play with the poem; we post those possibilities next to the poem. The students are invited to sing the poem to a familiar tune or chant it with a group of other students. A display like this often gets kids having fun with poetry early in the year and promotes further conversations about poetry.

Conversations Around Books

We keep our eyes open for books with pages that can be used as wall displays. For example, Bruce McMillan's book *Puniddles* uses photographs as clues for word riddles. We purchased an extra copy of the book to cut apart and display. The book sits under the display. Our board of word riddles gets kids talking and having fun with words.

A nonfiction series we like is National Geographic Kids *Weird but True!* books. These books contain great facts and visuals for kids. We use an extra copy and hang interesting pages around the room with a sign that asks, "What surprises you about this information?" Again, this kind of display not only gives students a great invitation into the series, but is also a place where kids gather to read and discuss the information displayed.

Wordplay

We want our students to see that words can be fun, so we're always on the lookout for great word games that can be enlarged as a classroom display. For example, the Cleveland Indians programs often have terrific crossword puzzles and other word games dealing specifically with baseball. There are also several word games in each issue of *American Girl* magazine. The books that go with the Bananagrams game give us great ideas for beginning-of-the-year wall displays. We want word games that invite kids to gather, problem solve, and laugh through their thinking about words. A display like this is often hung directly above a basket of books about wordplay.

We struggle with wall spaces in the room that don't lend themselves to being used as often because they are not in the normal flow of daily activity. For those spaces, we try to find permanent things to hang that give kids messages about the learning that will occur. For example, we've used four postcards that we've framed and hung near the classroom door. Each postcard has a single word on it: "smile," "celebrate," "laugh," and "create." These postcards remind kids about the best ways to work together in the classroom. The small frames give the words more importance than they would have had if we had just hung the postcards on the wall. We've also found great postcards with quotations about learning that we've framed and hung above the bookshelves. These displays will not be replaced during the year, and they'll continue to give kids great messages about learning.

Books with Pages to Display Throughout the Classroom

Title	Author	Feature
The Girls' Book of Wisdom	Catherine Dee	Quotes for girls
Craft a Doodle: 75 Creative Exercises from 18 Artists	Jenny Doh	Drawings to try
Puniddles	Bruce McMillan	Picture riddles to solve
Grapes of Math	Greg Tang	Challenging math problems
Brain Waves Puzzle Book	Rick Walton	Variety of puzzles to solve
The Kid Who Invented the Popsicle	Don L. Wulffson	Stories behind everyday inventions
Big Book of How	Time for Kids	Fun visuals and text about how things work
Sports Illustrated Kids: Big Book of Why, Sports Edition	Editors of *Sports Illustrated Kids* magazine	Facts and information about a variety of sports topics

Books That Invite Students to Think About Words

Agatha's Feather Bed by Carmen Agra Deedy
I Yam a Donkey by Cece Bell
Animal Soup by Todd H. Doodler
Take Away the A by Michael Escoffier
A Chocolate Moose for Dinner by Fred Gwynne
Alphabet Riddles by Susan Joyce
There's a Frog in My Throat by Loreen Leedy
A Huge Hog Is a Big Pig: A Rhyming Word Game by Frances McCall and Patricia Keeler
Word Play Fruit Cake by Roger Priddy
I Scream, Ice Cream: A Book of Wordles by Amy Krouse Rosenthal
And the Dish Ran Away with the Spoon by Janet Stevens
The Dove Dove: Funny Homograph Riddles by Marvin Terban
Too Hot to Hoot: Funny Palindrome Riddles by Marvin Terban

Extending the Classroom with an Online "Hub"

Look at your learning space with 21st Century Eyes: Does it work for what we know about learning today, or just for what we knew about learning in the past?

—The Third Teacher

Authenticity in the reading workshop is key, so we can no longer think about the environment only as the space within the four walls of our classrooms. In the last several years, we've realized that creating virtual spaces is as important as designing our classrooms. As digital tools become more important in our workshops, it is critical that we design sites that are accessible to students from both school and home. If we want to build digital reading habits in our students, designing a "hub" is critical. In her blog post "Have a Hub," Cathy Mere lists several benefits to having a hub for your readers. These include student accessibility to resources from one site, centralizing links, building connections, and communicating with parents. We spend a great deal of time creating a resource that supports reading beyond the classroom walls. We include links to websites that have accessible reading material for our students as well as links to author sites, our classroom social media sites, and more. This hub has become more and more important as digital tools have become more important in the lives of readers.

Making the Most of Our Time in the Classroom: Why Workshop?

Our daily schedule always includes a block of time (forty-five to sixty minutes) for reading workshop. We know that big blocks of time for workshop are important. Once we have the school's master schedule, we work within its parameters to fit in the workshop structures, which are described here.

Mini-Lesson

Mini-lessons are planned based on what we know about our students. We continuously observe students to determine each one's greatest needs for that time. Mini-lessons are focused on a topic or skill that we know many of our students need. The length of time devoted to mini-lessons will vary, but the majority of them should be short (ten minutes). We monitor the length of lessons over time and strike a balance between shorter and longer mini-lessons.

Independent Reading Time

During independent reading time, students read books of their choice. This is the time for students to explore the classroom library and choose books that are engaging or recommended by other readers in the classroom. Student choices are not dependent on reading levels and reflect a wide range of texts and genres. We establish a reasonable amount of time for independent reading time. We often begin the school year with short periods of time and increase it as students develop more stamina. We may even plan a mini-lesson to help students recognize what independent reading looks like and sounds like.

Individual and Small-Group Work

During independent reading time, we have individual conferences and organize small-group instruction. This is when explicit teaching is the most evident in our classrooms. It is also the time for authentic formative assessment. We may work with students at their reading level, but our individual and small-group work also includes reading skills that are not dependent on a reading level. Each encounter helps students understand themselves as readers, focuses on improving a skill or strategy, and sets goals for their reading.

Stools provide a comfortable spot for small-group work.

Share Time/Closing Conversations

We end the reading workshop time with a whole-class conversation. The focus of these conversations is on reader identity and agency. Often students share a skill or strategy, something they learned as readers, or an insight into being a reader.

Read-Aloud

Read-aloud occurs outside of the forty-five-minute reading workshop. We set aside time during the day when we can come together as a community to enjoy a book. Read-aloud time offers many opportunities for conversations about the story as well as what it means to be a reader. It offers opportunities to have conversations that strengthen understanding and develop strategies for independent reading.

Some years, we're able to set aside a two-and-a-half-hour block for literacy. In other years, we've had to break literacy time into shorter sessions scattered throughout the day because of how related arts, lunch, and recess are allocated in the school's master schedule. The schedule for the students' day

Genius Hour

According to the website geniushour.com, "Genius hour is a movement that allows students to explore their own passions and encourages creativity in the classroom. It provides students a choice in what they learn during a set period of time during school." In our classrooms, we begin our morning with a form of genius hour that we sometimes call "wonder workshop." During this time, students can choose to learn about anything that interests them. They can use the time to learn, create, or build something based on individual goals they have set. The time each day is devoted completely to students' inquiries that are interest-driven but provides opportunities to apply many of the skills they are learning. More information about genius hour can be found at the website.

may not be ideal because of the compromises we have to make as part of the master schedule. But we can still prioritize what we do in the classroom to support whole-group lessons, independent reading time, small-group instruction, thoughtful conversations, mini-lessons, and read-aloud time each day. We believe that every element of the reading workshop is critical, because each plays an important role in developing independence in our readers. We believe that reading workshop is critical for teaching and learning, because it creates opportunities for each child to learn and grow. The workshop also focuses on building agency and reader identity.

Here are examples of daily schedules that have worked for two different school years:

Sample A

8:55–9:40	Writing workshop
9:40–10:00	Class meeting and word study
10:00–10:45	Related arts
10:45–11:45	Math
11:45–12:30	Lunch and recess
12:30–1:00	Read-aloud
1:00–1:45	Reading workshop
1:45–2:45	Science/social studies/health
2:45–3:00	Recess
3:00–3:30	Genius hour/wonder workshop

Sample B

9:10–9:30	Genius hour/wonder workshop
9:30–10:50	Math
10:50–11:40	Related arts
11:40–12:10	Read-aloud
12:15–1:00	Lunch and recess
1:00–1:45	Science/social studies
1:45–2:35	Writing workshop
2:35–3:25	Reading workshop
3:25–3:35	Closing/#classroombookaday

Our classroom schedules are much more flexible than they appear. We know we have limited time in each school day, and we know there will be some days when the reading lesson will take more or less time than the schedule says. If setup or cleanup for a science experiment will be an issue, we rearrange the day to fit our needs. We respond to these changes easily because we know that our daily schedule is a flexible guide for the learning experiences in our classroom. It provides a framework for thinking about our day at school, but it can be changed in response to instructional needs. The structure of our day is flexible because we have self-contained classrooms. This instructional delivery model gives us the flexibility we need to modify our schedule when it meets the needs of our learners.

Thoughts for Literacy Leaders: Creating a Master Schedule

As a teacher, Karen was also always eager to get the school's master schedule from the principal so she could begin to think about how she would use blocks of time for instruction. She looked for the longest blocks of time for reading and writing workshops, because she wanted her students to be able to dig deeply into literacy. She was disappointed when the master schedule reflected small (fifteen- to thirty-minute) blocks of time. It was difficult to plan meaningful instruction in those brief moments of the day.

When she discovered that her schedule would have a twenty-minute block of time between art and lunch, she wondered what she would do with that time that could make a difference in her students' learning lives. When the class returned to the classroom after art class, it would take time to gather on the rug or gather the needed supplies for a learning activity. These short transitions were taking more time than the class had to learn together. There was little time to accomplish anything significant in the learning process. Like most teachers, she tried to make the best of those short breaks in the school day, but what she really needed were the longer blocks of time for deliberate and responsive teaching and learning.

She celebrated when she noticed that her schedule included long blocks of time when her students could dig deeply into learning. She was excited to see the long blocks of time for reading and writing workshop. She would guard this time for meaningful instruction and plan thoughtful routines for learning. She needed the time to help her students understand that they would have time for reading and writing each day. The habits developed in reading and writing workshop are critical to successful learning. The extended time promoted student choice, a commitment to reading and writing time, and reflection.

Building a Master Schedule That Works

Later, as a principal, Karen wanted to collaborate with staff to create a master schedule in which every teacher had optimal times for in-depth learning and teaching. The members of the school's Advisory Team worked hard to create the best possible schedule for students and teachers. The collective goal was to create the largest blocks of instructional time possible for each teacher and to reduce the number of short blocks that would break up the day with ineffective flashes of time. Karen wanted teachers to think hard about how they would structure their day in purposeful ways that promoted powerful and sustained opportunities to learn. Each year, the Advisory Team did its best to establish a master schedule that would promote thoughtful instruction.

Important Considerations for the Master Schedule

As the Advisory Team created the master schedule, everyone made sure that the schedule honored our beliefs about learning and teaching:

- Collaboration is critical to building a master schedule.
- Large blocks of time promote purposeful learning and teaching.
- Short blocks of time do not support meaningful instruction.
- The workshop model is nonnegotiable, and word study is a critical part of literacy instruction.
- Teachers should have a common planning time for grade-level collaboration.
- The schedule should represent our resolve for effective instruction.

Questions That We Ask Our Students to Think, Talk, and Write about Throughout the Year

The following questions are ones we use throughout the school year to deepen students' understanding and extend their thinking. These questions help our students name the things that they are doing so they become more aware of their own use of strategies.

Knowing yourself as a reader

What did you learn about yourself as a reader?
How have you changed as a reader?
How will this affect your independent reading?

Reading difficult text

Where did you get stuck? What did you do to help yourself?
What made that part/text difficult to understand?
What are you wondering?

Using evidence from the text to support your thinking

What in the text makes you think that?
How does this evidence help you understand the text more deeply?

Changing your thinking while reading

Where did you notice that your thinking had changed?
Why do you think that your thinking changed?
What in the book led to your change in thinking?

Rereading (reading again, reading differently)

When you reread, how did you read differently?
What did you notice when you reread that you didn't notice the first time?
How did rereading help you understand the text better?

The power of writing and talk

Did anything in your conversation today help you understand something about the text more deeply?
Did writing cause you to think about something you hadn't thought of before?

Building Routines That Make the Most of Our Time in the Classroom

Students deserve instruction that moves them forward as readers and thinkers and values their unique experiences and needs. Finding the balance is not impossible. We can teach students how to read closely and fall in love with reading.

—Chris Lehman and Kate Roberts

We try to design our classroom space to nourish and challenge readers and writers. We set aside large chunks of time to immerse our students in reading and writing and to promote thoughtful conversations and rigorous learning. But, perhaps most important, early in the year we strive to establish routines that support students' growing independence as readers. Many of these routines include common questions and conversations around texts and the use of reading notebooks and other formats to extend the conversations in writing.

Writing About Reading: Building Habits of a Reader

Although we do not give written tests or use end-of-chapter comprehension questions, we do want a place for our students to record and reflect on their growth as readers. During a visit to Judy Davis's classroom at the Manhattan New School, we saw how powerful reading notebooks could be. We have used reading notebooks ever since and have revised them often to meet the goals we have for our students. These notebooks give us the information we need to plan whole-class activities as well as small-group and individual instruction. We refer to them continuously to analyze and assess student needs.

During the summer before we began using reading notebooks with students, we each started one of our own. We knew that having a model to show our students would be important, and we also knew that many mini-lessons could come from our own reflections as readers. We purchased fun spiral notebooks from a local stationery store and separated them into sections. We spent the summer filling these sections with thoughts and responses to our reading. We discovered the power of keeping a reading notebook, and keep-

ing one ourselves helped us think of new ways to work with our students in the area of reading.

When we began, we had our students divide the reading notebooks into five sections (Reading Log and Response, Books I Want to Read, Read-Aloud, Me as a Reader, and Mini-Lessons and Goals). These five sections support the reading behaviors and habits that we want our students to practice. The notebook served as a place for each child to capture his or her thinking and reading experiences throughout the school year.

Since our visit to Judy's classroom, a lot has changed about the way we record and respond to our reading. We both use Goodreads to log our reading and to keep track of the books that we want to read. Franki blogs regularly at A Year of Reading, often responding to and reviewing books that she's read recently. She often uses the camera on her phone to take photos of books that she wants to add to her "to read" list when she discovers one in a bookstore or library. We realize

Students use various tools and devices to track their thinking while reading.

that the notebook gave us a way to scaffold these habits for our readers. We are still committed to the habits of readers and want our students to have routines in place to plan and reflect as readers. But just as we do, our students have more choices in the ways that they do these things. We build these habits into the classroom mini-lessons and conversations in a variety of ways.

In each section below, we share the way that we would begin conversations and give students the option of using notebooks to record their reading and thinking. We also include alternatives we have more recently shared with students that give them authentic ways to build these particular behaviors as readers.

Many students read with their
notebooks or other tools nearby.

Reading Log and Response

We do not believe in the idea of mandatory reading logs as an accountability tool. Instead we want students to keep track of their reading so that it becomes a tool for reflection and goal setting. The Reading Log and Response section of the notebook is a place for students to keep track of books completed as well as those started and abandoned. This section is where they can write assigned and unassigned responses, and is also a place for them to record favorite lines of text, questions they have as they read, and thoughts about books they've read during independent reading. This section of the notebook is a great way for students to begin their reflective thinking about reading. We encourage them to look at this section to consider what they have been reading and to notice what genres they have not read yet. By keeping track of their reading over long periods of time, students can see how they are changing as readers and can easily set goals for themselves. Over time they can see patterns in their reading.

Students organize this part of the reading notebook in different ways, depending on the purpose. At the beginning of one year, Franki asked one group of fourth-grade students to write information in their reading log each time they finished a book. (A form for this type of organization is provided in the appendix.) After a few weeks, Franki realized that her students were not consistently using the log and were forgetting to record their reading. She changed the log to a daily record of their reading. At the end of each reading workshop, students took a minute to complete their logs. They recorded the date, the name of the book, and the pages they read that day. (See Figure 3.1.)

We no longer require each student to keep a log in his or her notebook. Instead we may ask students to post to a class or individual Padlet page or use a tool like Kidblog to share books with others. Apps such as Biblionasium and Bookopolis are other digital alternatives for student book logs. We have learned that matching our purpose to the tool is critical, and we want our students to find tools that work for them.

There is no one right way to keep a reading log. If you want students to begin reflecting on favorite authors, you might have them include the names of authors they have read in the log. If genre balance is important, you might want to have a column where students list the genre of each title. Have the log match your instructional goals, which in turn are based on student needs.

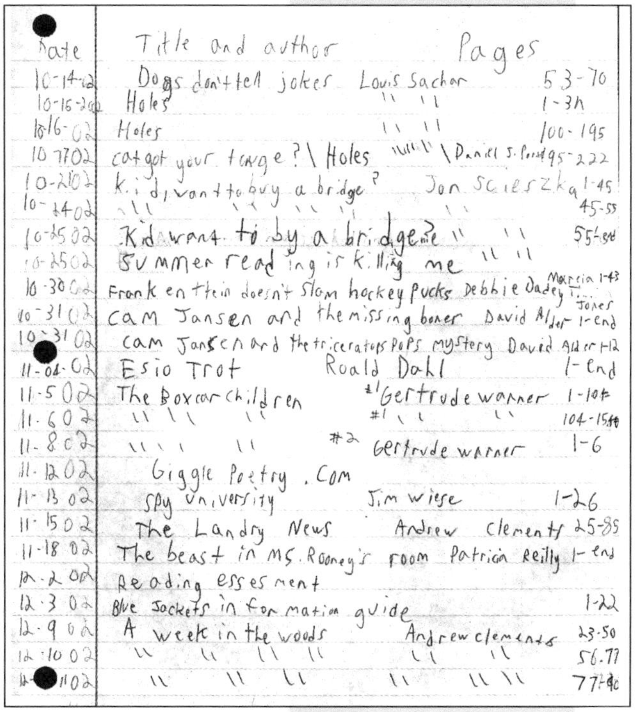

Date	Title and author	Pages
10-14-02	Dogs don't tell jokes Louis Sachar	53-70
10-16-02	Holes " "	1-34
10-16-02	Holes " "	100-195
10-17-02	cat got your tonge? \ Holes " " \ Daniel S. Pinkwater	95-222
10-20-02	kid, i want to buy a bridge? Jon Scieszka	1-45
10-24-02	" " " " "	45-55
10-25-02	Kid want to by a bridge " "	55-end
10-25-02	Summer reading is killing me " "	
10-30-02	Frankenstein doesn't slam hockey pucks Debbie Dadey Marcia Jones	1-43
10-31-02	Cam Jansen and the missing boxer David Alder	1-end
10-31-02	Cam Jansen and the triceratops pops mystery David Alder	1-12
11-04-02	Esio Trot Roald Dahl	1-end
11-5-02	The Boxcar children #1 Gertrude warner	1-104
11-6-02	" " " #1 " "	104-154
11-8-02	" " " #2 Gertrude warner	1-6
11-12-02	Giggle Poetry.com	
11-13-02	Spy university Jim wiese	1-26
11-15-02	The Landry News Andrew Clements	25-85
11-18-02	The beast in Ms. Rooney's room Patricia Reilly	1-end
12-2-02	Reading essesment	
12-3-02	Blue Jockets in formation guide	1-22
12-9-02	A week in the woods Andrew clements	23-50
12-10-02	" " " " " "	56-77
12-11-02	" " " " " "	77-90

Figure 3.1
Jordan's reading log

Books I Want to Read

The Books I Want to Read section of the reading notebook helps students look ahead in their reading. It helps them plan what they might read next and is a place for them to think about the books they want to read in the future. Here, students can make a list of books they may want to read, paste any book reviews they've cut out and want to keep, or include photos of book covers to support them in choosing books. This section of the notebook helps them think ahead in reading as well as pay attention to ways that their tastes are changing and expanding.

In our own reading notebooks, we keep lists as well as book reviews that we cut out of magazines. Franki even has a napkin taped into her notebook from a visit to a local bookstore. The napkin was the only thing she had to write on when she found several books to add to her list. A great resource for students is the website www.kidsreads.com, which has hundreds of book reviews and summaries.

By sharing entries in our own reading notebooks, students learn ways to think ahead in their reading. We also encourage them to note where they can find the book when they are ready to read it; it may be in the classroom or the school library, or perhaps a friend has it. (See Figure 3.2.)

For some readers, seeing a stack of books is more helpful than looking at a list of books. Our students have individual book bins that house books they are

Figure 3.2
Kelsie keeps track of books she wants to read in her notebook.

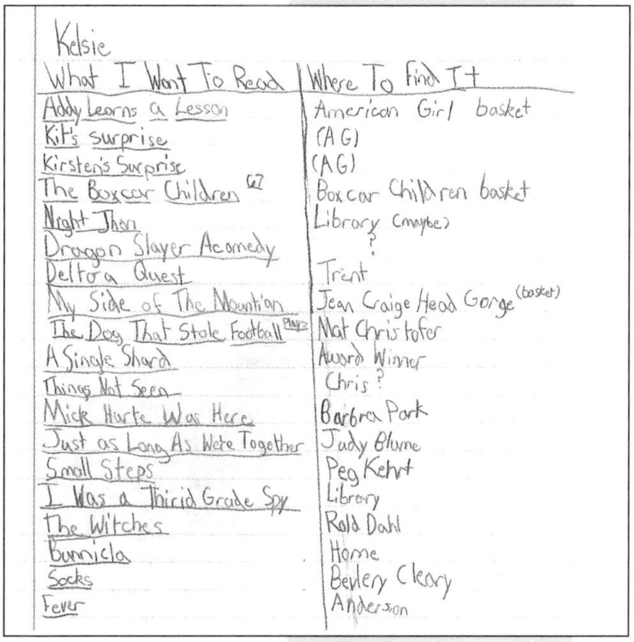

Kelsie

What I Want To Read	Where To Find It
Addy Learns a Lesson	American Girl basket
Kit's surprise	(A G)
Kirsten's Surprise	(AG)
The Boxcar Children 67	Boxcar Children basket
Night Thon	Library (maybe) ?
Dragon Slayer Acomedy	?
Deltora Quest	Trent
My Side of The Mountian	Jean Craige Head Gorge (basket)
The Dog That Stole Football Plays	Mat Christofer
A Single Shard	Award Winner
Things Not Seen	Chris ?
Mick Harte Was Here	Barbra Park
Just as Long As We're Together	Judy Blume
Small Steps	Peg Kehrt
I Was a Thirid Grade Spy	Library
The Witches	Rold Dahl
Bunnicla	Home
Socks	Bevlery Cleary
Fever	Anderson

currently reading as well as books they want to read in the near future. Some students keep lists of books they want to read in a notes section on their phones. Others carry small notebooks around so they can jot down book titles that they notice. Again, tools like Bookopolis and Biblionasium allow students to tag books they may want to read.

It isn't the writing about books we want to read that is important; we are more interested in helping kids think ahead as readers. Building the habit of thinking about books they want to read is our big goal, and we've found many ways to support it.

Read-Aloud

The Read-Aloud section of the notebook is dedicated to whole-class read-aloud books. Children respond to each book in different ways, depending on the instructional focus. This section helps students keep track of their thinking and practice a strategy. Although informal, it can spark purposeful conversations and support a more thoughtful view of reading aloud. After finishing a read-aloud of *Wringer* by Jerry Spinelli, one class made a list in their notebooks of all the types of responses they had during the session. Their notes showed them how responses to the same text may vary and how writing can help develop one's thinking about a book. Later in the year, we might choose to focus on specific types of responses (as Tessa has done in Figure 3.3), but encouraging open-ended responses in the notebooks helps students develop their own thoughts around a book.

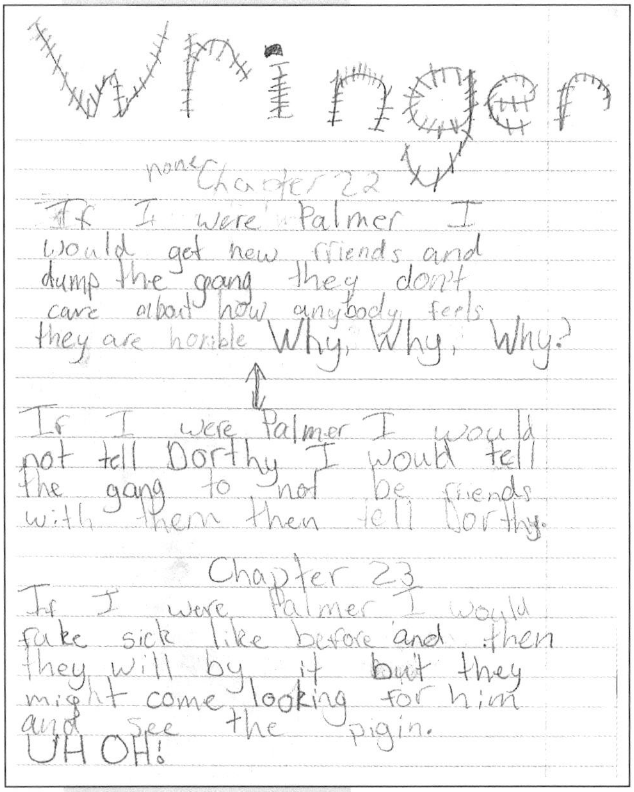

With the inclusion of digital tools, our readers have more choices in the ways they respond to text. Tools like Popplet allow students to web their thinking about various aspects of their reading. A Padlet board allows us to collect thoughts and reorganize them as new information arises. Google Docs and Google Draw are always an alternative to the reading notebook. Our goal is for our students to experience a variety of tools that help them understand text more deeply.

We also want our students to learn the annotation tools available to readers of e-books, so we often use annotation tools on the Kindle or other apps as we read aloud an e-book version.

We have also used this section of the reading notebook to serve as a record of the books the class has read together. One year, after each read-aloud, students looked back through the book and chose a page that they wanted to keep in their reading notebooks. We made a copy of that page for each student to paste into

Figure 3.3
Tessa decides to focus her response to *Wringer*. Each day she asks herself, "What would I do in Palmer's place?"

his or her reading notebook as a reminder of the read-aloud experience. Students then responded to the part of the book that they remembered most vividly or the scene that meant the most to them.

Students keep book preview information in this section. For example, before beginning *The Tiger Rising* by Kate DiCamillo, students previewed it by studying the front cover, back cover, inside flap, and first page and by thinking about what they already knew about the author. Then they wrote their thoughts about the book in this section of their reading notebook. This not only teaches students previewing skills but also gives them a place to track their thinking over the course of the book. As an alternative to using a notebook to preview, we often post preview pages and thoughts on a Padlet board or post things into a Google Doc for students to respond to and comment on.

Me as a Reader

We sometimes include a section in the reading notebook called Me as a Reader, where students write their thoughts about themselves as readers. They reflect in this section at least once a week as part of a mini-lesson or whole-class conversation. They may reflect on a quote about reading, a book we've shared, a question posed to them, or something they noticed in their own reading. At certain times during the school year, we ask our students questions about their reading or have them reflect on their reading log. These reflections help them define and redefine themselves as readers throughout the year. (See Figure 3.4.)

> **Books That Have Great Quotes to Write and Talk About from Our Histories as Readers**
>
> *Life Is So Good* by George Dawson and Richard Glaubman
> *Reading Magic: Why Reading Aloud to Our Children Will Change Their Lives Forever* by Mem Fox
> *What the Dormouse Said* by Amy Gash
> *Looking Back* by Lois Lowry
> *How to Read a Story* by Kate Messner
> *Where Are My Books?* by Debbie Ridpath Ohi
> *How Reading Changed My Life* by Anna Quindlen
> *For the Love of Books* by Ronald Shwartz
> *Red Knit Cap Girl and the Reading Tree* by Naoko Stoop

> **Types of Responses in Reading Notebooks During the Reading of *Wringer* by Jerry Spinelli**
>
> Things that surprised me
> Predictions
> Things I wondered/questions
> New things I figured out
> Important things
> Evidence for an interesting question I stuck with for a while:
>   Is Beans a good friend?
>   Would Palmer keep Nipper?
>   Would I do what Palmer did?
>   Will Beans find out about Nipper?
>   Will Beans ever change?
>   Does Henry want to be part of the group?
> Summary of chapter
> What would I do in the situation?

Figure 3.4
Karyn writes her first entry in the Me as a Reader section of her notebook.

> Dear Mrs. Sibberson,
>
> I like to read in my own special way. Sometime I have to be in the mood to read. I like to read nonfiction books. I really like to read more things that are like people that do things as people would do now.
>
> Sometimes I will sit on the floor and read, or sometimes in my seat. I really like to have someone read to me. At home I read books from the library, and books that my mom recomends to me that I like to read.
>
> I hope you like my letter,
> From,
> Karynn

Mini-Lessons and Goals

> *Children should leave school with a sense that if they act, and act strategically, they can accomplish their goals.*
>
> —Peter Johnston

The fifth section of the notebook, Mini-Lessons and Goals, overlaps the other areas. We use it to keep track of specific lessons using primarily short text. For example, when we read a book and ask students to question the text, those questions are recorded in this section of the notebook. When students work through a newspaper article or if we model a particular strategy, the article and sticky notes that students use are placed in this section of the notebook. Students use this section of the notebook during whole-class, small-group, or individual conferences. Some of the lessons are not necessarily strategy based. When we realized that one group of fourth graders thought that all poetry rhymed, we had them pore over stacks of poetry books, jotting down things they noticed that they never knew about poetry. (See Figure 3.5.) This section can also capture much of the learning that is not connected to independent reading or read-aloud.

We always have a place for our students to record their reading goals. This could be in a notebook, on a sticky note, or on a device that changes and grows. As our students learn about themselves as readers and become aware of their strengths and challenges, goal setting becomes natural and a habit we want our students to cultivate. As students learn more strategies and skills during mini-lessons, goals often come from what they see is possible for readers.

Because we have to grade our students, we are always tempted to grade the responses in the reading notebook. When we asked our students how they would feel about their notebooks being graded, they were candid with their responses. Andrew said, "If you graded our notebooks, every time you write, you'd be so concerned whether your thinking was good enough." Glen told us, "If you graded our notebooks, we'd be more worried about getting an A than about our thinking." Although we sometimes give points or credit for keeping a reading log updated or for children's identifying places in their log where they have changed their thinking, we know that if we started to put a grade on the writing in their notebooks, the purpose of the notebooks would change. They would no longer be a safe place for students to develop and deepen their understanding of reading, which is our main goal of the notebooks.

Figure 3.5
Mia discovers new things about poetry.

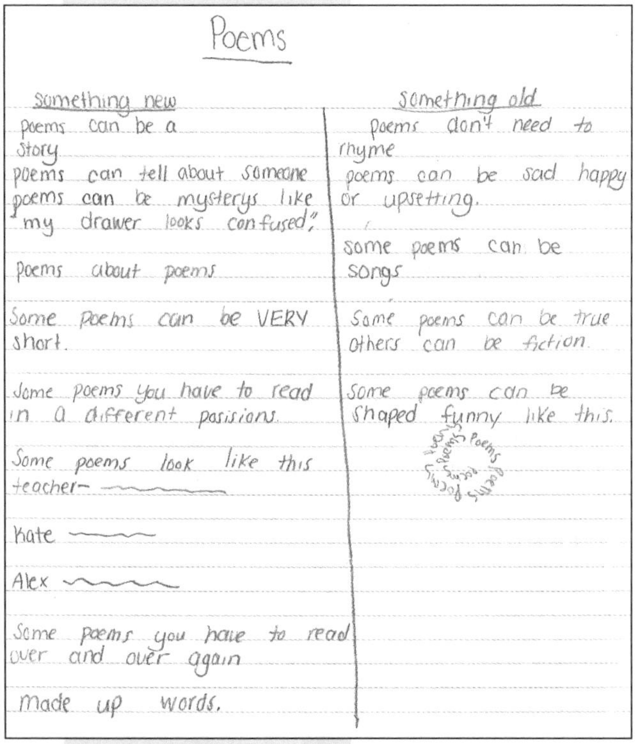
Poems

something new	something old
poems can be a story	poems don't need to rhyme
poems can tell about someone	poems can be sad happy or upsetting.
poems can be mysterys like "my drawer looks confused."	some poems can be songs
Poems about poems	Some poems can be true others can be fiction.
Some poems can be VERY short.	Some poems can be shaped funny like this.
Some poems you have to read in a different posisions.	
Some poems look like this teacher	
Kate	
Alex	
Some poems you have to read over and over again	
Made up words.	

We have learned that writing in response to reading can no longer be the end product. When children are asked to talk and write about their thinking about their reading, they often develop new ideas *because* of the writing and talk. We want our students to see the power of both writing and talk as tools for thinking.

Since the first edition of this book, our thoughts about notebooks have broadened. Our priorities for the conversations we have about reading have not, but our classrooms are now filled with many options for other formats. Our students are becoming more comfortable using digital tools as readers. Those digital tools provide a variety of ways to think about reading that were not possible when we wrote the first edition of this book. Now students easily engage with digital tools that will do many of the things we used notebooks for in the past.

There is no magic notebook format that works for all students and teachers. In the first edition we shared what was working for our students at the time. Fortunately, we now have a wide variety of digital tools that affect the way we share our thoughts about reading. Digital tools offer students more choices in the ways they annotate what they read.

Our goal each year in setting up our classroom is to create an inviting environment that will engage learners. We know we will be fine if we always design and redesign based on what we value the most about teaching and learning.

Teacher as Reader as a Component of Planning

We have learned that a critical part of our planning is our own reading. If we are to take on the job of teaching young children to read, part of our work must be reading books that may have a place in our classroom. The importance of discovering new books for the classroom library, to use in mini-lessons and to support students in small-group instruction, cannot be overlooked. Reading books with a teacher's eye is part of our ongoing planning. Our students deserve teachers who know the best books and have a menu of books to choose from during all components of the reading workshop. We cannot plan purposeful and thoughtful reading instruction if we do not continue to expand our menu of books.

We spend a lot of time in libraries and bookstores browsing books. We subscribe to and read review magazines such as *The Horn Book*. We are active on Twitter and follow hashtags such as #bookaday (created by Donalyn Miller) and participate in Twitter chats such as #titletalk (hosted monthly by Donalyn Miller and Colby Sharp). We also spend a lot of time online checking out book recommendations from people who love children's books as much as we do. Here are some of our favorite sites that help us stay up-to-date on books:

John Schumacher's blog, *Watch. Connect. Read.*
   http://mrschureads.blogspot.com
Anita Silvey's *Book-A-Day Almanac*
   http://childrensbookalmanac.com
Carol's Corner
   http://carolwscorner.blogspot.com
Jen Robinson's *Book Page*
   http://jkrbooks.typepad.com
Seven Impossible Things Before Breakfast
   http://blaine.org/sevenimpossiblethings/
Travis Jonker's blog at School Library Journal, *100 Scope Notes*
   http://100scopenotes.com
Colby Sharp's blog, *Sharpread*
   https://sharpread.wordpress.com
Teri Lesesne's blog, *The Goddess of YA Literature*
   http://professornana.livejournal.com
Nerdy Book Club
   https://nerdybookclub.wordpress.com
Donalyn Miller's site, *The Book Whisperer*
   http://bookwhisperer.com
Katherine Sokolowski's blog, *Read. Write. Reflect.*
   http://readwriteandreflect.blogspot.com
Alyson Beecher's blog, *Kid Lit Frenzy*
   www.kidlitfrenzy.com
Jen Vincent's *Teach Mentor Texts*
   www.teachmentortexts.com/#axzz3kED2ZyTe

Chapter 4

Slowing Down During the First Six Weeks

Confessions of a Reader

Almost spring
A spider
Stakes a claim
On a corner
Of the eight-foot window
In our living room.

Each morning
I admire
Taut guidelines
Carefully placed spokes.
Dancing gown threads,
Architecture unrivalled.

My mother
Would not tolerate
Such slovenly housekeeping.
She would get a broom
And knock down
This errant squatter's palace.

I do not.

I am waiting for Charlotte
To leave a message.

—Carol Wilcox

In these days of mandated standards and high-stakes testing, it is often difficult to remember our overall goals for our students. Of course it is important for them to pass high-stakes tests and meet the educational standards set by our state and nation. However, we want much more for our students than to merely pass tests and meet standards. Like the reader in the poem above, we want our students to live joyfully literate lives. We find it is sometimes most difficult to remember this in September, when school begins. As teachers, we enter the school year knowing what our students are capable of and want to jump right in, teaching those skills that are necessary at their grade level. We worry that someone will think we are wasting time when we take the time to build a community and have conversations about books. We worry that our time should be spent teaching the skills and strategies that will be tested in the spring. But we believe that helping our students develop new attitudes and behaviors is an important step in building new skills and strategies for understanding the texts they read.

We believe strongly that if we want each and every one of our students to see themselves as readers, we must be extremely intentional during the first six weeks of school. We agree with Peter Johnston when he says, "Building an identity means coming to see in ourselves the characteristics of particular categories (and roles) of people and developing a sense of what it feels like to be that sort of person and belong in certain social spaces" (2004, 23). Knowing our beliefs and our vision for the classroom is critical as we set up the routines that will grow throughout the year.

We believe that all students deserve the following.

Daily Time for Independent Choice Reading

All students deserve daily time for choice reading in a classroom filled with great books, one in which a "just-right" book is not defined by level. Our readers need books they can read, understand, and enjoy. And just as important, they have to be able to choose among those books.

We strive to build classroom libraries that include many genres, levels of difficulty, and topics of interest to meet the needs of all readers. For this to happen, the classroom has to be a place that values all kinds of reading. If success in the classroom is measured only by the length of a book, some children will be pushed into books that are too difficult. It is not easy for a child to be reading a short chapter book if everyone else in the classroom is reading a Harry Potter–length book. For every child to really engage in books that are right, they need to be in a classroom where many kinds of books are valued for a variety of authentic reasons.

Honest Conversations About Their Reading Lives

One of the most important things we can do for our students is to encourage a growth mind-set. It is hard not to want to build kids up by praising all that they do and telling them how great they are doing, but honesty has to come first. That means we can't use any inauthentic or general praise. Our comments of praise as well as our suggestions for improvement have to be honest and specific. We have to be up front about what is going well and what challenges we notice in our work with students. So instead of saying, "Great job!" we name something they've done that we hope they will continue to do. We might say, "Wow, I know comprehension has been hard for you as you move to longer books, but I noticed that today, you really stopped to think about what happened yesterday before you began reading, and that helped you hold on to the story. Is this the first time you've tried that?" Honest talk with honest feedback is the key for our most-struggling students.

Whole-Class Lessons That Target Their Individual Needs as Readers

If we do not plan carefully, too many students lose out on whole-class lessons. If instruction is over their heads, or the pace is too fast for them to keep up for some reason or another, they lose out on meaningful learning. Every child requires a different level of scaffolding, so we need to plan our lessons and choose our texts for mini-lessons so that all children can access the learning.

Opportunities to Read Books That Are Not "Just Right"

Franki's youngest daughter read one page of a Junie B. Jones book every night at bedtime for months in first grade. The book was much too hard for her, and it took a great deal of work every single night. Her daughter would read aloud to herself, and Franki would hear her struggle from her room next door. The book wasn't just right for her, and she knew it. But she also knew she could work through it a bit at a time. This was an important piece of her reading life. She spent a bit of time each day stretching beyond her comfort level but not at the expense of books she could enjoy more.

Some students will pick up a nonfiction book that is well beyond their ability when it comes to making sense of the text, but it provides them an opportunity to access the many features of nonfiction reading. We never want reading levels to define what a child chooses to read during independent reading. We think we've taken the idea of "just-right" books a bit too far. Of course every child needs time each day to read books that are at the right level. But our students do not have to spend every minute of every day reading a "just-right" book.

Opportunities to Talk with Others in the Reading Community

Franki heard Dan Feigelson, author of *Reading Projects Reimagined*, talk at the 2015 All Write Summer Institute. He told conference participants that the words "Say more about that" are often our best friends during reading conferences. We have found this to be true. We have also noticed that the combination of honest feedback and giving students time to talk helps us better support them. Students are more apt to tell us things that they know they are confused about but that they've been covering up. They are much more comfortable talking to us about their reading—the celebrations and challenges—when we give them time to talk and we give ourselves time to listen.

We plan opportunities for students to talk throughout the reading workshop. Whether it's during read-aloud, a whole-group lesson, small-group

Thoughts for Literacy Leaders: Shared Reading

In our classrooms, students benefit from the conversations they have around books. It enriches their learning as they listen to the ideas and experiences that others have as they read. It's the conversations around reading and books that build a literate environment in the classroom.

There is a similar outcome when a staff or small group of educators reads a book together. The experience of coming together to read builds common conversations from which everyone can learn. Whether the group chooses a professional book, an adult book, or a children's book to read, the conversations will be rich with ideas of how to help the students in their classrooms. Often, adults' reading experiences mirror the struggles and challenges of students in their classrooms. They offer important insights that can promote a deeper understanding of what happens when children are learning to read.

A grade-level team may choose to focus on a book that is essential to an instructional focus such as word study. Another group might choose a professional resource to gather strategies for supporting struggling students. The shared experience of reading together builds a common language that strengthens the conversations around reading and books.

In similar ways, a school or several grade levels can participate in a shared reading. At Karen's school, the students in grades 4–5 read the book *Wonder* by R. J. Palacio. It promoted many thoughtful conversations among students and even led to a schoolwide theme: Choose Kind.

work, or individual conferences, we always encourage students to talk about their reading experiences and to have thoughtful conversations with other readers in the classroom.

To Feel Part of a Community of Readers with Shared Experiences

Every reader in our classroom must be equally important to our community. For all students to feel part of the community, each one needs opportunities to learn from and give to the community in some way. Every reader has a voice in the classroom, and every reader contributes to the conversations we have.

To Participate in Small Groups That Have Purpose and Intent

Small-group work is critical for all students, including those who are struggling as well as those who are ready for new challenges. But we are careful to do more than guided reading in our small-group instruction so that students have time to talk, process, and take charge of their own reading.

Explicit Instruction Based on Individual Need

We use the first several weeks of school to begin to live with the beliefs we have about readers. We look at each routine in the reading workshop and make sure our practices come from beliefs. We build in routines that allow all students to engage during mini-lessons. We work hard to help every child find books that engage him or her for the duration of the independent reading time. We choose read-alouds that invite all readers into powerful conversations. We plan interactive share sessions to let our students know that their ideas matter. And we confer with students about their individual strengths and needs.

In her book *What You Know by Heart: How to Develop Curriculum for Your Writing Workshop*, Katie Wood Ray says, "Filling a classroom up with possibilities for how this work might go is really at the heart of teaching writing" (2002, 80). We believe that this is just as important in the teaching of reading. Our role as teachers is to fill our classroom with the possibilities of being a reader. Doing so lets children find their own identity as readers—to discover their preferences as well as the strategies that work for them. The beginning of the year is the perfect time to validate the possibilities of the reading work-shop, establish routines, and begin conversations that will be important throughout the school year.

Where Do We Begin?

Early in the school year we need to do many things, and we plan to accomplish a lot in our reading workshop. We are tempted to rush right in and begin rigorous instructional plans that focus on the many skills we need to teach throughout the year. As Lucy Calkins writes in *The Art of Teaching Reading*, "In September, the challenge is not deciding what to teach, but deciding what not to teach. The art of teaching reading is always about selection, but this is never more true than at the start of the year" (2000, 342). The conversations we start in September will be the foundation for the critical conversations we have and the learning we do throughout the year. We need to go slowly. That doesn't mean we are not teaching. Taking the first steps toward learning who our readers are and establishing the routines that will promote thoughtful reading practices is the strong teaching we need to have at the beginning of the school year. It's this slow, thoughtful, and purposeful beginning that establishes a reading community that will support all readers throughout the school year.

We usually spend the first several days talking informally with students, both individually and as a class, about their reading. These first conversations help us find out where our teaching must begin. Every child comes into our classroom with different strengths, challenges, interests, and experiences as a reader. Taking the time to find out who they are makes our teaching throughout the school year strong and effective. The time we invest at the beginning of the school year promotes each child's independence as a reader. Now is the time to slow down and learn from our students. As Karen has always said, "Listen carefully to children, because they tell us all there is to know about teaching wisely and well."

Our district requires some beginning-of-the-year assessments during a window of time in the fall. We used to rush to fit in our district assessment during the first few weeks of school. The information we gain from the district-mandated assessment is valuable. But the information we gain from informally conferring with our students about their reading is just as important at the start of the year. When we take the time to ask students questions about reading, we not only learn about our students, but also establish for them what is important and valued in our classroom. We have found that many intermediate students still believe that reading is about "getting all of the words right." When we give the more formal reading assessments before we have had time to talk to our students individually, we reinforce that definition with them. However, when we begin the year by chatting with our students about their likes and dislikes and struggles and strengths as readers, we teach them that reading is more than getting the words right and answering questions. Most importantly, we also teach them that we are interested in what they have to say and that they have a voice in their learning.

When we talked recently to a group of fourth-grade students about their lives as readers, we asked questions such as "How do you choose books?" and "What do you do when you get to a word you don't know?" As we listened to each child, we began to build a profile of each individual. We also listened for patterns that would help guide our teaching. Here is what we learned:

- Many of the students were interested in "reading harder books—books that were long and had hard words in them."
- Few students mentioned favorite authors or series.
- Students thought texts were hard when they couldn't say the words correctly.
- A very small number of students read and enjoyed poetry and nonfiction.
- Most students had few strategies for dealing with unfamiliar words.
- Students had never been asked these questions about themselves as readers.

As early readers, children measure their success as readers by their decoding skills. But as they move into the upper elementary grades, they need to understand their lives as readers. They are ready to begin learning the strategies, behaviors, and attitudes that shape their reading lives.

Building the Stamina for Independent Reading Time

We know that one of the most important things we need to have in place early in the year is a long block of independent reading time. We believe that independent reading time is the most important part of a child's day, and we know it needs to be in place before we can run good conferences and small-group lessons. But that block of independent reading time does not magically happen on the first day of school. Our students need to discover what is in the classroom library, find spaces to read that work for them, and learn that reading quietly is worthwhile. Many of our mini-lessons revolve around these topics:

Do you have enough books in your book bin each day?
Where is a good spot for you to read? Why?
Which books kept you engaged today? Which ones didn't?

Beginning by Knowing Yourself as a Reader

I read differently now than I did fifteen years ago. I have moved from a passive to an active stance. I am acutely aware of my own reading process, the questions and challenges I have for authors I read, the awareness I have of moments of confusion and disorientation in the text, and the tools I use to confront that confusion.

—Ellin Keene and Susan Zimmermann

Much of what we know about teaching reading we have learned through our own experiences as readers. Teaching reading in the upper elementary grades is a constant process of monitoring our own strategies with the texts we enjoy and the texts with which we struggle. As we learn more about our reading, we can use this knowledge to help our students. The challenge is to keep the conversations natural and the connections unforced between our reading and the behaviors we want to see in our classrooms.

Richard Allington (2000) notes the gap between the ways adults talk about books and conversations in classrooms:

Imagine that you are talking with a friend. Imagine that you ask a known-answer question. You ask for the location of the nearest hardware store, even though you already know the answer. Your friend replies, correctly, and you give her a sticker and say, "Good job, you've got your thinking cap on." Would your friend be pleased with your reply and the sticker? Or confused, wondering whether you've gone mad? We do not quiz friends on the newspaper articles they've read. Nor the books they've read. However, we do discuss the articles and books. We engage in conversations about the text, typically focusing on ideas in the texts. (88)

As readers, we anticipate our future reading and watch for books by our favorite authors. Karen has been reading reviews and is eagerly waiting to get her hands on a copy of *All the Light We Cannot See* by Anthony Doerr. Franki was recently looking forward to the upcoming release of a book by one of her favorite authors, Brené Brown. We both have marked books as "Want to Read" on Goodreads. We share our anticipation with students so they will recognize that we all have certain behaviors that support our reading. It is not just the strategies we use while we are reading that we want to share with our students. We want to show them the behaviors and attitudes that make us unique as readers as well as the ones that we share, the ones that bring us together as members of a wider reading community. Anna Quindlen, in her book *How Reading Changed My Life*, writes, "Part of the great wonder of reading is that it has the ability to make human beings feel more connected to one another" (1998, 39).

In our first whole-class mini-lessons, we often take a few minutes to share our own experiences as readers to provoke informal talk about the ideas and concepts in books, as well as reading behaviors. We will continue these lessons about our experiences throughout the year. Just as we considered our own book-shopping habits when we organized our classroom library, we do the same when we are planning how to teach a skill, strategy, or behavior to our students. When we read a book or magazine at home and have insights about our own reading that we think may someday help our students, we bring that book to school. There it sits on a shelf in the classroom, so that we'll have it when we see the need to use it with students.

For example, when Franki was reading *The Red Tent* by Anita Diamant, she found herself constantly going back to the second page of the book, the page that introduces four of the main characters. For the first fifty pages of the book, Franki could not keep track of who was who in the story. She knew that to understand the rest of the book, she would need to clarify her understanding of the characters and their relationships. The second page supported her until she knew the characters well enough. Franki now keeps this book on her shelf because she knows that keeping track of characters in novels is a skill that many transitional readers struggle with as they become more independent. We want to encourage our students to share with other readers in our classroom their own stories as they struggle with texts. These are important conversations to have as a reading community.

When Franki finds that many of her students are moving into books with more characters and are having difficulty keeping track of them, she shares the strategy she used in *The Red Tent*. While reading that book, Franki kept a sticky note on the inside cover and added notes about characters as they were introduced. She could refer to this sticky note throughout the book whenever she couldn't remember a character. This likely will lead to talk about other strategies that readers can use to keep track of characters in books. Franki's experience with *The Red Tent* often becomes the beginning of a series of lessons on character development. By starting with her personal experience, Franki lets her students know that keeping track of characters can be a challenge for any reader and that they can develop strategies for making their way through books with complex character development. The focus of these lessons from our lives as readers is always to encourage our students to learn strategies that will help them when they read independently.

As we work with students and recognize opportunities to teach behaviors or skills, we share our saved texts with them. These are not books that we would read to children; they are usually adult books. Yet we show them to our students and use them intentionally to share what we noticed about our own reading. We share why we struggled and what we did to help ourselves as readers. We share text features that helped or challenged us. Students benefit when their teachers share their own stories as readers, and it encourages them to begin sharing with each other.

Franki's and Karen's List of Books to Share with Students

Franki's Books

Title and Author	Focus for Sharing
Wanderer by Sharon Creech	Linger longer with a story by reading favorite lines and passages that have been marked in the text.
Sister of My Heart by Chitra Banerjee Divakaruni	Shifting scenes, characters, and narrators between chapters.
The Power of Habit by Charles Duhigg	Reading this nonfiction book on the Kindle and highlighting important things that she wanted to go back to and remember.
Beholding Bee by Kimberly Newton Fusco	Learning to choose audiobooks by previewing or based on audiobook narrators she already loves.
Where the Heart Is by Billie Letts	Living with a story and its characters long after you have finished reading the book.
Crossing to Safety by Wallace Stegner	Rereading to notice new things about the story and understand it more clearly.
Anna Karenina by Leo Tolstoy	Has the skills to read it, but needs a longer stretch of time (like the summer) to read it.

Karen's Books

Title and Author	Focus for Sharing
Portrait in Sepia by Isabel Allende	Becoming familiar with a complex set of characters and the connections among them with a family tree.
Life Is a Verb by Patti Digh	Reading beyond the text to learn from graphics, quotes, and boxed information on the page.
All the Light We Cannot See by Anthony Doerr	Understanding the story told from the perspective of multiple characters and in different time periods.
A Memory of Violets by Hazel Gaynor	Using a dictionary to unravel the meaning of unusual words in the text.
The Girl on the Train by Paula Hawkins	Keeping notes to build a profile of characters so meaning remains clear.
My Dream of You by Nuala O'Faolain	Noticing text features and reading without typical supports (quotation marks).
Empire Falls by Richard Russo	Recognizing a possible theme in the story and continuing to read to sustain or revise thinking.

We use not only our own stories, but also each other's stories and the stories of children we have known in our teaching. We keep stories of former students in our heads. We remember how hard it was for Christy to choose a book after finishing *Wrinkle in Time* by Madeleine L'Engle because she couldn't find one that was "even close to being as good as that!" Sharing Christy's story with our current students helps them learn about other readers' habits and behaviors. We can then help them decide whether they want to read a book of a totally different genre to avoid disappointment or try another book by the same author. When we share other readers' stories, it reminds our students how important it is to talk to other readers. Sharing stories also lets our students know that others often struggle with the same kinds of things they are struggling with. It also lets them know that even good readers sometimes get stuck. They begin to learn that good readers are not people who never get stuck, but people who know what to do when that happens.

We invite other adults in to share their reading life. We invite administrators and parents and guidance counselors and art teachers. We want our students to know many readers and to begin to use what they learn from readers to reflect on their own reading. When readers come in, we learn that some have favorite series, others love to give books as gifts, and some read the news on their phone each morning before they leave for work. Knowing other readers is important in knowing yourself and setting goals as a reader.

We also share our professional reading with our students. We know that work-related reading is an important part of who we are as readers. Our children are fascinated by the fact that there are books written about how to teach students! They are also interested to see that our reading affects what we do in the classroom. Sharing our professional reading helps students recognize that teachers can continue to learn and that our focus is on becoming better teachers as we read.

Although Franki may share her experiences about the way she kept track of characters in *The Red Tent* with one class, she may find that another class does not need that lesson. Because our students and their needs can vary so much from year to year, our own reading experiences become a crucial guide for designing instruction. That's why it is so important to know the readers in our classroom well as we plan thoughtful and effective instruction. Each class of students brings to us a new set of needs and challenges, and we want our teaching to be responsive to their uniqueness.

Students Reflect on Their Reading Lives

We spend several weeks at the beginning of the school year helping our students learn as much as they can about themselves as readers. As students get to know themselves as readers, we are able to begin to build a profile of each reader in our classroom. Early in the year, when we ask students questions about their reading, their answers are usually somewhat shallow. Often we get blank stares, a quick comment such as "I don't like to read," or a puzzled response such as "I don't know. No one has ever asked me that before." We always worry when we get these responses that maybe this group of students won't be as thoughtful or as reflective as previous classes. Somehow, each September, we forget that it takes time and conversations to help students become reflective about their learning.

Because we know it is important for children to know themselves as readers, many of our lessons during the first few weeks of school invite the students to think about different aspects of their lives as readers. We start the year reading books about reading, such as *The Library* by Sarah Stewart. We also read them Ellen B. Senisi's *Reading Grows*. This picture book follows children through reading development, from their being read to as infants to their becoming proficient readers on their own. It is a simple book, but it gets students thinking about their growth as readers. They begin to build the habit of thinking about themselves as readers by responding to questions and quotes about reading. Their responses help us learn about how they see themselves as readers. The responses also help us continue the conversations and thinking that we began with our informal reading interviews. (See

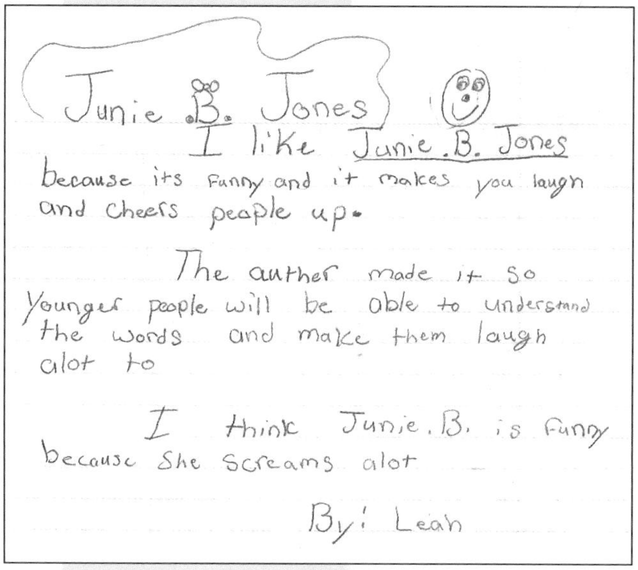
Junie B. Jones
I like Junie. B. Jones
because its Funny and it makes you laugh and Cheers people up.
The auther made it so Younger people will be able to understand the words and make them laugh alot to
I think Junie. B. is Funny because She Screams alot
By: Leah

Figure 4.1
Leah thinks about a series that she enjoys.

Figure 4.1.) We encourage them to think about their literacy lives as they reflect on their earliest memories as readers. Here are some questions that we have found useful to get children thinking about their reading:

> Which series books do you like? Why?
> Is there a book from your childhood that you asked your parents to read over and over and over?
> Which books do you remember from the years that you were just learning to read?
> What was your favorite book when you were little?

We sometimes send students home to do some research. They ask family members what they remember about the student as a reader. What were they like when they were toddlers? Which books did their parents remember reading over and over and over? (See Figure 4.2.) A form for such an interview is contained in the appendix.

Franki embeds these conversations into many of her early mini-lessons. A favorite lesson is one she calls "100 Things About Me as a Reader." She creates a list titled "100 Things About Me as a Reader" and lists as many things as she can about herself as a reader (including tastes, habits, quirks, and so on). She then shares her list with students and invites them to begin their own list in their reading notebooks. Franki's list never consists of more than ten to twelve things and she doesn't expect to get to 100, but she knows that the number 100 invites kids to continue to pay attention to who they are as readers and to add to the list (mentally or in writing) when they notice new things.

Figure 4.2
Kelsey learns about her reading history by interviewing her family.

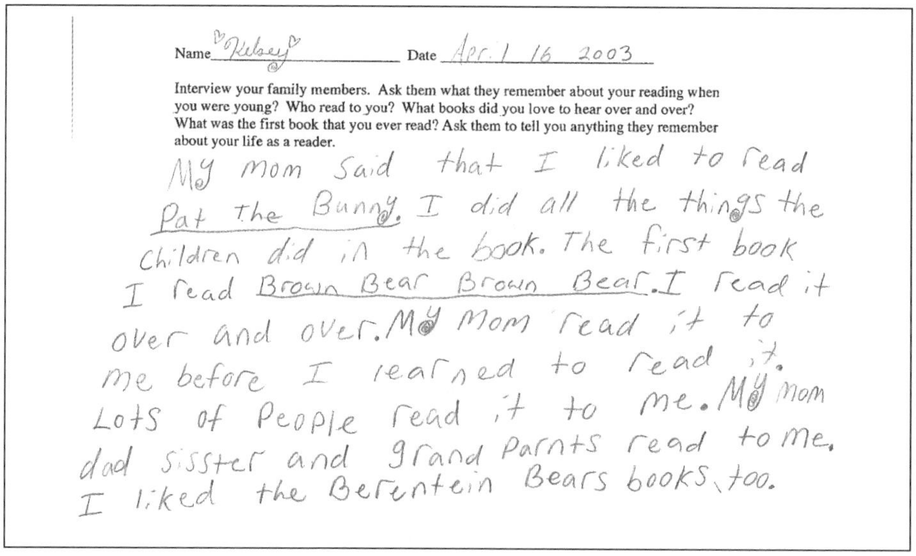
Name Kelsey Date Apr. I 16 2003

Interview your family members. Ask them what they remember about your reading when you were young? Who read to you? What books did you love to hear over and over? What was the first book that you ever read? Ask them to tell you anything they remember about your life as a reader.

My mom Said that I liked to read Pat the Bunny. I did all the things the Children did in the book. The first book I read Brown Bear Brown Bear. I read it over and over. My Mom read it to me before I learned to read it. Lots of People read it to me. My mom dad sisster and grand Parnts read to me. I liked the Berentein Bears books, too.

After several conversations about their lives as readers, we ask students to look through the entries in their reading notebooks and write a piece that puts it all together. A form along the lines of the "Reflecting on Reading" page in the appendix may be used. The students celebrate growth and change as they reflect on who they are as readers. This experience not only helps students get to know themselves, but also lets them get to know their classmates as they share their reading journeys with each other. It is an important piece in building the reading community. When students in our classroom know each other as readers, they are poised to help each other become more independent and support each other as readers.

During these early weeks, one of the quotes that we often invite students to respond to is from Mem Fox's book *Reading Magic: Why Reading Aloud to Our Children Will Change Their Lives Forever*: "Most of us think we know what reading is, and that's not surprising. After all, we can read. But reading is tricky. Reading is complex" (2001, 75). When we ask students to read this quote and to write their definition of reading, they are sometimes confused. They groan that this kind of thinking is "too hard." It is clear that they haven't thought much about what reading actually means to them or that they have a very limited definition of reading. Most of the students write just one or two sentences, almost always mentioning "figuring out words" or "getting the words right" or "sounding it out." Only a few students mention understanding or meaning. Redefining reading is the next step for these students. We begin to plan experiences that will help them think more deeply about their own reading.

One good resource to help students redefine reading is *Bark, George* by Jules Feiffer, a hilarious picture book meant for very young children. With upper elementary readers the challenge is getting them interested in a book that clearly looks as though it was written for preschool students. But the humor and the conversation about the book hook them. In *Bark, George*, the text and the illustrations work together to tell the story. For a mini-lesson in September, Franki read the text aloud, one page at a time. After each page, she asked the students what they were thinking. Students shared their responses, predictions, changes in thinking, and inferences. (The surprise ending elicited the best responses.) Franki ended the lesson by asking the kids to remember all the thinking they did. Then she said, "Wow: if you did that much thinking in *this* book, imagine how much thinking you must be doing in the books you are reading during reading workshop." Instead of defining reading for the students, Franki hoped that this lesson would begin to make them curious about what readers do. Franki could have taught her students all about the habits of effective readers. Instead, she decided to help them gradually discover for themselves what readers do and to uncover their own lives as readers.

On the following day, Franki read *Click, Clack, Moo* by Doreen Cronin, another amusing picture book that engages readers. She read the book aloud

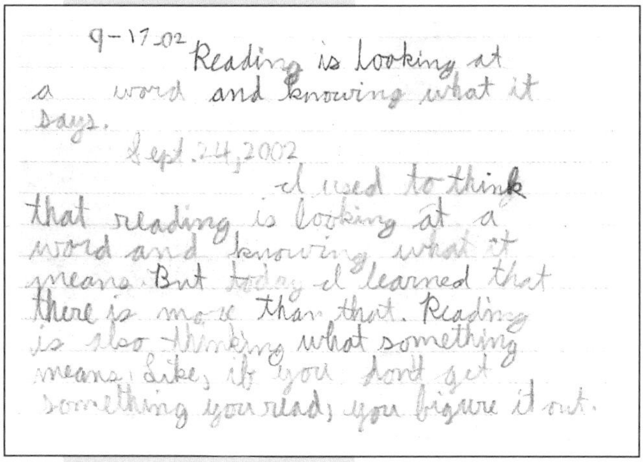

9-17-02 Reading is looking at a word and knowing what it says.

Sept. 24, 2002 I used to think that reading is looking at a word and knowing what it means. But today I learned that there is more than that. Reading is also thinking what something means. Like, if you don't get something you read, you figure it out.

Figure 4.3
Courtney changes her definition of reading.

and asked students to write down their thinking as she finished each page. Once in a while, they would stop and discuss the kinds of thinking they were doing. The students were amazed at how much thinking they were doing along the way. The last page of *Click, Clack, Moo* is critical to the story, but it contains only an illustration, no words. After finishing the reading, Franki turned again to the last page and asked, "Was this reading?" The children started talking all at once. Some were saying, "Yes!" Some were saying, "No!" Some were saying, "Yes and no." Some children were frustrated by the question. They argued that it couldn't be reading because there were no words. They argued that it had to be reading because without that final page, the story would be different. The conversation over that one page lasted twenty to thirty minutes, with Franki saying very little. The students' definitions of reading were beginning to change. They were developing a deeper understanding of what readers do. Finally Franki stopped the conversation and asked the students to go back to the entries in their reading notebooks where they had defined reading a few days earlier. She asked them to look at their earlier definition of reading and to write what they were thinking about it now. (See Figure 4.3.) The students were beginning to realize that reading was much more than just "getting the words right."

We've found that wordless picture books are very powerful to use with our intermediate students. As they learn that reading is thinking, digging into complex wordless books helps them see the level of thinking needed for deep understanding. We've used wordless picture books early in the year to help students monitor their thinking while they read, to begin to find evidence to support thinking, and more.

Early in the year, it is the deep thinking we do around simple texts that sets the stage for future learning. Lessons like these invite kids to redefine reading for themselves and to continue to think about what reading means to them. And we listen in to add all the things we are learning about the ways our students define reading and respond to books. We have found that sharing wordless books on the screen using the iBooks app invites powerful conversations early in the year.

At the end of the first six weeks, we begin goal setting with students. Although the goals are often simple

Easy Books to Help Redefine Reading

Grandpa's Teeth by Rod Clements
Click, Clack, Moo by Doreen Cronin
Bark, George by Jules Feiffer
I Want My Hat Back by Jon Klassen
Bamboozled by David Legge
Ring! Yo? by Chris Raschka
Don't Let the Pigeon Drive the Bus! By Mo Willems

Wordless Picture Books

Window by Jeanie Baker
Journey by Aaron Becker
Flashlight by Lizi Boyd
Inside Out by Lizi Boyd
A Circle of Friends by Giora Carmi
Hank Finds an Egg by Rebecca Dudley
The Farmer and the Clown by Marla Frazee
Sidewalk Flowers by JonArno Lawson and Sydney Smith
The Flower Man by Mark Ludy
South by Patrick McDonnell
Float by Daniel Miyares
The Boy and the Airplane by Mark Pett
The Girl and the Bicycle by Mark Pett
Coming Home by Greg Ruth
Where's Walrus? by Stephen Savage
Bluebird by Bob Staake
Chalk by Bill Thomson
Fossil by Bill Thomson

and based on their developing version of what it means to be a reader, we find that it is important for our students to begin to use what they've been learning about who they are as readers, and to have a voice in deciding where to go next. Goal setting is an important part of our classroom routine throughout the year, so we start setting and recording goals early.

Literary Connections

We also want students to begin to appreciate the literary connections in their world. We want them to be part of the community of readers beyond their classroom and the school walls. For example, we often see cartoons in the paper that relate to stories or fairy tales. We recently found a card with a picture of three bears and a little blond girl on the front. The card says, "Happy Birthday, Oldilocks." We have seen ads for mortgage companies that show the three little pigs building houses. These types of things are part of our daily lives, and they remind us how much a part reading plays in them. We keep our eyes open for these things so that when the time is right, we can share them with our students. In an early issue of *Time for Kids*, one of the students spotted an article about a very large pig. A caption with a picture accompanying the article read, "Some pig!" Another student immediately noticed the connection to *Charlotte's Web* by E. B. White. This connection led us to set up a new bulletin board in the classroom for the children to display similar items. Throughout the year, they were on the lookout for literary connections. They found them in newspapers, books, and magazines.

We use the routines of the reading workshop to listen to our students during the first six weeks of school. One year, during read-aloud, Franki noticed that each time she asked her students to stop and talk, they merely retold what had happened. When she asked them about it, their understanding was that readers retold and summarized when they had read. That seemed to be the only thinking they were aware that they did independently. For the next several weeks, Franki did a lesson cycle on "Readers Think While They Read." This was a focus during mini-lesson time as student dug into picture books and wordless books. It was a focus during read-aloud as they learned to notice different ways readers think in the midst of a text. And it came up in conferences and share sessions. Franki knew that it was the most important way to spend the first six weeks of their school year.

Conferring with Kayla

During an early reading conference, Kayla shared that she would like to do more thinking about characters while she read. She was reading the Babysitters Club Graphix and discovering that in each book, a different character was most interesting. She decided to use sticky notes during her reading to think about two characters. Then she would analyze those notes to determine who was the more interesting character in this particular story. Kayla's goal grew from all the conversations we had had in the first six weeks of school. She knew readers thought when they read, and she knew they often thought about character. She had discovered a new series and format that she loved in this Babysitters series. And she had seen several possibilities during read-aloud of collecting thoughts during reading. She took what she was learning and made it work for her own reading life.

Students keep an eye out for literary
connections to add to the board.

Readers Get Stuck

One of the first things we want upper elementary readers to understand is
that all readers get stuck. Most of our students believe that reading is about
getting the words right, and that if they get all of the words right (quickly!),
they are good readers. They don't realize that all readers get stuck in their
reading. We need to help our students understand that experienced readers
have strategies to help them get unstuck.

Our goal for students in upper elementary classrooms is for them to
become strategic readers. We have benefited by reading professionally from
works published by some of the leaders in literacy education. In *Strategies
That Work*, Stephanie Harvey defines strategic reading as "thinking about
reading in ways that enhance learning and understanding" (2007, 23). She
and other educators at the Public Education and Business Coalition in
Denver began to focus on the strategies proficient readers use, as identified
by researchers. For example, P. David Pearson et al. (1992) identified the most
critical strategies that readers use when they construct meaning from text. In
Mosaic of Thought (1997), Ellin Keene and Susan Zimmermann describe the

thought processes of proficient readers and the strategies that help children become more flexible, adaptive, independent, and engaged readers.

Here are some of the strategies proficient readers use:

- They make connections between what they know and the texts they read.
- They ask questions as they read.
- They visualize to enhance their understanding.
- They draw inferences during and after reading.
- They determine the most essential ideas in the text.
- They synthesize information.
- They monitor, correct, and clarify their understanding.

Stephanie Harvey writes, "Comprehension means that readers think not only about what they are reading but what they are understanding. When readers construct meaning, they are building their store of knowledge. But along with knowledge must come understanding" (2007, 15). We have had many conversations with Cris Tovani, author of *I Read It, but I Don't Get It: Comprehension Strategies for Adolescent Readers* (2000), and Debbie Miller, author of *Reading with Meaning: Teaching Comprehension in the Primary Grades* (2002), about the kinds of teaching and learning that encourage strategic reading. We know we need to do more than teach comprehension strategies in order for students to apply them independently. We realized early on that students aren't often aware of what works for them or when they need to stop reading to clarify meaning. They know the comprehension strategies and can talk to us about them. They can tell us they are making a connection or making an inference, but they don't always know how and when to use that strategy when reading difficult texts independently.

Strategy instruction will be new to some of our students. Others may know the strategies but be unable to use them when needed to help them understand what they read. They can make a connection to a text, but they do not necessarily make connections that help them understand the text at a deeper level. They can make a prediction, but not always one that is likely to happen based on what they have already read in the story.

We caution teachers about teaching a skill and a strategy from a list and moving on. When we teach reading strategies as a daily lesson, checking skills off as we go, our students suffer. But when we think about the year as a whole and the kinds of behaviors and habits we want our students to have when they leave us, it is easier to see what is truly essential. We want to teach in ways that help them become more independent and promote strategies that will help them read complex texts. We also want our students to see the joy in reading and to become lifelong readers. We want them to know that it is important to be part of a reading community. But many young readers have come to see reading as a chore because it is not purposeful or because they do not have the strategies and behaviors in place to understand the types of texts they are encountering.

We've asked many readers in grades 3–6 what they do when they get stuck. Almost all of them talk about getting stuck at the word level. They say that getting stuck means getting to a word they don't know. But as texts become more difficult, getting stuck means more than not knowing a word. As students begin to encounter more complex texts, meaning may break down beyond the word level. Getting stuck in their reading means many more things to the upper elementary grades. We've learned from Cris Tovani (2000) that older readers may

- daydream while reading (getting to the bottom of the page not knowing what they just read).
- lose track of the characters as they come up again in the story.
- get confused by the format or structure of the text.
- fail to recognize when the setting or narrator has changed.
- not be able to infer the less literal meaning in the text.
- not pause in their reading to ask questions and monitor their comprehension.

Students need to know that they will always get stuck in their reading, but that throughout the year, they will be learning strategies for getting unstuck. Cris Tovani tells her students, "A strategy . . . is an intentional plan that readers use to help themselves make sense of their reading. Strategies are flexible and can be adapted to meet the demands of the reading task. Good readers use lots of strategies to help themselves make sense of text" (2000, 5).

We have found that a great way to begin a conversation about reading strategies is to start a chart that lists ways that students got stuck when they were learning how to read. We then use the chart to contrast those early reading experiences with the ways students get stuck in their current reading. After writing their own ideas down (see Figure 4.4), one fourth-grade class created the following chart:

Readers Get Stuck

Then	*Now*
Said the wrong words	Read too fast and don't know what happened
Didn't know a word	
Bigger words	Not concentrating on the book
Skipped words or sentence	Get distracted
Didn't understand	Too tired
Confused	Skip paying attention for a couple of pages (This doesn't make sense!)
Couldn't find books I'd like	
Distracted	Words you don't know

Read things over and over   Don't know what it means
Didn't pay attention to detail   Reading names
                                 Lose my place
                                 Change in setting

Once students realize that all readers get stuck, they will be more open to the strategies needed to understand difficult texts. If we want our students to practice strategies that will help them when they do not understand, we must first make it okay for them to get stuck. We have found that students welcome this piece of learning. They are always relieved to find that they aren't the only ones who get stuck in their reading. These lessons are critical; they show students that being a good reader doesn't mean "getting all the words right," and they help them see how much more complicated higher-level reading can be.

By the end of the first few weeks of school, students have redefined reading and understand that all readers get stuck sometimes. They have learned that throughout the year reading will be important and that their lives as readers matter. We can then move on to the following broad goals for our students during the remainder of the school year:

- Having students continue to think about themselves as readers.
- Having them begin to identify reading that is difficult.
- Having them learn to support their thinking with evidence from the text.
- Getting them to extend and sustain conversations during read-aloud.
- Having them use their reading notebooks in increasingly sophisticated ways.
- Helping them develop new skills in selecting texts.

Because we know that these goals will be the foundation for many other lessons throughout the year, we launch into them slowly. Instead of jumping in with difficult texts and teaching children strategies for getting through them, we have students spend weeks paying attention to the kinds of reading that are difficult for them. They begin to realize that different texts are difficult for different readers, and they learn to identify the kinds of texts that they struggle with. It's critical that we start these lessons when students are ready and continue to revisit them throughout the school year. Sustaining strategy instruction throughout the school year will support our students, and they will change as readers.

Figure 4.4
One student's notes on getting stuck

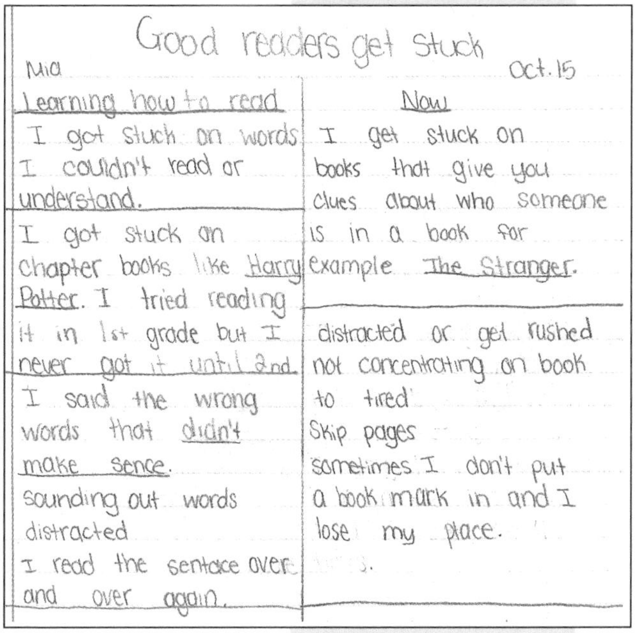

Good readers get stuck

Mia   Oct. 15

Learning how to read	Now
I got stuck on words I couldn't read or understand.	I get stuck on books that give you clues about who someone
I got stuck on chapter books like Harry Potter. I tried reading it in 1st grade but I never got it until 2nd.	is in a book for example The Stranger.
I said the wrong words that didn't make sence.	distracted or get rushed not concentrating on book to tired
sounding out words distracted	Skip pages sometimes I don't put a book mark in and I
I read the sentace over and over again.	lose my place.

We notice behaviors in the first weeks of school that can make a big difference throughout the year. When one group of students began to read each day, we noticed that they spent several minutes flipping through their books. After a few conversations, we realized that most of these students were reading novels without using bookmarks! This was an easy fix. Reminding kids about bookmarks and showing them how index cards and sticky notes can serve as bookmarks took just a few minutes. This is an example of why we can never stop observing our students carefully. This simple lesson gave students several more minutes of actual reading time each day.

We always go into a bit of a panic in mid-October. Up to then, we have been patient and have spent long periods of time having great conversations with students about reading, but then we realize it is almost November, and we fear that our students haven't accomplished anything. So we try to take some time in October to figure out what our students have learned. We invariably realize that they have accomplished quite a bit (thank goodness!). And we know exactly where to go next with instruction.

For example, by mid-October one year, Franki's fourth-grade students had learned many things:

> They could think and talk about their lives as readers.
> They could think about how they were changing as readers.
> Reading is about understanding, not merely getting the words right.
> Different readers like different books, but readers behave in similar ways.
> All readers struggle with some text.
> Getting stuck now is different from getting stuck while they were learning to read.
> They could identify easy and difficult texts.
> There are strategies to use when the text is difficult.
> Reading nonfiction is difficult for most students.
> Features in nonfiction are intended to support the reader.
> Authors leave clues in the text to help with understanding.
> Conversations around books help readers think of ideas they wouldn't think of on their own.
> Readers choose books in different ways.

At this point, after taking stock and realizing that our students have learned a great deal about reading, we make a new list of goals for the following several weeks. We always try to be intentional in our teaching, so we reflect what our students have learned and plan ahead based on what we know about them as readers. Franki knew she would continue to work with her students on strategies for understanding hard text, supporting thinking with evidence from the text, and choosing good books. She also had some new goals, which were related to the following observations:

- Many of her students talked about "reading it again," but doing so didn't seem to be improving their comprehension.
- During conversations, many students were still just taking turns talking instead of building on things others had said to deepen their understanding.
- Students were not remembering to write in their reading logs. Franki thought they would need to be changed to daily logs.
- Students made predictions to be "right." They did not see how predictions, whether right or wrong, could help them understand the text better.
- Students still seemed to be bopping aimlessly on several websites, not using the same skills they did with traditional text. They did not use tools to stop and think with digital texts.

Working on these issues involves ambitious goals, but these new goals are attainable over the course of the year. And they all fit into the standards that the state and district establish. We know that if we help students learn to reread in different ways and to predict in ways that will enhance their understanding, they can use these skills when reading any text.

The stakes are high. Our students are going to be asked to perform at higher levels than we have asked them to do up to now. But we know that it is possible for them to do so—that our students constantly exceed even our highest expectations. If we look at the whole year and think about the over-all goals we have for our children, it is easier to teach well. And if we remem-ber these goals, a slow but deliberate start always pays off in the long run. Yes, we know that by late fall, we will always panic, thinking students haven't learned anything. But we force ourselves to sit down each year and remind ourselves how far our students have come. And at the same time, we need to keep the end of the year in sight so that we remain aware of where our stu-dents can go if we take it slow and give them more ownership and more responsibility for their learning.

Chapter 5

Grouping Beyond Levels

Students deserve instruction that moves them forward as readers and thinkers and values their unique experiences and needs. Finding the balance is not impossible. We can teach students how to read closely and fall in love with reading.

—Chris Lehman and Kate Roberts

We're in a busy reading workshop one morning in March in Franki's fourth-grade classroom. Franki gathers a group of four students together to talk about how to recognize a change in setting as they read. She knows these particular students struggle with this issue in their independent reading because of the conversations she has had with them during individual conferences. Before she begins working with the group, she announces to the rest of the class, "This is a group that is going to work on finding clues for when the setting changes in a story. Who else thinks they need to join us?" From across the room a boy calls out that he wants to join the group. Another girl walks over and silently joins the circle as Franki begins to talk with them about changes in setting and hands out texts to read. Together, the group starts finding places in the text where they get confused about the setting and looks for clues in the text that would signal a change in setting.

Our goal is to be at this point by late October in our reading workshops. By October, we have completed beginning-of-the-year assessments and met with students about individual goals. We have routines in place and been able to observe our students in each of these routines. We are using assessments and observations of our students to know what skills to focus on in groups. We have goals for each of our students, and our students know enough about their own needs as readers to join a group that is working on a reading skill that they too need help with. Through instruction, planning, assessment, and observation, we have come to know our students well enough to match what they need with what we teach. There is a comfortable, relaxed feel to our whole-group instruction, the flexible groups form and change regularly, and the individual conferences result in productive conversations with students about their reading.

We make better instructional decisions when we know our students well. Before our discussions later in this chapter about planning lessons and organizing groups, we begin with our beliefs about assessment, planning, and instruction, which challenge many current practices in upper elementary classrooms.

A Close Look at Two Readers

As we mentioned earlier, our district requires us to give various assessments to gain insights about our students as readers. We also choose other assessments that we know will tell us a great deal about our children. The Developmental Reading Assessment (DRA) is one tool that teachers have found especially helpful. This assessment tool has students choose a book, make predictions about it, read it, and respond to it. Teachers take a running record of each child reading and listen to his or her retelling of the story to determine an accurate level of comprehension. The DRA is an excellent assessment tool that provides some direction for teachers as they plan instruction. But it gives us just one piece of information about our students as readers. As Clare Landrigan and Tammy Mulligan remind us in their book *Assessment in Perspective*, "Assessment needs to be the vehicle that moves us beyond defining our readers as a number. Assessment should not be about defining a reader but about piecing together information to help us design classroom experiences so we can observe our readers learning and understand what each one needs"(2013, 9).

Recently, we had conversations with two students, Anthony and Sarah, each of whom measured at level 40 on the DRA scale. If we considered only the level from this assessment tool to plan instruction, we might place both students in the same group and assume they needed the same instruction. In addition to administering the DRA, however, we interviewed each student. The interviews were simply informal chats. We didn't sit with a clipboard of questions next to us and check them off as we asked them, though we did have a list of questions as a guide. We have a menu of questions that we use to start conversations with our students:

How would you describe yourself as a reader?
What are you currently reading?
What kinds of things do you like to read?

What kinds of things do you *not* like to read?

What are you going to read next?

How do you choose the things you read?

What kinds of things do you read on a computer/phone/etc.?

Do you read any blogs or websites on a regular basis?

Do you read any type of e-book?

Have you ever read an audiobook?

What do you do when you get stuck?

What do you do when you start to read each day?

How do you keep track of the characters in the books you are reading?

What kind of reading is easy for you?

What kind of reading is hard for you?

We have found that conversations around just one of these questions help us discover more about the strengths, habits, attitudes, and needs of our students. Early in the year, we do not ask students to read aloud to us. We wait a few weeks until they have realized that reading is about more than getting the words right. If we were to ask our students to read aloud to us before we had time to learn about the other aspects of their reading, we would reinforce the notion that our main goal for them as readers is oral fluency. Although fluency is important, it is not the only goal, and certainly not the most important one for older readers.

These conversations give us crucial information that we use to plan instruction, and they continue all year long. We match what we learn about individual students' interests and histories in reading with what we know about skills that are essential for upper elementary students to acquire. We try to heed Shelley Harwayne's advice: "Make sure you can articulate why you're doing what you're doing. Our time with students is precious and never enough. We can't waste time on things that don't add up, that don't connect to students' assessed needs and their interests. Teachers must remain decision-makers, making wise choices based on professional know-how" (2002, 21).

We present this look at two readers to show how different students can be in their behaviors, tastes, interests, and abilities, even when they are reading at the same "level."

Anthony

Anthony began our interview by saying, "I like to read history and nonfiction. I read history to learn more about the past, and I read fiction to see how life is in other books." Anthony was a child who didn't necessarily read a variety of genres, but when we asked him what he was thinking about reading next, he said, "I might read some poetry, but I'm not sure what book or poet."

Anthony told us that when he gets stuck in his reading, he sounds words out, looks them up in a dictionary, skips them, or fills in substitute words. He told us proudly, "Some of the history books I read are like grown-up books." When he begins a new book, he checks the back of the book for a summary. He opens the book to the first page and reads it. If he doesn't get stuck, he reads another page. He said, "Sometimes I read as many as ten pages and the back of the book before I decide to read the book." When he reads books with several characters in them, he writes the characters down on a piece of paper as they come into the story. He said, "Sometimes I write things by the names of the characters to help me remember who they are."

Anthony said he has strategies he uses when he starts reading each day to help him sustain comprehension over time. He told us, "When I start reading each day, I go back and read the last page I read before to remember what happened and how it happened." He told us that when he finishes reading each day, he tries to stop at the end of a chapter. He looks ahead to the next chapter title and the pictures to get an idea of what the chapter might be about. He told us, "In second grade and at the beginning of third grade, my favorite author was Marc Brown." He was currently reading *Wayside School Gets a Little Stranger* by Louis Sachar.

We were glad to know that Anthony had set a short-term reading goal for himself. We noticed that he recognized getting stuck only at the word level. We began to think about which poetry books Anthony might enjoy that we could recommend to him.

Sarah

Sarah had been reading a few of the Pinky and Rex books by James Howe. In addition, she had recently read *Pirates Don't Wear Pink Sunglasses* and *Santa Doesn't Mop Floors* by Debbie Dadey. Sarah said, "I don't like to read thick books." When she chooses a book to read, she looks at the title to see if it sounds interesting, and looks at the cover and the back of the book. Sarah said, "The Pinky and Rex books are average for me. Books with one sentence on a page are easy, and books with no pictures are hard." When we asked her about keeping track of characters as she reads, Sarah said, "I like books with only a couple of characters because it is easy to keep track of them." She said that when she gets stuck, she looks for chunks or small words inside words, or sounds the words out. She never reads on when she is stuck on a word. When she starts reading each day, she starts right where she left off. She doesn't go back to think about what she read the day before. Sarah said, "I don't like to read. I would rather draw." Her favorite authors were Dr. Seuss and David Wisniewski.

Our interview with Sarah led us to believe that she was not very interested in reading and that she did not seem very confident as a reader. Our immediate goal would be to help her gain confidence and begin to see herself as a reader.

Instructional Implications

After interviewing these two readers, we quickly determined that grouping them together for instruction would probably not be the most effective use of their time. They didn't need the same kind of support or even the same degree of teacher involvement.

Although we use our conversations with students to help us plan instruction, we also want the conversations to help students identify their own strengths and needs in reading. Children can know all the best strategies for comprehending texts, but if they don't use them as they read, their understanding will falter. As Regie Routman reminds us, "Just because we teach our students strategies doesn't mean they apply them. They can 'do' the strategy, but they don't apply it when they read" (2003, 120). Children should recognize who they are as readers. It helps them understand how every one of their reading experiences sharpens their skills and moves them forward. Once they know themselves as readers, they can begin to take some responsibility for planning and assessing what they need next from us and from their classmates.

Thoughts for Literacy Leaders: Supporting Each Other

Fortunately, teaching is no longer an isolated experience. Teacher collaboration is becoming the norm in many of our schools. It provides the support we need in the challenging learning landscape. As teachers seek to help each child become a more accomplished reader, it often seems as though there aren't enough strategies in our toolbox. For some students, the struggle is real, and teachers seek to find any strategy or tool that can move them forward. On the other hand, for some of the most independent and accomplished readers, teachers need to broaden the experiences to enrich their reading lives. Each child deserves to be the focus of our most thoughtful instruction.

Making time for teachers and staff to share what challenges they face in their teaching can provide the support they need. Often, when collaboratively focusing on the needs of an individual student, clearer paths emerge and new student support strategies are developed. The teachers at Karen's school participated in small-group case-study conversations. Each teacher shared a narrative about a student who was struggling and opened a conversation about what strategies had been initiated with the student. The other members of the case-study group offered additional ideas, tools, and strategies that might support the student. After a few weeks, the groups would meet again to continue to follow the progress of the student and offer any additional support to the teacher.

Limitations of Levels

If we were using the guided reading levels as a planning tool for instruction for Sarah and Anthony, we might choose a book that is a level Q or R. But after getting to know Sarah and Anthony, we don't believe that basing instruction solely on book levels is the best way to help students develop new skills. To plan effective instruction, we need to know not only the readers well, but also the materials. By knowing our readers and our books, we will be better able to help students choose books that will help them grow as readers.

We worry about the level mania that is occurring across the country. It doesn't matter whether teachers are using guided reading levels, Accelerated Reader levels, or some other leveling system. Students and teachers in the upper elementary grades often measure progress in inappropriate ways. We worry that our children will not choose books because they are interesting or challenging, but simply because they are the "right" level. Students nowadays sometimes define reading as "getting through a book at my level" rather than enjoying and understanding great texts.

Fountas and Pinnell (2012-2013) promote a more thoughtful approach to teaching children to choose the books they read independently in an article for the *Reading Teacher*. "We want students to learn to select books the way experienced readers do—according to their own interests, by trying a bit of the book, by noticing the topic or the author. Teachers can help students learn to choose books that are right for them to read independently. This is a life skill. The text gradient and leveled books are a teacher's tool, not a child's label, and should be de-emphasized in the classroom. Levels are for books, not children" (17). We are careful not to choose books for instruction based on level alone. Although level is one consideration, we have learned that we have to be far more intentional about book choice than merely matching levels. There is much more to a book than level.

We've spent a lot of time looking at leveled books. Think for a moment about the strategies and behaviors that cannot be measured by a test or an assessment instrument but need to be taught to students in the upper elementary grades. As Jo Worthy and Misty Sailors (2001) write in an article for the *New Advocate*, "We have often seen these [leveled] lists used in place of teacher judgment and have heard teachers describe students' reading in terms of numbers (e.g., 'He's a level 21') rather than in ways that reflect the complexity of reading. Further, moving students step by step through text difficulty levels assumes that students progress in small, measured increments" (232).

Let's take a look at two books that are a Level Q on the guided reading list (Fountas and Pinnell 2001, Appendix 61). Although these books are the same level, they offer different supports and challenges.

Bunnicula by James Howe

Longer text that requires sustained comprehension over time
Fantasy genre
Very few illustrations to support the text
Several characters to remember throughout the story

***Grandpa's Face* by Eloise Greenfield**

Can be read in one or two sittings

Realistic fiction

Illustrations support the text

Two main characters throughout the story

Although Anthony would probably be successful with both of these books, Sarah may not yet have the skills needed to stick with a longer novel like *Bunnicula*. Instead, we might want her to try a book like *Judy Moody* by Megan McDonald, which has each character's picture listed in the front of the book. A book like this would help Sarah begin to read longer novels, which seem to be a stumbling block for her. *Judy Moody* provides the support of a character chart and can build Sarah's confidence as a reader. We also think that the humor in this book might appeal to Sarah; it might be a series that she could get hooked on.

Because Sarah's needs are similar to those of some of the other students in the class, it makes sense for us to put her in a group with those other students—for example, students who are struggling with keeping track of characters in their reading. Anthony's greatest need, however, is unique, so it makes sense to meet with him individually. Our focus is on what we can do to help each reader rather than making sure that everyone is in a small group. We guide and support our upper elementary readers in many ways besides assigning them to reading groups.

Levels are just one tool in a large array of assessments that can help us plan instruction. Once we have completed the informal reading interviews, we administer more formal assessments, such as the DRA. We also continue to observe students, have individual conferences, and review past test scores. One year, as she discovered insights about each student over six to eight weeks, Franki collected the information on a grid. (That form is provided in the appendix; a completed sample grid is shown in Figure 5.1.)

Name	Interview	Observation	DRA	Survey	Standardized Tests	Goal
Beth	disliked reading last year trying to enjoy reading again picky about what she reads	reads at recess always very engaged	Level 50 good comprehension and reflection has had no strategy instruction but uses strat. naturally	likes fantasy and popular titles	well above grade level	book choice strategy instruction set own reading goals
Cameron	"safe" reading likes funny, scary, small books difficulty with unknown words	very conscientious little risk taking	Level 38 goes on when test doesn't make sense plan/plane (miscue)	Bailey School Kids Henry Huggins Interested in the solar system	just at grade level	confidence expand reading choices take risks when stuck
Anthony	likes history and nonfiction good previewing skills keeps track of characters	engaged during reading brings books from home	Level 40 very few miscues good comprehension	reads only nonfiction no favorite authors	above grade level	poetry (Anthony's goal)
Doug	likes zoo animal books wants "hard" books "I don't get stuck"	chooses very difficult books distracted and unengaged during reading time	Level 38 very few miscues very little comprehension	likes Harry Potter, Lord of the Ring no favorite author	below grade level	know when he's stuck choosing books (maybe short stories)

Figure 5.1
Franki's grid

Strategy Lesson

Keeping Track of Characters

■ **Why We Teach It:** As students encounter more complex texts, one of the biggest challenges for them is keeping track of the characters when there are more than a few in the story. They often get confused, mix up one character with another, or continue reading when they know they have lost track of who everyone is in the story. Although "keeping track of characters" is not in itself a Common Core standard, it is part of what is needed to comprehend text and to understand characters.

■ **Possible Anchor Book:** *Judy Moody Was in a Mood. Not a Good Mood. A Bad Mood*, by Megan McDonald. This is one in a series of Judy Moody books published by Candlewick Press. The second is *Judy Moody Gets Famous*. Most of these chapter books have a "who's who" page at the front of the book with a picture of all the characters in the story along with their names. In *Judy Moody Gets Famous* the page also contains a brief description of each of the characters. These books are a good choice for children who are moving away from stories with just two or three characters in them.

■ **How We Teach It:** As students preview the book, it is important for them to discover the "who's who" page. We discuss how the page might be helpful as they read the story. As the group begins to read the book, we pause when a new character enters the story and refer to the "who's who" page. As they continue to read, we encourage the students to refer to this page when they are confused about any of the characters in the story. We suggest that they keep a list of characters on a sticky note or a bookmark as they read.

■ **Follow-Up:** Once the children have read the book for a few days, we often ask them to reflect on how the "who's who" page was helpful for them. We have them share the list of characters they were keeping as they read. We ask them what they learned that will help them the next time they are reading a book with several characters. *Amelia's Notebook* by Marissa Moss is a great book to share. When Amelia moves to a new school, she draws pictures in her notebook of the people she meets and writes about them. Students might want to do something similar in their reading logs.

■ ■ ■

Thinking Through Grouping

A planning form (see Figures 5.2a and b and the blank form in the appendix) often helps us with the instructional decisions we make. Some teachers have found it helpful to use such a form as part of their lesson plans. The form helps us see the broad picture of our instruction that students will receive in whole-class, small-group, and individual instruction.

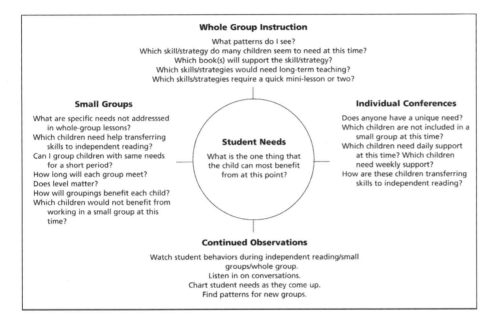

Whole Group Instruction
What patterns do I see?
Which skill/strategy do many children seem to need at this time?
Which book(s) will support the skill/strategy?
Which skills/strategies would need long-term teaching?
Which skills/strategies require a quick mini-lesson or two?

Small Groups
What are specific needs not addresssed in whole-group lessons?
Which children need help transferring skills to independent reading?
Can I group children with same needs for a short period?
How long will each group meet?
Does level matter?
How will groupings benefit each child?
Which children would not benefit from working in a small group at this time?

Student Needs
What is the one thing that the child can most benefit from at this point?

Individual Conferences
Does anyone have a unique need?
Which children are not included in a small group at this time?
Which children need daily support at this time? Which children need weekly support?
How are these children transferring skills to independent reading?

Continued Observations
Watch student behaviors during independent reading/small groups/whole group.
Listen in on conversations.
Chart student needs as they come up.
Find patterns for new groups.

Figure 5.2a
Grouping for instruction

Whole-Group Instruction

We look for problems that many of the students in our class are having when we think about the whole-group instruction we want to provide. What skills and strategies do many of the children seem to need at this time? Which text or texts will support the skill or strategy? What skills and strategies will we need to teach over a long period of time, and which will require just a quick mini-lesson or two? We look for patterns in the classroom that will help us plan whole-group instruction. Our whole-class lessons should always be based on what we have learned about our students as readers.

Early in the year, we often find that learning how to choose books and how to browse are the most common needs we see in our students. Other early challenges for many students include knowing when they are stuck, sustaining interest or comprehension, and writing in response to reading. Early in the year, students' needs seem more similar than they do later in the year. Their needs become more individual as the year goes on and we get to know our students better. Thus, we often spend more time on whole-class instruction early in the year and more time with small groups later in the year.

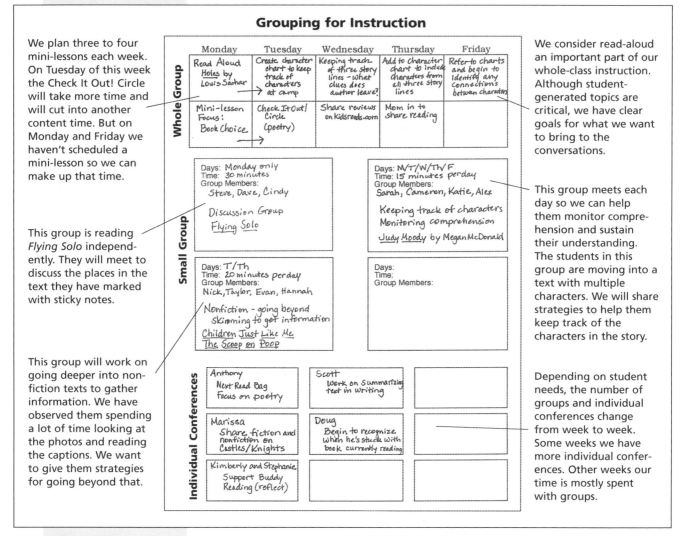

Grouping for Instruction

We plan three to four mini-lessons each week. On Tuesday of this week the Check It Out! Circle will take more time and will cut into another content time. But on Monday and Friday we haven't scheduled a mini-lesson so we can make up that time.

This group is reading *Flying Solo* independently. They will meet to discuss the places in the text they have marked with sticky notes.

This group will work on going deeper into non-fiction texts to gather information. We have observed them spending a lot of time looking at the photos and reading the captions. We want to give them strategies for going beyond that.

Whole Group

	Monday	Tuesday	Wednesday	Thursday	Friday
	Read Aloud Holes by Louis Sachar	Create character chart to keep track of characters → at camp	Keeping track of three story lines – what clues does author leave?	Add to character chart to include characters from all three story lines	Refer to charts and begin to identify any connections between characters
	Mini-lesson Focus: Book Choice	Check It Out! Circle (poetry) →	Share reviews on kidsreads.com	Mom in to share reading	

Small Group

Days: Monday only
Time: 30 minutes
Group Members: Steve, Dave, Cindy

Discussion Group
Flying Solo

Days: T/Th
Time: 20 minutes per day
Group Members: Nick, Taylor, Evan, Hannah

Nonfiction – going beyond Skimming to get information
Children Just Like Me
The Scoop on Poop

Days: M/T/W/Th/F
Time: 15 minutes per day
Group Members: Sarah, Cameron, Katie, Alex

Keeping track of characters
Monitoring comprehension

Judy Moody by Megan McDonald

Days:
Time:
Group Members:

Individual Conferences

Anthony
Next Read Bag
Focus on poetry

Marissa
Share fiction and nonfiction on Castles/Knights

Kimberly and Stephanie
Support Buddy Reading (reflect)

Scott
Work on Summarizing text in writing

Doug
Begin to recognize when he's stuck with book currently reading

We consider read-aloud an important part of our whole-class instruction. Although student-generated topics are critical, we have clear goals for what we want to bring to the conversations.

This group meets each day so we can help them monitor comprehension and sustain their understanding. The students in this group are moving into a text with multiple characters. We will share strategies to help them keep track of the characters in the story.

Depending on student needs, the number of groups and individual conferences change from week to week. Some weeks we have more individual conferences. Other weeks our time is mostly spent with groups.

Figure 5.2b
Planning form

We are careful not to try to teach too much in one mini-lesson. We focus on a particular skill, strategy, or behavior that we know will move our readers forward. We combine our knowledge of the children with what we know about experienced readers to determine what will help our students become more strategic in their reading.

Along with teachers all across the country, we have examined the Common Core State Standards and learned what is expected from students at different grade-level bands. Whether we agree with the standards or not, whether the standards remain or not, we have found that the conversations with colleagues around grade-level expectations have been worthwhile. As we dig into specific standards such as Standard RL 5.3 (Compare and Contrast two or more characters, settings, or events in a story or drama, drawing on specific details in the text [e.g. how characters interact]), we cannot merely ask students to "do" the things listed. Instead we have to break down the standards ourselves based on what we know about our students and what they bring to the conversation. Comparing characters in second grade does not look the same as it does in eleventh grade as characters become more complex. We have to think about our readers and where they fall on this continuum—how we can teach them to grow as thinkers about character in ways that will grow as books become more complex. To compare characters in fifth grade, students need to know characters in multiple ways. For students to compare settings, they need experience with and understandings of the ways settings add to a story in a variety of genres. Breaking down each standard and scaffolding teaching based on where our students are is the key to good instruction. Our teaching is a combination of knowing our students, the standards, and the texts well.

We don't want to spend so much time with whole-group lessons that we cut into our students' independent reading time. It is tempting to short-change independent reading time to teach a necessary skill. We try to remember that reading develops over days, weeks, and months, and that the best thing we can do for our students is give them time to practice during independent reading time.

Specific skills and strategies that readers use need to be taught. Stephanie Harvey shared her thinking in an article in the *Reading Teacher*. "We don't teach strategies for strategy sake. We don't teach kids to visualize so they can be the best visualizers in the room. We teach our kids to think strategically so they can better understand the world around them and have some control over it. We teach them to ask questions, to delve into a text, to clarify confusion, to connect the new to the known to build knowledge, and to sift out the most important information when making decisions" (2013, 433). We can no longer be satisfied with giving our students a list of questions or a packet of comprehension activities to complete after their reading. We know that we need to help them learn what to do *during* their reading of a text in order for them to understand it.

Early one year when Franki was teaching third grade, she listened to her students during the first days of read-aloud and realized that the talk they did while reading consisted of summarizing what was happening in the story. When Franki asked them about it, many assumed that thinking happened after you were finished with a book so that you could tell someone about it. When she pressed further, she found they weren't aware that they were also doing more complex thinking as they read. Franki knew that the ways in which her students were defining reading would be a roadblock if they didn't discover all the ways they were thinking *as* they read. She designed five or six whole-class lessons that helped students notice all the ways readers think in the midst of reading. She also embedded this talk into the next few weeks of read-aloud as she asked students to identify ways in which they were thinking each time they shared. As the conversation continued, they charted those ways on the easel. This collection of lessons led to the more standards-based cycle in which readers discovered ways to think about characters while they read. As we planned throughout the year, it became more important for us to focus on a cycle of lessons to deepen student understanding rather than a single lesson that might not be effective for all students.

Small-Group Instruction

Recently, Franki talked to her students about goal setting. She let them know that in her yoga classes, she has long-term and short-term goals. She let them know that doing a *chaturanga* was something that was far from her reach. She needed lots of skills that she didn't yet have to do it well, but she'd work at it, and ideally in a year or so, she'd have it. But there were other challenges, such as holding a balance pose for longer than she had in the past. She was really close to accomplishing this and thought that with some work and effort, she could accomplish it in the next few weeks. Then she transitioned to a conversation about reading goals. Which goals did students have that seemed to be long-term goals and which seemed to be short term—things they could do in the next few weeks if they put in some time and effort and had a bit of support?

Over the last several years, we have started our small-group instruction in this way. For years, we assumed our students understood the purpose of small-group instruction and individual conferences, but after many conversations, we realized that many of our students came to groups just because we told them to. It wasn't until later in the school year that we invited students to suggest topics for small groups or to determine which groups they needed. But if we truly want our students to have agency and to know the power of small-group instruction and individual conferences, they must understand that every small group is a way to support students in their particular needs and goals. If this is to happen, they must be involved in planning them in some aspect from early on in the year.

We start groups with this vision in mind, letting students know right off that small-group instruction is intended to help every student move forward as a reader. Before any groups begin, we complete beginning-of-the-year assessments and conduct goal-setting conferences with students, asking them about their latest goals as a reader. We create a list of groups together as a class and ask students to sign up for them. We explain that we'll work together to create groups based on what we notice. We are honest with our students about the patterns we see in their reading, and we find that they are honest with us about the things they notice if we begin in this way.

Some Whole-Class Lesson Cycles We Have Taught

Time	Strategy/Skill	Text Used to Begin Conversation
Early in year	What makes text hard	*Time for Kids*
Early in year	Self as reader	*Reading Grows* by Ellen B. Senisi
Early in year	Book choice	Variety of books
Midyear	Using evidence	*Table Where Rich People Sit* by Byrd Baylor
Midyear	Keeping track of characters	*Holes* by Louis Sachar
Midyear	Understanding powerful writing	*Because of Winn-Dixie* by Kate DiCamillo
Midyear	Rereading for understanding	*Emma's Rug* by Allen Say
End of year	Reading multiple sources	Various news articles
End of year	Author study	*The Tiger Rising* by Kate DiCamillo

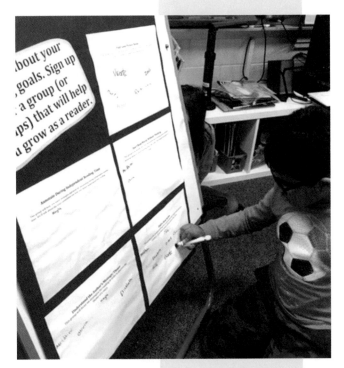

We often create groups based on student goals. This chart shows a list of goals that students brainstormed together.

The class then decided which goals required group support, and students signed up for groups they thought would be helpful.

We used to worry about needing to see children a certain number of times each week or making sure that every child was in a small group each week. Now we make decisions based on what the children need rather than the unnecessary pressures we've put on ourselves.

Flexible grouping provides a framework for meeting the needs of each reader in a systematic way. Just like Sarah and Anthony, each student comes to us with a unique array of skills, behaviors, attitudes, and reading experiences. Sometimes we have to resist the urge to focus on the skills and concepts that are listed in the standards and measured on a test. We have learned that knowing the standards well and teaching to the needs of our students is key to small-group work. As Regie Routman reminds us, "Instead of focusing on 'Is it right?' or 'What's the best way?' let's think about and focus on what's right and best for a particular student or group of students at this point in time as indicated by what we've read, the conversations we've had with our colleagues, valid research we've consulted, our teaching experiences, and our students' needs and interests" (2003, 6). We have learned over and over

Some Things We've Taught in Small Groups

Although we can't really be comprehensive in our thinking about small-group topics, we have found some patterns over the years in terms of strategies readers at this age typically need support with. The following is a list of lesson cycles we often teach in small groups in grades 3–6. The ways in which we teach these strategies vary based on specific student need.

Rereading
Keeping Track of Characters
Choosing Books
Expanding Tastes as a Reader
Sustaining Reading Over Time
Noticing a Change in Setting
Talking About Texts
Reading for Information
Pausing to Check for Understanding
Inferring Author's Message
Reading a New Genre
Discovering How a Character Changes Over Time
Annotating Thinking
Making Sense of a Website Organization
Deciding When to Click on a Link While Reading
Understanding Unfamiliar Words
Setting New Goals
Learning New Information from a Video
Thinking More Deeply About a Text
Visualizing a Text with No Pictures
Rereading for Various Reasons

again that teaching to the child is the only way to help kids meet the expectations of the standards.

When we plan small-group instruction, we look for patterns that emerge within groups of students. We look for several students who might benefit from the same type of instruction and group children who have similar needs. We think about the support small-group instruction can provide for our students and how they will benefit from reading and learning together. Is there a group of children with the same needs that can meet for a short time? Are there children who need help transferring skills to independent reading? As we plan for small groups, we think about how often and how long we will meet with each group. We think about whether the level of the text we use matters. We think about how the way we group children will benefit each child in the group.

We have no formula for the number of days, length of time, or size of groups when we plan small-group instruction. Some weeks, several groups are going on at the same time. Other weeks, we spend more time with individual students in conferences. We try to remain focused on what the children need, and we are flexible with the groups.

We might meet with a group of children who have trouble choosing books for one or two days until we think each has made a good choice and learned some strategies for choosing a book. For students who are working on understanding unfamiliar words, we might conduct small-group mini-lessons once a week for a few weeks. However, if we are meeting with a group that is having trouble sustaining comprehension over an entire novel, we need to meet with them every day to scaffold their understanding throughout the entire text. We try to determine the best use of time for our students and create a schedule that allows us to facilitate their learning.

Although we are often the ones to decide on the purpose of a group and who its members are going to be, we also ask for student input. We want children to be involved in their own learning, and we know that they often know themselves better than we do. So a few times each year, we ask our students to think about whether they would benefit from being part of a group and to let us know what they think they need to learn. We ask them to think about which reading skills they think they need more instruction on and which skills, strategies, and behaviors they would learn best as part of a small group. (See Figure 5.3.)

Figure 5.3
Casey and Ben reflect on ways that group work may help.

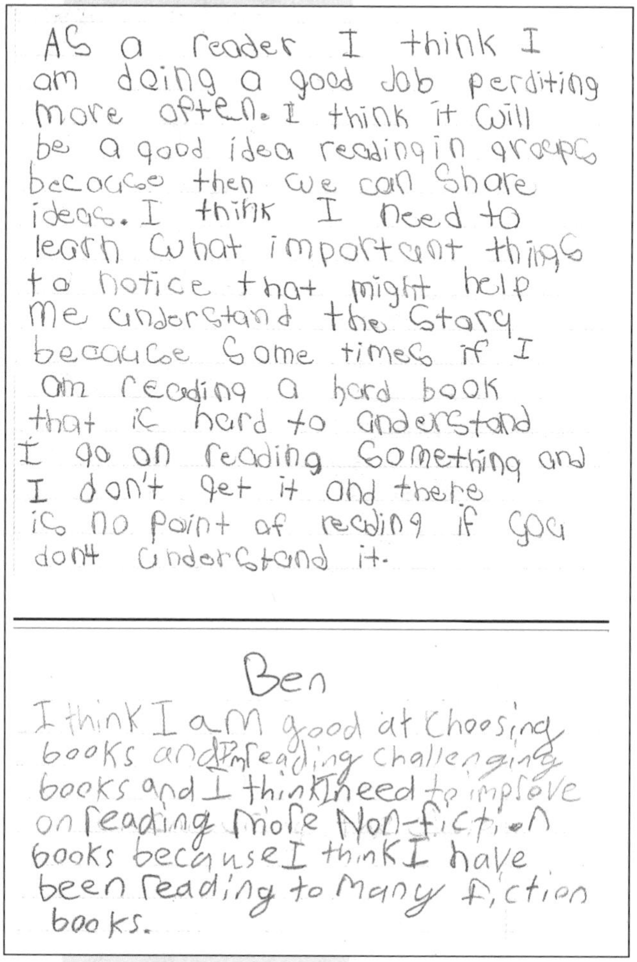

AS a reader I think I am doing a good job perditing more often. I think it will be a good idea reading in groups because then we can Share ideas. I think I need to learn what important things to notice that might help me understand the Story because some times if I am reading a hard book that is hard to understand I go on reading something and I don't get it and there is no point of reading if you don't understand it.

Ben

I think I am good at Choosing books and Preading challenging books and I think I need to improve on reading more Non-fiction books because I think I have been reading to many fiction books.

Early in the year, we may give our students some options during this discussion. We may say that we are thinking of offering groups on reading nonfiction, choosing books, and keeping track of characters. We personally invite those students who we know would benefit from the instruction. Then we open it up to others who are interested. As the year progresses, we leave the decisions about groups more open-ended, and students often tell us what lessons they need. When students tell us what they think they need to learn, their thoughts often match ours exactly! And if children ask to be in a group, they are often much more engaged and committed. (See Figure 5.4.)

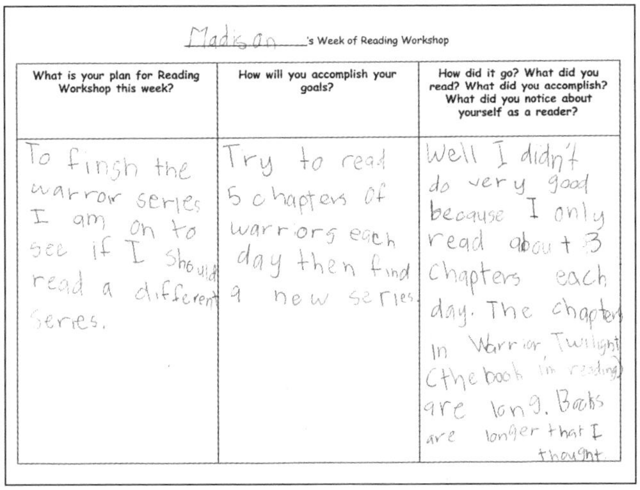

Madison's Week of Reading Workshop

What is your plan for Reading Workshop this week?	How will you accomplish your goals?	How did it go? What did you read? What did you accomplish? What did you notice about yourself as a reader?
To finsh the warror series I am on to see if I Should read a different series.	Try to read 5 chapters of warrors each day then find a new series.	Well I didn't do very good becaus I only read about 3 chapters each day. The chapters in Warrior Twilight (the book in reading) are long. Books are longer that I thought.

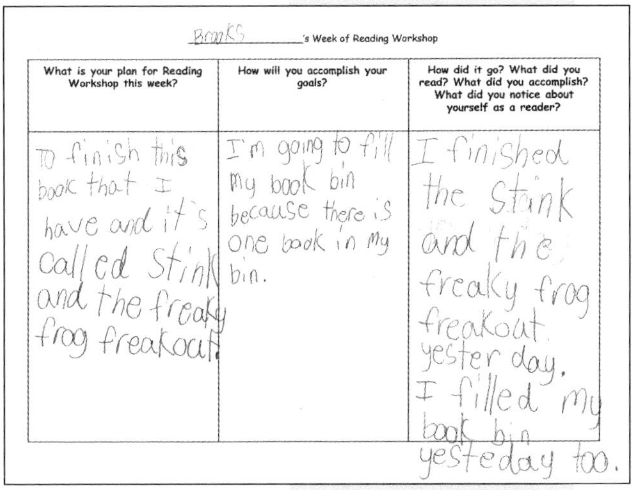

Brooks's Week of Reading Workshop

What is your plan for Reading Workshop this week?	How will you accomplish your goals?	How did it go? What did you read? What did you accomplish? What did you notice about yourself as a reader?
To finish this book that I have and it's called Stink and the freaky frog freakout.	I'm going to fill my book bin because there is one book in my bin.	I finished the Stink and the freaky frog freakout yester day. I filled my book bin yesteday too.

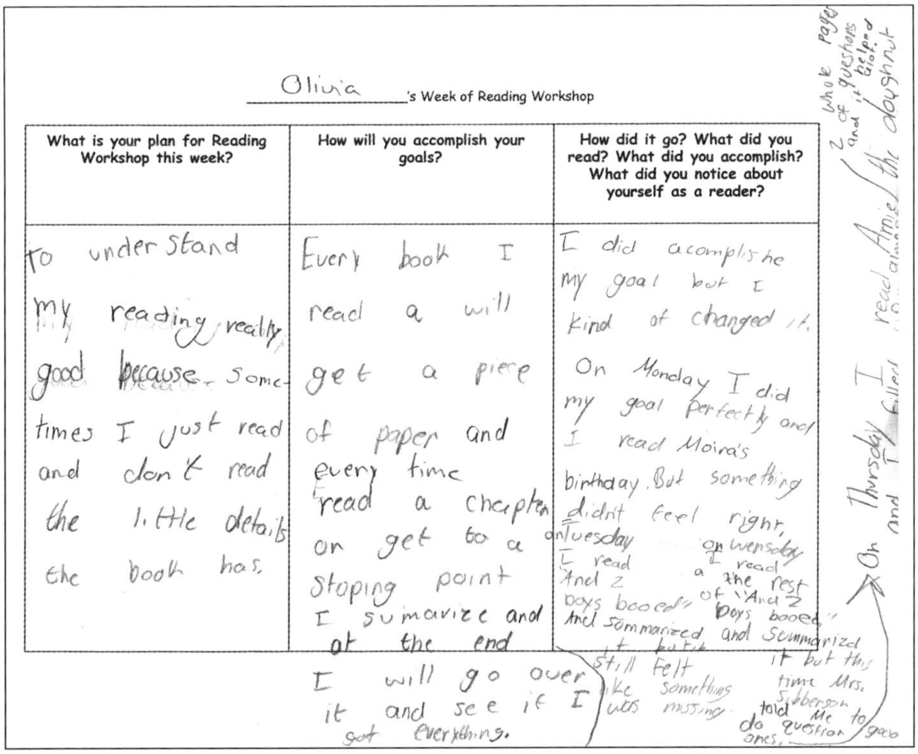

Olivia's Week of Reading Workshop

What is your plan for Reading Workshop this week?	How will you accomplish your goals?	How did it go? What did you read? What did you accomplish? What did you notice about yourself as a reader?
To under stand my reading really good because some times I just read and don't read the little details the book has.	Every book I read a will get a piece of paper and every time read a chapter or get to a stoping point I sumarize and at the end I will go over it and see if I got everything.	I did acomplishe my goal but I kind of changed it. On Monday I did my goal perfectly and I read Moira's birthday. But something didn't feel right. on tuesday I read And 2 boys booed. And summarized it but it still felt like something was missing. on wensday I read the rest of "And 2 boys booed" and summarized it but this time Mrs. Sibberson told me to do question ones. On Thursday I read Arnie the doughnut and I filled 2 whole pages of questions and it helped alot.

Figure 5.4
Students' weekly goal/reflection sheets

Individual Instruction

> *Our scaffolds should give students an opportunity to generate and explore new ideas, to change, and to grow. For children to truly reach independence, our interactions with them have to shift away from customary teacher-as-expert conversations with us simply telling students the answers.*
> —Terry Thompson

We also look for students who have needs that will not be met in the whole-class and small-group lessons, and we make time to meet with those students individually. When we know our students as individuals and take the time to build profiles of them as readers, we are much better prepared to meet with them individually about their reading. As we think about the children in our class, we look for the ones who have unique needs, because we want to consider what we can do in an individual conference that will support them. We consider those children who need daily support. Which children might benefit from a brief conference every day—one that leaves them prepared to engage in reading for the day and gives them the support they need? Which ones can move along with weekly support? Individual conferences give us opportunities to sharpen our image of the readers in our classrooms.

Looking at the planning chart (Figure 5.2b), we intend to meet with Marissa, who is disengaged as a reader but has recently shown an interest in castles and knights. We plan to introduce her to a selection of nonfiction books that would interest her. We also intend to meet with Doug. He doesn't always know what to do when he is stuck in his reading. We plan to show him several strategies for understanding difficult text.

We continually observe, and talk and listen to the children in our class. We watch them during independent reading and in small- and large-group lessons. We listen in on conversations. We consider the needs of each of our students and find patterns for new groups, and the cycle continues. Our thinking in response to what we know about our students is what helps us plan for short-term instruction and long-term teaching. We recognize what skills we can teach quickly and what strategies will take more time for our readers to develop, and we always have a clear picture of where we are going with our teaching in response to what we know about our children as readers.

We want our conferences to be worthwhile for our students, so we begin with goal-setting conferences. Asking students their insights about their reading and sharing the things we've noticed is always a powerful way to begin our yearlong conversations. We also want our students to go off and have the scaffolds necessary to work on their goal. With the ease of technology, we've used Google Apps for many of these things. Most recently, our students log their reading on a Google Form. We also keep conference notes on a Google Doc that can be shared with each individual child. In this way, the purpose of the conference is transparent and the transfer to independence is smoother.

What Instruction Does the Child Receive?

We often get overwhelmed by the management issues involved in grouping. We worry that all students aren't in a group or that we don't meet individually with one child as often as another. We need to think of our planning from the individual student's eyes. When we plan for whole-group, small-group, and individual instruction, we try to think about what each child will experience. How will his or her week look?

For example, we have decided that Sarah will benefit from all whole-group lessons. She has difficulty choosing books, and the mini-lessons dedicated to this will support her in her book choice. She will also benefit from the conversations in our read-aloud sessions. Even though these group lessons don't necessarily meet her immediate needs, they will support her as she becomes more sophisticated as a reader. Sarah will be part of a small group, but not part of individual conferences. This will guarantee that she has time each day to read independently. Sarah's days, planned this way, seem very balanced.

Anthony, too, will benefit from the whole-class lessons. The read-aloud could be powerful for him, and the book choice lessons will help him meet his own goal. Although he is not in a small group and we will meet with him only once this week, Anthony is at a point in his reading where we know he will spend his independent time well. He will have long periods of time each day to read independently. Because he isn't in a group or many individual conferences this week, we will make sure to pay close attention to his talk and his writing during whole-class lessons to determine what his next needs may be. Then we may put him in a group to help him meet the new need.

A Close-Up Look at Instructing a Skill in Whole-Class, Small-Group, and Individual Settings: Rereading for Understanding

One of the skills we want all of our students to develop is the ability to reread for understanding. Good readers reread, but they don't just read a passage again—they read it differently if they are to gain a deeper understanding. Regie Routman writes that "rereading is the strategy that is most useful to readers of all ages. When given opportunities to reread material, readers' comprehension always goes up. And research consistently shows that rereading is one of the most highly recommended strategies for struggling readers. Yet, we rarely teach rereading as a primary strategy" (2003, 122).

Students will use rereading as a strategy throughout the school year. It will come up in whole-group, small-group, and individual conversations. We use our first lessons on rereading to define it for our students and to give

Books That Invite Rereading

Sam and Dave Dig a Hole by Mac Barnett
The Skunk by Mac Barnett
The Summer My Father Was Ten by Pat Brisson
Voices in the Park by Anthony Browne
Walk On! by Marla Frazee
How to Heal a Broken Wing by Bob Graham
Annie and the Old One by Miska Miles
Emma's Rug by Allen Say
Stranger in the Mirror by Allen Say
The Wretched Stone by Chris Van Allsburg
The Other Side by Jacqueline Woodson

them the opportunity to see the power that it has. Because it is important for the whole class to have the same definitions and expectations for rereading, we always do the first several lessons on rereading with the entire class. Even students who reread successfully need to be made aware that this strategy will help them when they get to an unfamiliar genre and challenging text. We are also always on the lookout for books that encourage rereading. These are books in which a great deal of thinking is left up to the reader, books that don't end with a note of finality, so that when we finish them, we still have lots of questions. *Emma's Rug* by Allen Say is the perfect book to use to teach students the power of rereading.

Understanding That Rereading Is Reading Differently

We might introduce the whole class to the concept of rereading through a read-aloud that includes focused writing and discussion. When we read *Emma's Rug* to Franki's fourth-grade class, we read it aloud three times. Before we read it the first time, we told the students that we would be reading it to them several times. We told them that this was a book that could be more deeply understood by rereading. We wanted them to feel the power of rereading for themselves, and to record some changes in their thinking in their reading notebooks as they reread the story.

On the first read, the students enjoyed the book, but were frustrated at the end because of all the questions they still had. After the first reading, we asked them to respond in their reading notebooks in any way they wished. On the second day of this series of lessons, we asked our students to think about a place in the book that they wished they understood better. Blair said, "The thing that I didn't get was when she went outside and saw all her paintings and then the next day she started drawing again." Before we began to reread the book aloud, we asked the students how they would read (or listen) differently the second time. Blair wrote, "I'll be listening by thinking more creatively. I think she was imagining the drawings she drew before and that reminded her how fun it was to do art." After the second reading, Blair wrote, "This time, I actually saw the drawings all over the lawn and got to understand it better."

The children's responses were diverse. It was evident that they were beginning to understand the power of rereading. Shea mentioned that when we read the story the first time, he was anticipating the end of the book. Since he now knew how the book ended, he could listen for other things. Tessa talked about how she wanted this time to focus only on those things dealing with the rug, since that was an important part of the book. The children also talked together about the story, so that they could learn from others' thinking. On the third day, we again asked them to use their notebooks to think about the way they would read (or listen) differently. (See Figure 5.5.)

Rereading a book like *Emma's Rug* helps students understand that readers often have a different focus or purpose each time they reread. If we don't teach our students to stop before they reread and think about how the second or third reading will be different from the first, they may never find success in rereading. The power of rereading is in reading *differently*. *Emma's Rug* is a good anchor lesson for rereading. Throughout the year, when our students talk about reading again and reading differently, they often refer to *Emma's Rug*.

Another book that we use when introducing the idea of the power of rereading is *Walk On!* by Marla Frazee. At first glance, this is a simple story about a baby learning to walk. It is a fun read that children enjoy. Because we want students to know that often, when we notice new things in a reread, we have new information from the author that helps us understand more deeply, we begin our reread by noticing the dedication page, which says, "to my son, Graham, off to college." With this new noticing, we can read the book with new eyes and realize that the author is writing about more than a baby learning to walk. Rather she might be writing about becoming more independent at many stages in life. This is a great book with which to introduce the power of rereading for a deeper understanding, because every decision the author makes has the potential to add to our thinking as readers.

At other times during the year, to support rereading during independent reading time, we might pull volunteers together into a group. We would look for students like Anthony, who we know is already rereading to support his reading—he told us that when he starts reading each day, he rereads the last page from the previous day. To form the group, we would ask which students find that rereading really helps them. This past year, a group of four volunteers met to discuss rereading. At the first meeting, the students chatted informally about rereading. They talked about the times rereading was helpful to them

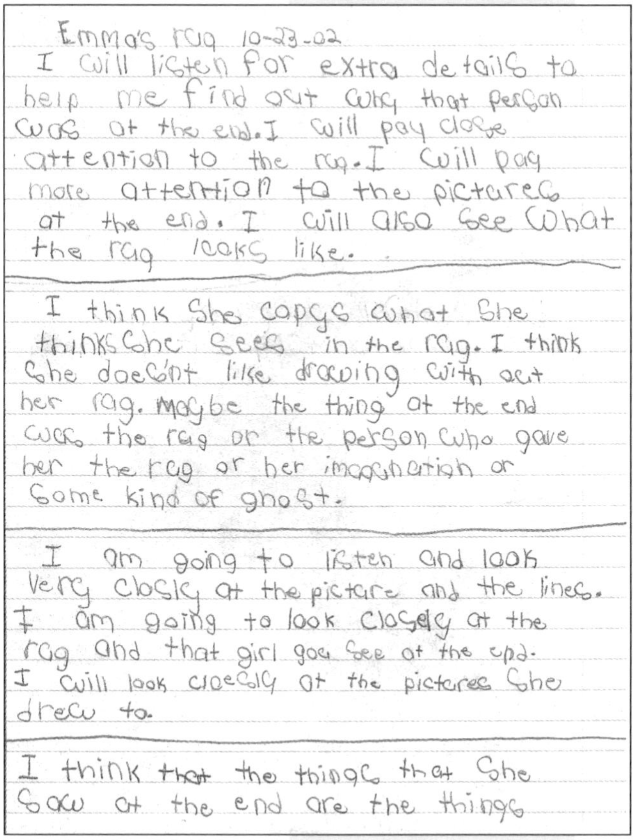

Figure 5.5
Casey tracks the changes in his thinking as he reads and rereads *Emma's Rug* by Allen Say.

Rereading with a Read-Aloud

Sometimes, instead of choosing a new book, we read a book to our class that many of the students have previously read. We use this as an opportunity to teach strategies in rereading. In one class, several of the students had already read *Holes* by Louis Sachar before we read it to them. We met with these students before we started the book and asked them how this time might be different for them. Just as we did with *Emma's Rug*, we asked these readers to think about how they would read or listen differently based on questions they had after they had read it on their own. We charted their responses to remind them of what they could do while experiencing the book for a second time:

Pay attention to details.
Try to answer questions that weren't answered.
Try to understand parts we didn't get.
Listen for things we missed the first time.
Listen to the end—there was so much information in it.
Listen for any clues we missed leading to the surprise at the end.

and times it wasn't. Sam said that rereading was helpful when he found he had read something too quickly. Brooke mentioned that she often rereads to find evidence in the text that she may have missed. Casey said that rereading did not often help him when he got to names he couldn't pronounce.

Then we gave each group member six arrow-shaped sticky notes (these can be purchased at office supply stores; they are often used when signatures are required on documents). We asked the students to keep the sticky notes handy as they read over the next several days. We asked them to mark the places in their book where they reread so they could share them with the group.

The group met again about a week later to share what they had discovered:

- Sam said that he caught himself rereading a nonfiction book, *Ancient Rome* by Simon James. He read something that surprised him, so he reread the passage to make sure he had read it correctly.
- Brooke reread a line from *Mick Harte Was Here* by Barbara Park that didn't make sense to her. She reread the line and thought about the way the words were put together to figure out what the sentence meant.
- Kelsey reread the first page of the second chapter of a book about an animal hospital, because a new character was being introduced on that page. She had thought that the entire book would be about one character and then realized that a new character was going to be introduced in each new chapter.
- Casey reread a few pages of *Lewis and Clark* by George Sullivan when he started reading one day. He had not picked up the book for a few days and had forgotten what had happened. He read the previous few pages again to remind himself.

To encourage the rest of the class to begin using rereading as a strategy, we asked these four students to share their experiences with the class. Each child also made a small poster about his or her rereading for a class bulletin board. Other students in the class would add to the board as they found instances when rereading was helping them.

After this group shared their rereading experiences, we asked if there were any students in the class who thought they weren't very good at rereading for understanding and could benefit from a group on rereading. Five students joined the group and began learning how to reread independently. (Sarah would benefit from joining a group on rereading; it might help her learn to reread to keep track of characters.)

Individual Conferences

Glen approached Franki a few days after he started to read *Castle in the Attic* by Elizabeth Winthrop. He realized that the character of Mrs. Phillips kept coming up in the story and he didn't really know who she was. He said, "She keeps being mentioned a lot and I think that she is going to be an important character. I can't figure out who she is." Obviously, Glen had missed some of the clues in what he had read that would have told him who Mrs. Phillips was. After Glen and Franki had talked a bit, Franki gave him a stack of sticky notes and asked him to reread, looking for any mention of Mrs. Phillips—clues about the character. She asked him to meet with her the following day to discuss what he had figured out. Glen went back to his independent reading and marked sentences such as "Mrs. Phillips was waiting for William at the kitchen door" and "Mrs. Phillips had been with William's family since he was born." During the conference the following day, Franki and Glen read through all of the marked text and inferred that Mrs. Phillips was the housekeeper in the story. Because Glen had been part of whole-group instruction about rereading, he understood the power of rereading. But his need was specific to his situation. For Glen to understand the book he was reading, he needed some support and scaffolding. This conference gave Glen a reason to use rereading for a specific purpose—a strategy that will help him with this book as well as future books.

Even when there were no specific lessons on rereading for the whole class or in small groups, rereading continued to be part of classroom conversations in read-aloud sessions, mini-lessons, and small groups. It is easy to build on conversations about rereading when the whole class has been involved in them. Throughout the year, we can add to the list of reasons students may find rereading helpful.

The decisions we make about whole-group, small-group, and individual instruction are challenging. If we want our students to know themselves and their needs, we need to get them in a variety of groupings. We have often found that students who are quiet in whole-class conversations come to life in a small group. Others are more comfortable in one-on-one settings. By thinking through individual students' needs, looking for patterns among students, and planning accordingly, teachers can enable students to benefit from a variety of instruction.

So Many Skills, So Little Time

There is only so much time in a school year. We constantly struggle with deciding how best to use that time so that our students can fulfill the expectations of the grade-level standards and meet the mandated standards for student achievement. Regie Routman reminds us to make every moment in the classroom count. She writes, "When I suggest that we need to 'teach with a sense of urgency' I'm not talking about teaching prompted by anxiety but rather about making every moment in the classroom count, about ensuring that our instruction engages students and moves them ahead, about using daily evaluation and reflection to make wise teaching decisions.

Complacency will not get our students where they need to be. I am relaxed and happy when I am working with students, but I am also mindful of where I need to get them and how little time I have in which to do it. I teach each day with a sense of urgency" (2003, 41).

It is tempting to make a list of all the concepts and skills that our students need to learn and check them off as we teach them. But these strategies are complex, and we expect our students to use them all their lives. We can't expect children to be able to use these strategies independently, without support, after just a few lessons. As teachers, we work to design whole-class, small-group, and individual experiences that model and scaffold our students' learning and give them the time they need to develop independence.

Threads of Learning Throughout the Year

When we focus on a few critical threads of learning throughout the year, our teaching becomes more purposeful. If we want our students to become life-long readers who are proficient readers who are also joyful readers, we must create conversations that go beyond tests and mandates. We want students to move beyond the words on the page and to develop a deeper understanding of what they read. We want our students to have thoughtful conversations with others about what they read. We want them to be strategic readers who are well aware of their own challenges in making sense of texts and to develop a reader identity that will carry them through the rest of their reading lives. Our goal is to build on previous reading experiences and to help students read a variety of genres and more complex texts with deeper understanding. We feel it is important that these ideas be more than a unit of study and instead build through the entire school year. The following threads of learning provide a focus for our teaching throughout the year.

Conversations and Writing That Grow Thinking

In her book *The Art of Teaching Reading*, Lucy Calkins says, "The mark of a good book talk is that people are not just reporting on ideas they've already had; they are, instead, generating ideas together" (2000, 235). When students are able to use conversations and writing to express their thinking, their understanding deepens. We need to create opportunities for students to talk and write about the books they are reading and their experiences as readers to help them clarify their thinking and support their independence.

Intentional Reading Choices Throughout the Year

Students who know themselves well are more capable of choosing books, knowing when texts are easy or difficult, monitoring their comprehension, and sustaining their reading. When we help them become aware of who they are as readers, the skills, strategies, and behaviors that they learn will be applied to their independent reading.

Reading Complex Texts

Students will continue to experience texts that are difficult for a variety of reasons throughout their lives. As our students grow as readers, fiction and nonfiction texts will become more complex, and we want our students to have the skills to deal with them. The texts may be complex because of the topic, the writing style, or the genre. They may be complex because the reader cannot concentrate because of something else going on in his or her life. The types of texts that are difficult for a reader will change as they become familiar with the complexities in text. We can scaffold learning experiences for our students that support their reading of fiction and nonfiction. Our goal is for students to have the skills to recognize when text is hard for them and to be able to use strategies to construct meaning from the text.

The Role of Close Reading in Grades 3–6

If our students can defend their thinking about their reading by using evidence from the text, they will be able to think through most texts. Because students in grades 3–6 often have been exposed to reading strategy instruction, providing evidence asks them to go a step further. We want our students to know how and when close reading will help them understand and deepen thinking. Often readers change their thinking as they read because of new information they find in the text. When readers make predictions and inferences, synthesize, or analyze, evidence from the text will give them confidence and a stronger identity as a reader.

The remainder of the book focuses on these threads of learning. These threads are anchors in our classrooms throughout the school year in whole-class, small-group, and individual instruction.

Finding Themes: "The Summer My Father Was Ten"

http://sten.pub/sltr2

Franki works with a small group during a discussion about theme.

Part 2
Threads of Learning Throughout the Year

Chapter 6

Read Aloud to Foster Writing and Conversations That Grow Thinking

Listening is the foundation of conversation and it requires that we are open to the possibility of changing our thinking. A turn and talk is not simply an opportunity to say what you have to say and allow someone else to do the same.

—Peter Johnston

In the middle of the year, Franki's fourth graders were working on independent research projects. During one of the mini-lessons, Franki was modeling on a chart a way for Trent to consider organizing his information about the Eiffel Tower. As she wrote on the chart, she wasn't sure how to spell "Eiffel." She asked Trent, who started with "I–F–E–." Franki said, "I think it starts with an *E*. Can you check it somewhere?" Several other students working nearby piped in, saying, "No, I'm pretty sure it's an *I* at the beginning." Franki asked Trent to find it in a book so they could write it correctly on the chart. The other children continued to insist that the word started with an *I*. Thinking that this was a great time for a quick impromptu lesson on how one's life experiences can inform one's literacy, Franki said, "You know, I am pretty sure it starts with an *E*. I read about the Eiffel Tower quite a bit because I took French for five years." Chris said, "Yeah, but how long ago was *that*?" Amused, Franki realized just how comfortable her students had become in conversations with her about reading and writing.

We are all learners in the classroom, working together to extend our thinking and learn from the conversations we have with one another. These conversations help our students reshape what they know about themselves as readers and give them the opportunity to develop the skills they need to become more competent readers. Writing in response to their reading experiences helps students clarify their thinking, develop new ideas, and recognize their unique qualities as readers. We can develop daily whole-class instruction to support and extend students' reading in a variety of ways through conversation and writing.

Rethinking Whole-Class Books and Read-Aloud

There are times when it is important for the whole class to read the same text because this common reading experience provides opportunities for shared conversations. However, we have never found a book that was the right match for every reader in the classroom at the same time. Although a book may be a good fit for most of the students in the class, it will probably be too difficult for a few or too easy for some. Also, reading a book together takes a huge amount of classroom time and often cuts into independent reading time, when each reader can have a more appropriate text. Rather than asking students to read the same book, we can better meet the needs of a wide spectrum of readers through read-aloud. When our students are engaged in whole-class lessons, small-group discussions, and read-aloud, reading whole-class books together isn't a necessary part of our reading time.

In the past few years, we have revised the way we use our read-aloud time to meet the needs of a wider range of readers in our classroom. We knew that reading aloud to children is engaging and is often a favorite activity of both students and teachers, so we wanted to develop ways to use our read-aloud time even more effectively. We never want to change the feel of read-aloud time—we always want our students to approach read-aloud expecting to listen to a great story in a relaxed setting. Surprisingly, we have found that when we want the children to learn something specific during read-aloud time, and when we stop to chat and listen to them throughout our reading of the book, they are even more engaged than they were before we put an instructional twist on read-aloud. Conversations and writing during read-aloud time draw our students deeper into the story and promote more thoughtful reflection and response. We no longer view read-aloud as just the time after lunch when we can get our students quiet and ready for the afternoon. We also don't worry about choosing books that are above their independent reading level to help them build their listening vocabulary. Our goals for read-aloud are much different now.

In her book *Reconsidering Read-Aloud*, Mary Lee Hahn writes, "Each book is thoughtfully chosen to support the skills the students are acquiring in their own reading, their own writing, or their own thinking and learning" (2002, 3). Because sustaining comprehension and interest throughout an entire book is often a challenge for students at this age, read-aloud time is a great way to model and teach the strategies that promote persistence and stamina.

Now that we are more aware of the possibilities of read-aloud, we select books differently. We still want to choose books that represent the best in literature, but we also consider the match between the book and what our students need. We no longer choose books for the entire year before school begins. How can we? We know books well, and we think ahead of time about those that would make good read-alouds. However, we also watch and listen to our students, because when we recognize what will help them become better readers, we are in a position to choose the best books for reading aloud.

Encouraging children to talk and write or to interject a thought or a question during a read-aloud session is often unfamiliar to them. Of course, when we first decided that talk might be an important feature to add to our read-aloud time, it was new to us, too! We knew that we wanted to have student-directed conversations, but we didn't realize how much patience it would take on our part. We were used to a relatively peaceful, after-lunch read-aloud, when we read and the children listened. Making changes required us to set the stage at the beginning of the year to allow thoughtful talk during read-aloud time.

For the first several weeks of school, we often choose short novels to read aloud to students. We look for novels that will not take long to read but will encourage students to think and talk about layers of meaning. Choosing several short novels instead of one longer one helps students learn the routines of read-aloud with a variety of engaging texts. By the end of the first few weeks, the children have shared several novels. These early experiences with read-aloud and the books they know in common will be important throughout the year.

> **Titles from Series We've Read in the First Months of the School Year**
>
> *Heroes in Training: Zeus and the Thunderbolt of Doom* by Joan Holub
> *Shelter Pet Squad: Jelly Bean* by Cynthia Lord
> *Ranger in Time: Rescue on the Oregon Trail* by Kate Messner
> *Galaxy Zack: Hello, Nebulon!* by Ray O'Ryan
> *The Time Warp Trio: Knights at the Kitchen Table* by Jon Scieszka
> *The Quirks: Welcome to Normal* by Erin Soderberg
> *Lulu and the Brontosaurus* by Judith Viorst

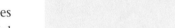

Students sit in a circle during read-aloud to better facilitate conversation.

Short Novels That Promote and Invite Great Conversations

Francine Poulet Meets the Ghost Raccoon by Kate DiCamillo
The Tiger Rising by Kate DiCamillo
Half a Moon Inn by Paul Fleischman
Fig Pudding by Ralph Fletcher
Stone Fox by John Reynolds Gardiner
Because of Anya by Margaret Peterson Haddix
Everything on a Waffle by Polly Horvath
A Dog Called Homeless by Sarah Lean
A Handful of Stars by Cynthia Lord
Waiting for Magic by Patricia MacLachlan
Firefly Hollow by Alison McGhee
How to Steal a Dog by Barbara O'Connor
Tiger Boy by Mitali Perkins
Van Gogh Café by Cynthia Rylant

Although some of what we teach during read-aloud is planned because we have anticipated what will come up in the books we read, conversations and insights are often spontaneous. Once, when students were previewing *Because of Winn-Dixie* by Kate DiCamillo for a read-aloud, they were confused by the use of the word "melancholy" on the front flap of the book. Some of the students thought it meant "sad times," whereas others thought it meant "good times." They reread the sentence that used the word: "And ultimately, Opal and the preacher realize—with a little help from Winn-Dixie, of course—that while they've both tasted a bit of melancholy in their lives, they still have a whole lot to be thankful for." After rereading the sentence, many of the students noticed the word "still" and recognized that it was an important word to use when inferring the meaning of "melancholy" in this sentence. We didn't plan for this conversation, but we made time for it when it came up.

During read-aloud, we often stop at the end of a chapter or at some other natural stopping point and give students time to reflect and jot down their thinking. At other times, we ask students to chat with the classmates next to them before they write. Students are usually free to respond in a way that makes sense for them. However, we often ask them to respond to questions and thoughts such as these:

What new information did you learn about the character in that scene?
Did you change your thinking at all during this chapter?
Where do you think the author is going with this story?
What questions do you have?
What did the author do in his or her writing to make us feel like this?
What would you have done if you were the character in this scene?

Figure 6.1 shows some examples of students' responses during read-aloud.

Scaffolds for Read-Aloud

We usually start the year with very few scaffolds in place for the writing and talk around read-aloud. We want to observe our students to see which, if any, scaffolds they need for talk. We want read-aloud to be worthwhile and accessible for all of our students, and we know this is an important time for our reading community. During this time, our students learn to talk about books, to change their thinking, to track thinking in various ways, and to experience

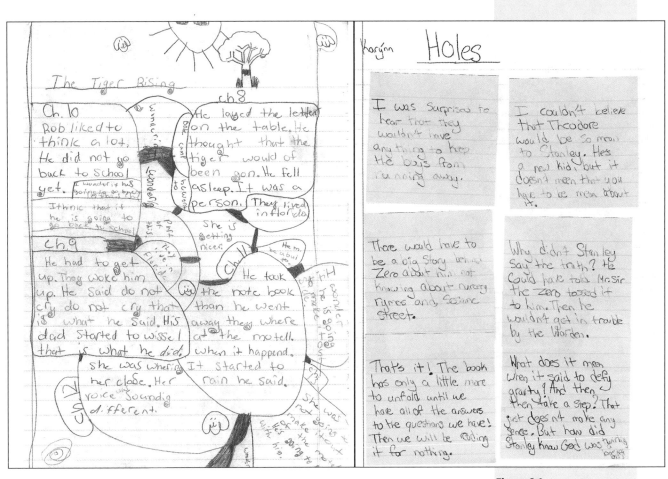

Figure 6.1
Students find many ways to respond in their reading notebooks.

the power of collective thinking around a book. We are not so worried about students understanding a particular book but instead focus on raising the level of talk and thinking across the year.

Small Notebooks

Sometimes a full-size reading notebook is overwhelming for younger students, so when Franki taught third grade, she didn't use the reading notebook as it is described. Instead, she started the school year having students use a very small notebook for read-aloud. Her goal of getting kids in the habit of writing during read-aloud—to keep track of their thinking in various ways—had to start small for a group of kids who hadn't had much experience talking or writing while they read.

Franki gave each child a 2-by-3-inch spiral notebook to use to jot thinking as they read. These mini-notebooks were the perfect way to help students get comfortable with writing without the stress of a big blank page. After a few days, students shared all the ways they were recording their thinking in their mini-notebooks. Franki discovered that they were recording their thinking in

We often use mini-notebooks when we launch read-aloud time. This gives students a way to begin writing about reading without feeling intimidated by a large blank page.

a variety of ways, partly because the size invited an easy way to try some things. After a few weeks, the students were given larger notebooks and transitioned easily.

Anchor Charts

We know that read-aloud is a time for our students to learn to dig deeper into their reading. Eventually, we want students to transfer these strategies to their independent reading. We've found that using anchor charts during read-aloud time is a way to raise the level of conversation and to help students become more independent with the skills we are learning during read-aloud.

As Marjorie Martinelli and Kristine Mraz say on their blog *Chartchums*, "Charts are the footprints of teaching, and all charts gear towards growth mindsets because they say, 'Look, here is a way to do this tricky thing.' They aid in flexibility and persistence, and they foster independence." We often build charts together during read-aloud so that students have access to them during all components of the reading workshop. One recent chart that was used early one year reminded students of all the ways readers think *while* they read. Franki noticed that this particular group of students was confident summarizing and thinking about a book after they had finished it, but they weren't aware of all the ways readers think while they read. This became the focus of their talking for the first several weeks of read-aloud time, and the chart they created together grew as students noticed new ways they were thinking and writing during the story.

Booklet and Preview Pages for Specific Read-Aloud

Sometimes we find that having access to the pages we preview when we start a book is an important tool for students to have while they read the book. Students who are new to longer chapter books often struggle with keeping track of the stories and characters over several weeks. The inside flap, the table of contents, the first page of the story, and other features are all tools readers can use to go back to as needed.

To help students get comfortable using these regularly as they make sense of a story over time, we sometimes give them copies of these preview pages and create a separate small construction paper booklet to accompany a single read-aloud title. For example, one year, Franki had students put together a small notebook for the read-aloud *The Quirks: Welcome to Normal* by Erin Soderberg. Students created the booklet with a copy of the cover, the table of contents, and the first page of the book. Franki also gave them a copy

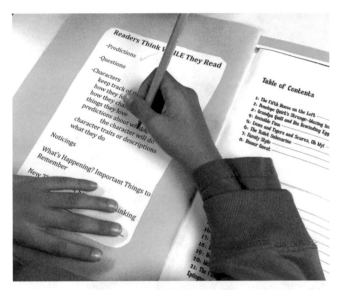

Each student had a place to annotate for a read-aloud of *The Quirks: Welcome to Normal*. The inside cover was a duplicate of a chart we had been creating on how readers think while they read. They also had a copy of the table of contents to refer to when reading. These pages were followed by several blank sheets of paper for jotting down thinking.

To scaffold writing about reading, we often create individual notebooks for a specific read-aloud.

of a chart they had created together about ways readers think while they read. Following these pages were several blank pages for students to jot their thinking. Having these materials at their fingertips scaffolded students as they became comfortable going back and forth from the text to the booklet and back to the text again to clarify their thinking. They could refer to the table of contents to make predictions or use the other features of the small booklet to help them understand what they were reading.

Thinking Partners

Turning to talk to a partner and growing thinking as a result of listening to someone else's thinking is an important skill for our readers. Some groups of students are very comfortable talking to each other, whereas others need some support and practice. We want our students to see not only the power of talk to grow thinking, but the power of talking with a variety of people. We want them to see that different people help us see different things as readers and as learners. We often use some form of a partner chart during the first half of the year to help with this skill.

We find that assigning partners often takes the pressure off students who are not confident enough to find a partner or to talk to someone they don't know well. But we don't want to spend too much time deciding on or assigning partners. Franki has a board in her room titled "Who are you thinking with today?" The board has individual photos of all the kids in the classroom so she can quickly manipulate them to form partners and groups.

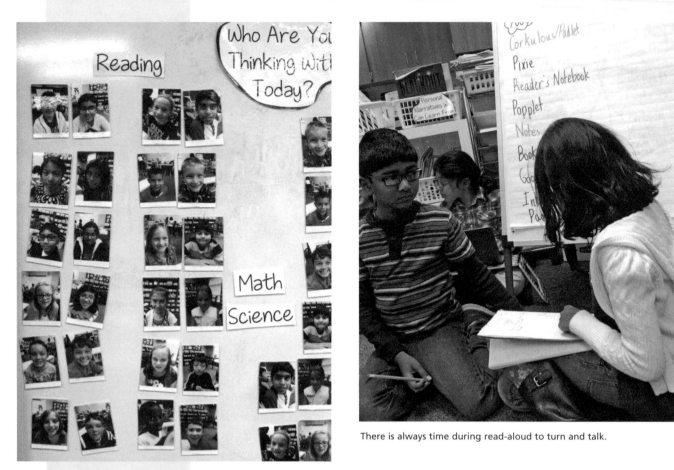

We want students to have experience thinking and talking with a variety of people. This magnetic board helps with that.

There is always time during read-aloud to turn and talk.

Early in the year, Franki will set up partners before read-aloud time and say, "Make sure when you find a seat today that you're sitting with your partner," and kids can glance at the board on their way to the floor. These partnerships can be short term or long term. By having this routine, we find that students focus more on the talk than on who their partner is. And they get comfortable learning from and with everyone in the class.

Copy of the Book/Various Ways to Track Thinking

We love reading notebooks, but we also want students to be flexible and intentional with the tools they use to track thinking while they read. To scaffold the various ways in which readers can record their thinking, we often get multiple copies of the read-aloud book and invite students to use sticky notes to track it right in the book. We also invite readers to use their devices to track thinking so that they experience the power of different tools. Our students have had success with digital tools such as Popplet, Padlet, and Corkulous.

Instruction during read-aloud time is really focused chat. We choose books to read aloud that inspire children to think deeply and respond orally during reading. Richard Allington has noted that class-room talk is critical to reading instruction: "The class-room talk we observed was more often conversational than interrogational. Teachers and students discussed ideas, concepts, hypotheses, strategies, and responses with one another" (2002, 744). Read-aloud time is the perfect place to begin this type of talk. Although students often use sticky notes or reading notebooks to record their thinking, there are no tests or paper-and-pencil responses here—only a focused discussion to address things that we think will help move kids forward in their reading. The discussions in read-aloud provide a foundation for more thoughtful independent reading.

Together the class created a chart of annotation tools and the ways each tool supports readers differently.

We used to try to align our read-aloud books with the content we were studying. We still do that when possible. For example, when we teach life science, the book *Handle with Care: An Unusual Butterfly Journey* by Loree Griffin Burns seems a perfect fit because it ties into our unit of study and at the same time allows us to teach skills our students need for understanding nonfiction, such as finding the most important information in the text. However, this kind of match isn't usually possible. For example, there isn't always a book for read-aloud that matches reading skills students need at the time with the study of our city's history. And we don't want to have our reading goals take a backseat to our content goals.

Choosing Books for Read-Aloud

People often ask us which books we read aloud or ask us for a suggestion for their own classroom. As much time and energy as we put into planning our read-alouds, we rarely know for certain which book we'll read next until a few days before we begin. Much of our read-aloud work is building conversations over time. We have to see where the conversations go and respond to student need with each read-aloud choice.

Instead of planning out our read-alouds for the year, we try to build a menu of books that seem to be a match for the age and the standards we are teaching. For example, building toward longer books, following plot, and analyzing characters are important skills for third graders. We read a variety of books and think about whether a particular book will invite conversations related to what is important for our students. This menu of possible read-alouds grows and changes as the year goes on and we see where students go in conversations and writing.

A record of the books we've read together helps us refer to them in our conversations.

If we have copies of the books, students can choose to use one to follow along and/or to comment using sticky notes.

A Year of Read-Aloud

Choosing books for a year of read-aloud is purposeful and intentional. The time of year, the concepts we are trying to teach, and what we know about our students all play a role in choosing books throughout the school year. Here are the books Franki chose one year.

Franki always starts the year with a few very short books so that she can get a sense for the way students think and talk while they read the book together. *Lulu and the Brontosaurus* by Judith Viorst is the first in a series and a fun read. Setting the stage with the sense that read-aloud is a fun, happy time is important, so having a fun book with a fun character who changes throughout the story are two reasons she chose this book.

The Meanest Birthday Girl by Josh Schneider is a very short book that requires a great deal of inferring. Franki chose this book to see how the class dealt with inferring and whether they were able to pick up on the message. What she learned about her students helped her make smart choices for read-alouds throughout the year.

Kate DiCamillo is one author Franki tries to include in read-aloud each year. Many of her students read the Mercy Watson books during independent reading early in the year, and she knows they would be able to build on that series when talking about *Leroy Ninker Saddles Up: Tales from Deckawoo Drive*. Franki also wanted to introduce the author as one whose work they would visit again.

Bink and Gollie: Best Friends Forever was the second book by Kate DiCamillo and focuses on the relationship between two characters. Many books that readers will encounter depend on the relationship between two different characters. We could also use this to begin to look for similarities to the other books we'd shared by Kate DiCamillo and discover that even though the two books are very different, there are things we can come to expect from this author. *Chicken Squad: The First Misadventure* by Doreen Cronin was another short read that was also a simple introduction to characters solving a mystery.

Later in the year, it seemed the students were ready for a longer book like *The Quirks: Welcome to Normal* by Erin Soderberg. Keeping track of several characters, keeping track of a plot across a longer book, and using the table of contents to keep track of the story and predict are all possible with this book. Franki knew that this was a series that many kids in the class could read independently as the year progressed.

Sometimes we choose books because our school is having an author visit and we want kids to be familiar with books by the author before he or she arrives. That was the case for *Tuesdays at the Castle* by Jessica Day George. Because the book was a bit difficult for third graders, we front-loaded it with previewing and conversations about what we might expect as readers based on the cover, inside flap, and first few pages. We listened to the audio version of the book because we wanted kids to have a variety of experiences during read-aloud.

The Miraculous Journey of Edward Tulane was the third book written by Kate DiCamillo that Franki chose as a read-aloud. One big understanding that Franki wants students to take away from a year of read-aloud is that we come to books with expectations. Once we've read a few books by an author, we come to expect certain things from him or her and carry them into the book we're currently reading. Franki knew at this point in the year that students were ready for a book with more depth and a bit of sadness, which seemed to make it the best choice for the next read.

El Deafo by Cece Bell is a graphic novel. Franki chose this book for a few reasons. First, it is based on Cece Bell's childhood and is the story of an amazing character. It is also a book that changes readers. Franki wanted her students to experience a graphic novel together and understand the ways in which the words and visuals work together to create a powerful story. They read the Kindle version and used an Airplay tool to project it onto the Smartboard.

The Terrible Two by Mac Barnett and Jory John was another book Franki's class read because one of the authors, Mac Barnett, was coming to their school. The book was brand new when they read it. It was a good choice for this time of year for a few reasons. The class hadn't read much humor. Understanding humor takes a different kind of comprehension. Franki also thought that the two characters gave the class lots to talk about and to build on from their other character conversations.

The Thing About Georgie by Lisa Graff is a book that often changes the conversation in a classroom. After reading *El Deafo*, Franki thought the students were ready to dig into a different character with different struggles and that this read-aloud would be more of a character study than a story. She wanted the conversation to move beyond plot and to focus on changes in the character. Franki knew this book (or any book by Lisa Graff) could do that.

How to Steal a Dog by Barbara O'Connor is a book Franki has used several times. Barbara O'Connor is an author who gives middle grades readers things to think about that do not have easy answers. In this book, the main character, Georgina, makes bad choices for good reasons, and Franki knew those choices would make for good discussion, because there are no right or wrong answers. Franki anticipated that her students would be able to agree and disagree with each other at a higher level than other books allowed.

Rump: The True Story of Rumpelstiltskin by Liesl Shurtliff was the final book of the year. Franki wanted to build on all the thinking students had done as readers throughout the year. See below for the thinking behind this choice.

Choosing *Rump*: Building on a Yearlong Conversation

Franki always struggles as the year comes to an end and she has to choose the final read-aloud of the year. With so many books and so little time, she doesn't want to make a poor choice, because she knows the last read-aloud can be a powerful experience for the students as they bring the year's worth of reading and conversation to the book. Franki uses the following questions when choosing all of the read-alouds but thinks about them more carefully when she knows the year is coming to an end:

- How can this book expand the conversation?
- How can this book help students meet the standards?

- How can this book meet the needs of students at different levels of reading?
- What have we read that they can build on?
- What charts might support good talk?
- Why is this the best "next read"?

After looking at all the options, reading reviews, and talking to colleagues, she decided on *Rump: The True Story of Rumplestiltskin* as the final read-aloud that year. *Rump* is a fabulous fantasy that tells the "true" story of Rumplestiltskin from Rumplestiltskin's perspective. Franki knew students could stretch their thinking when they got a new perspective on a story they knew well. She also knew they'd come to the story with lots of expectations as readers that they could build on. Meeting the standards of character development and perspective while enjoying a great story made this perfect for the last read-aloud.

Charts/The Read-Aloud

As Franki thought about the read-aloud, she planned the prereading days to invite talk that built on where the class had been as a reading community. She wanted kids to think about where they had been as readers and what, because of our experiences, they might expect from the book. Franki also wanted them to do what they always did when starting a new book. She

Before beginning the read-aloud of *Rump*, the class charted the things they expected as readers and the questions they had before they read.

The class also brainstormed Rumpelstiltskin's character traits from earlier reading. Then as they read Rump's perspective, they added new thinking to traits they believed this character possessed.

Strategies to Model, Teach, and Practice During Read-Aloud:
Some Questions to Start Conversations

Previewing: What can you do before you start a book to help you understand it?

Visualizing: What are you picturing in your mind as you read?

Predicting: What do you think will happen next? What in the book makes you think that?

Making connections: What does this remind you of from your own life? How might that help you understand the book better?

Making literature connections: Does this remind you of anything else you've read? How might that help you when you are reading this book?

Seeing character development: What did you learn about the character during this reading? How do you know? How is the character changing?

Sustaining comprehension: What strategies help you remember what you have read? What do you do when you start reading each day?

Noticing literary elements: What do you notice about the way the author wrote the book? What makes it effective?

Recognizing powerful language: What are the powerful words or phrases that the author used? What makes them powerful?

Books to Use in Modeling and Discussing Reading Strategies and Behaviors

Previewing a Book to Gain Information Before Reading

Flying Solo by Ralph Fletcher
Stone Fox by John Reynolds Gardiner
Baby by Patricia MacLachlan
Shiloh by Phyllis Reynolds Naylor

Using the Table of Contents to Support Comprehension Over Time

The Pinky and Rex series by James Howe
The Toothpaste Millionaire by Jean Merrill
The Quirks by Erin Soderberg

Making Personal Connections to Help Readers Understand the Text

26 Fairmont Avenue by Tomie dePaola
Fig Pudding by Ralph Fletcher
Sisters by Raina Telgemeier

Visualizing Settings and Scenes That Are Unfamiliar

The Lion, the Witch, and the Wardrobe by C. S. Lewis
Mrs. Frisby and the Rats of NIMH by Robert C. O'Brien
Tiger Boy by Mitali Perkins
Jack by Liesl Shurtliff
Milo Speck: Accidental Agent by Linda Urban

Understanding Character Development

Poppy by Avi
Circus Mirandus by Cassie Beasley
The War That Saved My Life by Kimberly Brubaker Bradley
Because of Winn-Dixie by Kate DiCamillo
Stella by Starlight by Sharon Draper
The Birthday Room by Kevin Henkes
How to Steal a Dog by Barbara O'Connor

wanted them to think of questions they had before they started it. Finally, Franki wanted to make visible the ways their thinking might change about a character they knew well from previous reading. The class made a list of all the things they knew about Rumplestiltskin on the left side of a two-column chart, knowing they were open to changing their thinking based on hearing the author's perspective. Setting the stage to keep track of their thinking in this way made for an amazing conversation.

When we noticed that most of the children in the class were not previewing books before reading and that this was having a negative effect on their comprehension, we spent more time previewing each read-aloud book before reading it. Franki told her students what happened when she went to see a movie without having seen a preview, commercial, or print ad for it. As a result, she was confused for the first several minutes of the movie, trying to figure out what was going on. Just as a movie preview sets the stage for us to fully understand the movie, explained Franki to her class, book previews do the same for readers. (See Figure 6.2.)

Similarly, when we realized that students were not reading the chapter titles in books to help them predict and comprehend, we chose *The Toothpaste Millionaire* by Jean Merrill to read aloud. The chapter titles are descriptive and provide a clear insight into what each chapter is about. In the course of our read-aloud, as we finished each chapter, we would read the title of the next chapter and ask students to write down their predictions in their reading notebooks.

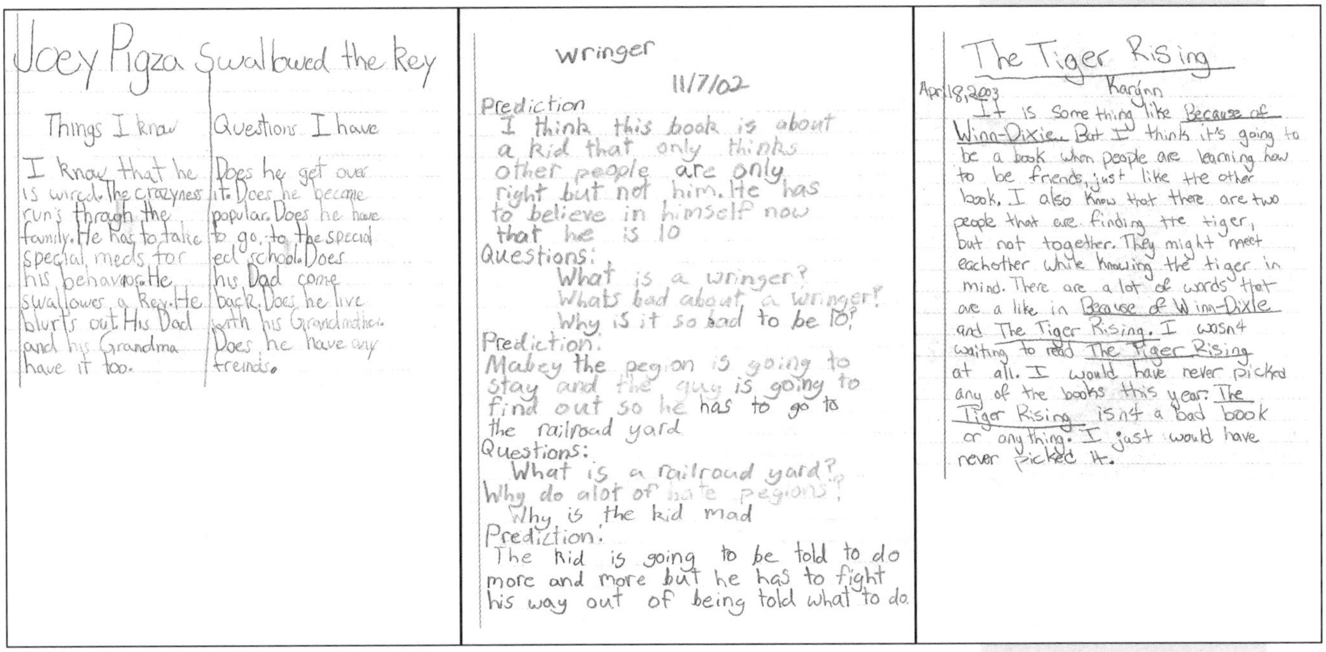

Figure 6.2
Students preview books in a variety of ways.

With the digital tools available to us, we try to do the things with students that we do in our lives as readers when previewing a book. We look at online reviews, watch trailers, visit authors' websites, and so on. Before we begin a new book, we often collect digital sources on a Padlet board to share with students. This can be a "read only" board or we can create a board on which students can share their thinking before they read. For example, we used a board to collect links before reading *The One and Only Ivan* by Katherine Applegate (http://padlet.com/Franki/iressibbreadaloud). During the read-aloud, we added a section of the board dedicated to ways students were writing to better understand and collected photos of student notebook pages about the book.

Many books may be used to support different skills during read-aloud. We want to keep read-aloud relaxed for the children, but we also know that we can get more mileage out of these sessions if we are thoughtful about book choice and the topics of our conversations during read-aloud time.

We use anchor charts with each read-aloud so we can track and grow our collective thinking. In the past several years, we have learned that there are many digital tools that help us support thinking during read-aloud. Corkulous is a digital tool that allows users to manipulate sticky notes and reorganize them as needed. Color coding and various shaped sticky notes also invite a variety of ways to track and make sense of thinking over time. Popplet, another digital tool, allows readers to create a web of ideas. These can be connected and color-coded in various ways. We have found that digital tools give students expanded opportunities for previewing books and annotating while reading.

Students are given the opportunity to use a variety of tools to track their thinking during reading. They can use these tools during read-aloud and independent reading time.

Keeping Track of Characters During Read-Aloud

During our reading of *Holes* by Louis Sachar with fourth graders, we knew how important the relationships between the characters were for understanding the text. In this book, there are really three stories going on at once, and readers need to keep track of the characters in each story. After the first several chapters, the class created two charts. One chart listed the characters at Camp Green Lake, including each character's name, nickname, and general information. A similar chart listed the characters in the story line about Stanley's great-grandfather.

Later, when the class read the chapter telling the story of Kissin' Kate Barlow, they created a third chart listing the characters from that story.

During our read-aloud sessions, we referred to the charts often to remember various characters as they reappeared in the story. The charts served as a way for the class to keep track of the characters and, later, to see the connections between characters in the three stories. After this activity, many students found other ways to keep track of characters in their reading notebooks (see Figure 6.3).

Figure 6.3
Chris, Trent, Tessa, and Ben each found a way to keep track of the characters in *Holes*.

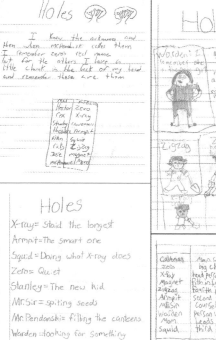

We referred to these character charts during our reading of *Holes*.

Conversations During One Read-Aloud

Franki decided to read *Because of Winn-Dixie* by Kate DiCamillo early one January. The class had just finished *Wringer* by Jerry Spinelli and was ready for the writing style of a different author. Franki's students were beginning to realize that there are layers of meaning in books, and she knew *Because of Winn-Dixie* would help them dig deep into the text for meaning. One of her goals was to have students pay attention to the powerful language that Kate DiCamillo uses in the book. Franki knew the children would also bring their own ideas to their conversations about the book.

Early in the reading, Franki began to write some of the more powerful phrases from the book on chart paper. Often these phrases were used to help the group begin their talk. Students were thus made to see that another way to respond to text is to think about the most powerful lines in a story, and that the most powerful words are those that provoke strong feelings in the reader.

The students had several questions early in the book. They wondered why the author had chosen the title she had. They wondered whether Opal's mother would come back. They wondered why Opal called her father "the preacher." Students returned to these three major questions throughout their reading of the text.

As students wondered why the book was called *Because of Winn-Dixie*, many of the story's themes emerged in their conversations. Students did not, however, realize that they were discussing what are known as "themes": the chart they created listed "things that keep coming up in the book." The list included friendship, losing things, holding on to things you love, sorrow and sadness, and Opal's mother coming back. Each day after read-aloud, the class referred to the chart to see if these themes were still strong parts of the story.

In the beginning chapters of the book, Opal refers to her father's "turtle shell." She mentions it again a few chapters later. The students picked up on the term. They predicted that the image would come up again as they kept reading. The students started another chart to keep track of the lines where Opal's father was compared to a turtle in his shell.

Throughout their reading of the book, Franki listened to her students for conversations that would lead to deeper understanding and revisited them in the days that followed. By charting their ideas, students were able to think in a more focused way about the text. Although Franki didn't take control of the conversation, she helped her students move the conversations forward and modeled the kind of writing that would clarify their thinking. When Courtney changed her mind and predicted that Opal's mother would not come back, Franki pointed out that this was a change in her thinking and asked Courtney what had caused her to change her mind. Because she had recorded her thinking in her notebook, Courtney could go back and track her thinking and the way it had changed. When Kevin noticed that each chapter could be its own short story, Franki asked the class to think about what ideas held the chapters together.

After the read-aloud, students focused on one area for written response. Brooke wrote the following:

> The preacher is changing. The preacher has lost his turtle shell and he doesn't want it back. The preacher used to use it all the time. He didn't want to lose it. The preacher has let his turtle shell go and has pulled himself back together. He used to not want to talk about things that had to do with Opal's mom or something sad until Winn-Dixie gave him a smile and sneezed and changed his life. The preacher has really changed. He has made it through the dark and finally found his first bit of light. The preacher and Opal weren't connected yet. There was a missing piece and Winn-Dixie fit perfectly. They just needed someone to show them the way out of the darkness. The preacher and Opal are connected now all because of Winn-Dixie.

Peter wrote this response:

> I thought Winn-Dixie made a big change in Opal's life. Now I think it was Opal herself who made the change. Winn-Dixie helped her on the way. First of all, it was Winn-Dixie who found Gloria Dump, but it was Opal who made friends with her. And, it might be Winn-Dixie who got Opal and Miss Franny Block together, but it was Opal who got to know her. Winn-Dixie brought everyone together, but Opal kept them together.

Figure 6.4
Kelly understood *The Tiger Rising* at a higher level.

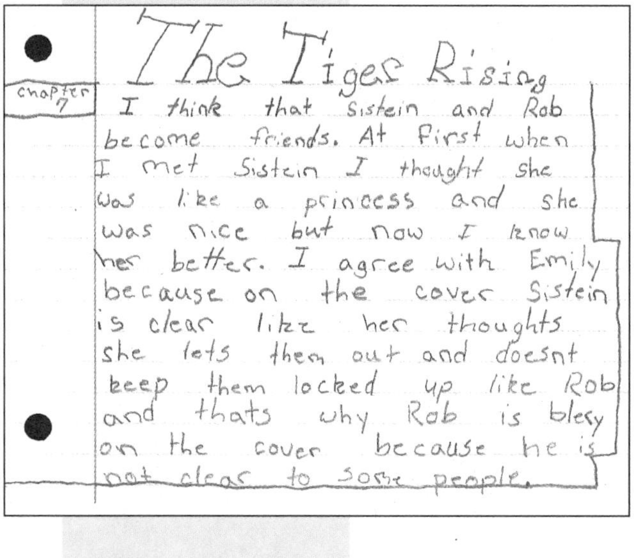
The Tiger Rising

Chapter 7

I think that Sistein and Rob become friends. At First when I met Sistein I thought she was like a princess and she was nice but now I know her better. I agree with Emily because on the cover Sistein is clear like her thoughts she lets them out and doesnt keep them locked up like Rob and thats why Rob is blesy on the cover because he is not clear to some people.

It was clear that these children understood the text at a deep level. Their conversations and daily jotting supported their thinking and helped them do what most of them could not have done on their own. By providing several experiences like this throughout the year, we helped our students move forward so that they could begin to read deeply on their own.

Conversations that are part of the classroom environment clarify children's thinking. As students sit side by side and talk about what they are reading, they learn about themselves and they learn from the thinking of other readers. An interactive classroom that promotes conversation can provide opportunities for our students to raise the level of their thinking, to dig deep into texts, and to grow as readers. (See Figure 6.4.)

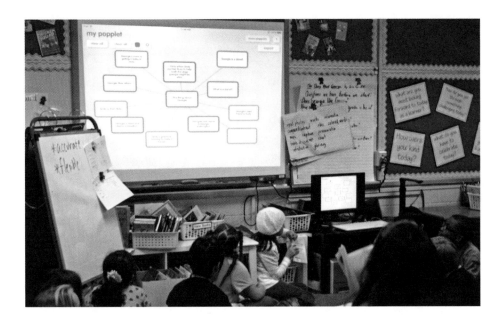

A shared Popplet helps students track and organize thinking about the read-aloud *The Thing About Georgie* by Lisa Graff.

We take every opportunity to make connections between thinking and writing. Our students use their reading logs to record their responses to the texts they read and what they discover about their own reading. Charts generated in whole-class lessons or small-group sessions show students that writing can clarify thinking and help us understand what we read.

Conversations and writing are the foundation that supports more sophisticated readers. As our students encounter more texts, they are supported by the conversations we have together and the thinking we generate together as we write. They become more confident and more competent in their reading.

Strategy Lesson

Sketching for Deeper Understanding

■ **Why We Teach It:** Many students are taught the strategy of visualizing before they reach the upper elementary grades. We want to support this strategy as a way for them to comprehend text, and we want to extend it by helping our students see how the text can help them visualize. We know that writing helps our students clarify and extend their thinking. We want them to see that sketching can also help them extend their thinking and better understand what they read.

■ **Possible Anchor Books:** *Holes* by Louis Sachar and Chapter 8 of *Stanley Yelnats' Survival Guide to Camp Green Lake* by Louis Sachar.

■ **How We Teach It:** After a read-aloud of *Holes* by Louis Sachar, we read Chapter 8, "How to Dig a Hole," from *Stanley Yelnats' Survival Guide to Camp Green Lake*, also by Louis Sachar. In this chapter, Stanley describes the steps necessary for digging a hole at Camp Green Lake. After reading the chapter together, we ask students to sketch a picture of someone at Camp Green Lake digging a hole based on Stanley's directions. We ask them to use as much information from the text as possible. When they are finished drawing, we ask them to go back into the text and highlight the phrases or sentences that are represented in their sketch. They can also label those parts on the sketch with the language from the text. (See Figure 6.5.)

Figure 6.5
Sketches based on "How to Dig a Hole"

Strategy Lesson

Talking About Word Choice

■ **Why We Teach It:** Students often encounter words or phrases that are used in a way that they haven't encountered before. Often these phrases are used in a poetic way that helps the reader compare one thing to another. We want our students to recognize them and add this as a way to talk about text during read-aloud time.

■ **Possible Anchor Books:** *Creatures of Earth, Sea, and Sky*, a collection of poems by Georgia Heard (and then possibly taking the conversation to the read-aloud discussion).

■ **How We Teach It:** Our favorite poems for teaching this lesson are from Georgia Heard's *Creatures of Earth, Sea, and Sky*. The poems in this book are not difficult to read, but they are great examples to use in introducing students to descriptive language and words used in new ways. We often start with the poem "Dragonfly." After reading and enjoying the poem together, we ask students to find words that the author used in different or surprising ways. We look at each of the words and reread parts of the poem to determine what the author meant by using the word or phrase. Then we carry that conversation to our read-aloud book. We often teach this lesson while we are reading a book by an author such as Kate DiCamillo or Ralph Fletcher who uses words in poetic ways.

■ **Follow-Up:** Using Heard's poems allows us to begin to talk with our students about how authors use words in new ways. Our students will encounter words and phrases used in unfamiliar ways in all genres. We are always on the lookout for fiction and nonfiction texts in which authors use language in interesting ways. We continue our conversation about word use throughout the year.

■ ■ ■

Previewing and Read-Aloud: *Greetings from Nowhere*

http://sten.pub/sltr3

A class of third and fourth graders previews the new read-aloud, *Greetings from Nowhere* by Barbara O'Connor.

Chapter

7

Intentional Reading Choices Throughout the Year

When a child brings us a book they've chosen, glance at the book, but then look into the child's eyes. If there is a light there, a proud joy of ownership, do whatever you can to keep it lit and not snuff it out.

—Cynthia Lord

Years ago, during the Harry Potter craze, we read an article written by Janette Barber (2001), who was a Harry Potter fanatic. She mentioned how upset she was because she had to wait so long for the next Harry Potter book to be published and how she couldn't imagine life without it. She wrote, "Let me just say at this point that I think certain people, whom I will not name (the writer J. K. Rowling), are very lazy and mean and think only of themselves. What could she possibly be doing? Eating? Shopping? Taking care of her family? These things are simply unimportant stacked up against keeping the world waiting for Harry Potter V" (42–43).

We talk to our students about this article and let them know that as avid readers, we understand Janette Barber's impatience. We let our students know that we too wait eagerly for books to be published. We tell them about the people we rely on to make good book recommendations, and we share our strategies for choosing the books we want to read. We want our students to know what it is like to be part of a reading community whose members talk about the books they are reading, share how they choose the books they will read, and recommend books to each other.

When we first started our reading workshop, we were committed to making sure that children spent time reading. We remember countless times when we'd see our students at the bookshelf, looking for their next book. We would worry about them being "off task" and too often said, "Hurry up and pick a book!" Then we would wonder why they weren't able to stick with the books they had chosen to read. We realized that young readers need to learn how to browse and choose books.

When we thought about our own book shopping, we realized that we spend hours browsing in bookstores and libraries. We look at covers, read book reviews, talk to friends, and read the front flaps and the first pages before choosing books. We get online and read reviews on Goodreads. We ask about it on Twitter. We find blog posts about the books and visit author web pages. Much of the joy of reading is in finding a book that we hope to love or one that we are eager to read. We can't take that part of reading away from our students. We can't expect our students to choose books quickly if we want their choices to be thoughtful or want them to read deeply. We need to give them the time to choose good books as well as the tools and strategies to do so. We value good book choice as much as we value other reading skills.

Book Choice Conversations Throughout the Year

The research base on student-selected reading is robust and conclusive: Students read more, understand more, and are more likely to continue reading when they have the opportunity to choose what they read.
—Richard Allington and Rachael E. Gabriel

We used to teach most of our lessons on book choice at the beginning of the school year. We believed that once our students felt part of a reading community and knew how to choose books, they'd be set for the year. But we've since realized that building community and lessons on book choice should not be limited to the beginning of the school year, because our readers are constantly changing. With each book we read, we learn new things about ourselves as readers. We may discover a new author we love; we may find that we are less interested in our favorite author than we used to be and aren't looking forward to that new book as eagerly as we thought we would. Our students need to know this. They also benefit from thinking about and talking about their shifting tastes as readers throughout the school year. They benefit from connecting with other readers in a variety of ways. We commit time all year to whole-class mini-lessons and individual conferences around these ideas.

We make sure that our students know about people in our lives such as Sally Oddi, owner of Cover to Cover, our favorite children's bookstore in Columbus, Ohio. They know that we try to shop at her store when we know she'll be there because we depend on her

Trying a New Genre

Franki talks to her students about the book *Ender's Game* by Orson Scott Card when she talks to her students about expanding the books they choose because this book changed her thinking about science fiction. Before she read *Ender's Game*, she was certain that she would not enjoy reading science fiction. A friend had recommended the Card book and told Franki that she had not enjoyed science fiction either, until she read the book. Franki took her friend's word for it, fell in love with *Ender's Game*, and went on to read the whole series. This experience taught Franki that she was probably missing some great books because of the limitations she had put on her own book choices; now she is more likely to try something different.

knowledge about books. Our students know that we ask Sally about books we want to read. They know we go to Sally for book recommendations and that we trust her completely when we are looking for books. They also know about friends who recommend books to us. They know we are both part of a Books and Brunch group that meets monthly to enjoy brunch and talk about new books. They know we learn about books from friends on Facebook and Twitter who recommend books. They know we often go to Goodreads to see which books our friends are reading and recommending.

We tell our students that we cut out book reviews from several sources and keep them handy when we go to the bookstore or library to choose a book. We keep lists of books we want to buy or borrow on our phones. We have the library app on our phones so that we can quickly reserve a book we might want to read. Our students know that we pay attention when we hear someone talking about books. We listen to see if there is a book that we might be interested in reading. We recently attended a professional-development workshop, and as people began to enter the room and choose their seats, we noticed that several of them had books with them. As they waited for the workshop to begin, some of them took advantage of the time to read. We are often compelled to talk with someone who is reading, to ask him or her about the book or peek at the cover. We too carry a book with us wherever we go. We make a conscious effort to bring up these reading habits and behaviors in the course of our classroom conversations.

Molly Foglietti has created a bookmark to support recommendations in her third-grade classroom. On the bookmark are the words "Thought of you when I saw this book!" Molly has made several copies of the bookmark, and when she sees a book that she thinks a student of hers might enjoy, she puts a bookmark in it and places it on the child's desk as an invitation to read the book. This is a great way to support student talk around book choice. The bookmark helps Molly model the fun of making individual recommendations to other readers. She also makes the bookmarks available to her students in case they want to recommend titles to other children in the class.

We recently read an article on the Nerdy Book Club blog in which Linda Kay shared a "Read It Forward" idea in which readers were encouraged to pass books along to other readers. Franki shared this article with her students, and they created a "Read It Forward"

Relying on Recommendations

Recently, a friend suggested that Karen read *Bel Canto* by Ann Patchett. During several trips to the bookstore, Karen picked up the book and read the blurb on the back. Every time she did so, she thought it just wasn't the book for her. Karen told her friend several times that she didn't want to read it, but her friend was persistent. She had known Karen for a long time and talked about books with her often, and she was convinced that Karen would like the book. She gave Karen a copy and told her to add it to the stack of books she was going to read, hoping that she would just pick it up and start reading it. Eventually, Karen did read *Bel Canto*—and loved it. Karen tells students that because she trusted this friend for book recommendations, she became convinced that the book would be worth reading.

Kayla fills in a "Read It Forward" bookmark telling a friend why she thinks she'd like the Owl Diaries series.

Mia recommends a book that she's just finished.

bookmark that a reader could leave in a book that he or she had read and wanted to pass along.

Because some books are so popular in the classroom that many students want to read them, Franki also designed a bookmark to keep track of who was "in line" to read the book next. Although this is a great management strategy, it is also another way to connect readers who enjoy similar types of books.

Franki's class also follows some Twitter hashtags such as #5bookFriday, #classroombookaday, and #readergrams to get recommendations from other classrooms that tweet.

We invite colleagues, parents, friends, and former students into our classroom to discuss their own tastes as readers with our students. We want our students to know that different people choose different books, but we also want them to know that most readers have similar strategies for finding books they want to read. Before school vacations we talk about the kinds of books we read when we have more time. We tell our students that sometimes we have a book we've been waiting to read, so we take advantage of the extra time we have during vacation to read it. We tell them that sometimes we save longer books to read when we'll have long stretches of reading time each day. We invite our students to use their reading notebooks to plan their own reading for holiday breaks. (See Figure 7.1.)

Figure 7.1
Julie and Mia plan ahead for their vacation reading.

My Plan for Winter Break

My plan for winter vacation is to read every day except for Christmas eve and christmas day. I'll try to read a lot in the car. I would like to finish the book I'm reading and start reading Walk Two Moons because my sister alread read it and said it was a good book to read. Also I would like to read Santa paws it sounds like a good book to read Or get on the internet for other books. Or I would like to read Fever and the series of Unfortunat Events.

Mia   My plan for x-mas vacation 12/18
1. Things not seen
2. Mick Harte was Here
3. Finish - Fever   My lis of what I
4. Unfortunate events 9 ")   want   to   read
5. Tuck Everlasting
6. Long Journey   - really want
9. Maybe Harry potter 4 ?   to read

I chose these books because I've heard they are really good and people recomended them for me. Especially Unfortunate events 9. I will keep track of what I read I will read I hour.

        I will make a chart

        1┐ 4-5-6┐
       2-3┘   7-8-┐
             9
            1-10┐
              11

Julia packs a bag for reading over winter break.

To keep conversations about book choice going throughout the year, we put up wall displays dedicated to book choice. We continually change and add to the display and place books in the basket by the wall. Posters on the following topics are below the board:

Book reviews
Author news
Recommendations
New books
If you liked_____, you might like . . .
Favorite websites

We sometimes have QR codes linked to many of these boards that take students to the sites with related information.

Kayla makes a QR code poster of book trailers for books she recommends (left).
Students use QR codes to get to various websites and articles for reading (right).

What We Ask Ourselves When Choosing Something to Read

Is it part of a series I've read or that someone has read to me?

Have I read anything else like this?

Did someone recommend it to me?

Do I like the subject?

Has anyone I know read it?

Have I talked to anyone who has read it?

Does the beginning sound good?

Does the back or the inside flap make me want to read it?

Do the visuals engage me in the topic?

Did I judge it by the cover without looking at the rest of the book?

Have I seen the movie?

Can I find out more about it on a website?

Is it by an author I like?

Is it a new book, blog post, or digital piece that I am eager to read?

Did I skim through it?

Does the title sound interesting?

Is it a best seller or an award winner?

How old is it?

Is it a piece I started a long time ago that I want to finish now?

Am I in the mood to try something new?

What genre am I in the mood for?

Am I in the mood for something short or long?

Am I in the mood for something funny or serious?

Am I in the mood for something happy or sad?

Am I in the mood for something easy or difficult?

If it is difficult, am I in the mood to work hard and stick with it?

Courtney chooses a poetry card from the poetry basket.

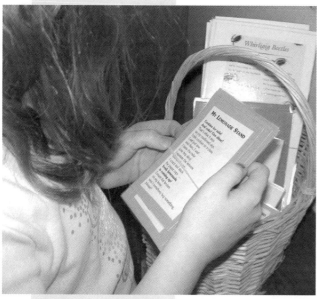

One class of students created a list of questions they ask themselves when choosing a new book (see sidebar). We posted this list in the same area as the posters listed above to support book choice and to remind students of great ways to choose books.

We share all of these experiences with our students so they can build their own circle of people they can turn to for book recommendations they can trust. And we make sure that these conversations happen throughout the school year. As Jackie said after one of these conversations, "It is kind of like when you ask the waiter what is good on the menu. I ask my friends about good books."

Poetry Cards

Poetry anthologies are often overwhelming to our students, so we have created poetry cards to help them choose poems to read. We have a wide selection of poetry anthologies on a shelf in the classroom. We choose an engaging poem from each of the anthologies to showcase for our students. We know that students find it fun to read poetry together, so we make six to eight copies of each poem and mount each copy on colored tagboard. We secure the copies with a rubber band and put them in a basket on top of the poetry shelf. Children can pull out several stacks of poetry cards to read together. On the back of each card we show a copy of the book's cover. Next to the cover is the sentence "If you liked this poem, you might like the other poems in the book _____ by _____." This helps children find a poem they like and then turn to the anthology that it came from for additional poems.

Check It Out! Circles

A Check It Out! Circle is another way to support book choice. We use this activity when we want to highlight a certain author or genre. If we notice that very few students have read a biography, for example, we will organize a Check It Out! Circle to introduce them to some biographies that we hope they will choose to read independently.

Often students have notebooks handy during a Check It Out! Circle so they can write down names of books they'd like to read in the future.

Students browse books in a Check It Out! Circle.

Before we begin a Check It Out! Circle, we collect the same number of books in the genre we are highlighting (such as poetry anthologies, biographies, or short novels) as there are students in the class. Then we have all the children sit in a large circle on the floor. We walk around the circle, give each child a book, and ask them to silently preview their book. After just a minute, we ring a bell and have the children pass the book to the child on their right. We continue doing this until every child has had a chance to look briefly at each book. We limit the amount of time because it gives students just enough time to find something interesting but not enough for them to read the book. As a result, they are often eager to get their hands back on the books that particularly interested them.

After the activity, we usually ask two questions: "Which books did you see that you want to go back to during independent reading time?" and "How did you go about previewing the book in such a short time?" Both of these questions are critical to the success of Check It Out! Circles. When students mention which books they want to revisit, it reminds others of the books they've seen. A Check It Out! Circle encourages conversations about books and reminds children that book choice is unique for each reader. And when we ask students how they checked out each book in a minute or less, everyone learns new ways to preview and choose books.

Book Recommendations

Several times each year, we have days that are dedicated to book recommendations. About a week in advance, we ask students to recall a book they think others in the class would like. We encourage them to think of a book that many students may not know about. Then we ask them to prepare an informal recommendation for the book and be ready to tell the class about it. This is an easy, informal way to encourage children to recommend books to one another. They understand how much more relevant it is to share books that are not well known by classmates. Students sit in a circle with their reading notebooks open to the Books I Want to Read section. When they hear a classmate describe a book they think they might enjoy, they write down the title. This session usually results in some lively discussions, with children asking lots of questions. Early in the year, we ask simple questions to introduce students to the kinds of questions that can help them know whether a book would be good for them—questions like these:

> Did it remind you of any other books we've read?
> Who in the class do you think would enjoy it?

Strategy Lesson

Taking Recommendations from Readers Like You

- **Why We Teach It:** Our reasons for teaching lessons on recommendations are twofold. First, we want students to learn to help each other choose books. Second, we know that students' tastes change throughout the year, so they will need ideas for new books to read.

- **How We Teach It:** We gather four to eight students who are reading or have read a similar type of book (fantasy, for example). Before the group meets, we ask each member to choose one book in that particular genre to tell the group about. During the meeting, the students share and ask questions about the books they've brought to the table. As the facilitator of the group, we ask questions such as "Is this book like another that you've read?" and "Is there anyone in particular who you think would enjoy this book?"

■ ■ ■

Supporting Individual Choice and Reflection

It is important for our students to be reflective about their reading. This is one of the reasons we ask them to keep detailed reading logs. About four or five times each year, we specifically ask our students to use their reading logs to see what they can discover about their book choices and their reading. Early in the year, we might give them a list of questions to guide their thinking (Szymusiak and Sibberson 2008, 85):

> What types of books have you read?
> Have you tried any books that were too hard? Which ones?

> Were most of the books on your reading list too hard, too easy, or just right?
>
> How do you know when a book is just right for you?
>
> How do you decide which books to read?
>
> How have you changed in the way you choose books?
>
> Is there a book that you know of that you'd like to read soon?
>
> What is one of your favorite books in your reading log? Why?

Alternatively we may share our reading logs to model what we noticed about our own reading. In January, for example, Franki showed her reading log to her students. She told them that she wanted to find out the kind of books she'd been reading over the last six months and to determine whether her reading was balanced. She also wanted to learn whether she read more extensively during certain months of the year. She made a transparency of the two pages in her reading log and shared them with her students. Then she gave her students time to look at their own reading logs, asking them to decide on their own what things they were curious about in their own reading. Some students made lists of what they noticed. Others created charts or graphs on certain aspects of their reading. Many noticed patterns in their reading. For example, Kelsie said she noticed "that I like to go short, short, short, long, short, short, short, long when I read." Casey said, "If I start a series, I finish it. I read a lot of the same author and then after a while I switch to another." (See Figure 7.2.)

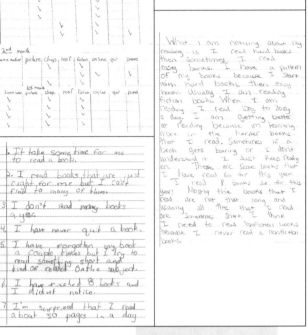

Figure 7.2
Students reflect on their reading using their logs.

Individual Needs

Individual conferences often revolve around book choice. For students who need support choosing books, we hold "next read" conferences. Students often initiate this type of conference because they need some help planning their future reading. If a conference is successful, the child is usually set in his or her reading for several months. When students come to a "next read" conference, we want them to think beyond just their next book. We want them to think about the next several books as well as the ways they choose books.

Before the conference, we ask students to spend some time at the bookshelves and choose eight to twelve books that look like good reads. When they come to the conference with their stack of books, we ask them to preview the books by reading the back cover and the first pages, and by looking over any other features that will help them learn as much as they can about the story. As they preview the books, they start two piles. One pile is for books they still want to consider; the other is for books they've decided they probably wouldn't enjoy reading after all. The books in the discard pile are returned to the shelf. We look at the remaining books together to determine which book looks like the one they want to read next. Then they choose two or three additional books to put in their "next read" bag—simply a plastic bag that holds the books they want to read in the near future. If the child has chosen more than three or four books, he or she writes the remaining titles in his or her reading notebook in the Books I Want to Read section. Once the conference is over, these readers are set for a long stretch of time and will not need to look beyond their "next read bag" for their next book.

Kelsie begins to look for possibilities for future reading. She sorts the books into two piles: those that look good and those that don't. She fills her "next read" bag and jots down other good titles in her reader's notebook. Kelsie can add to her "next read" bag throughout the year.

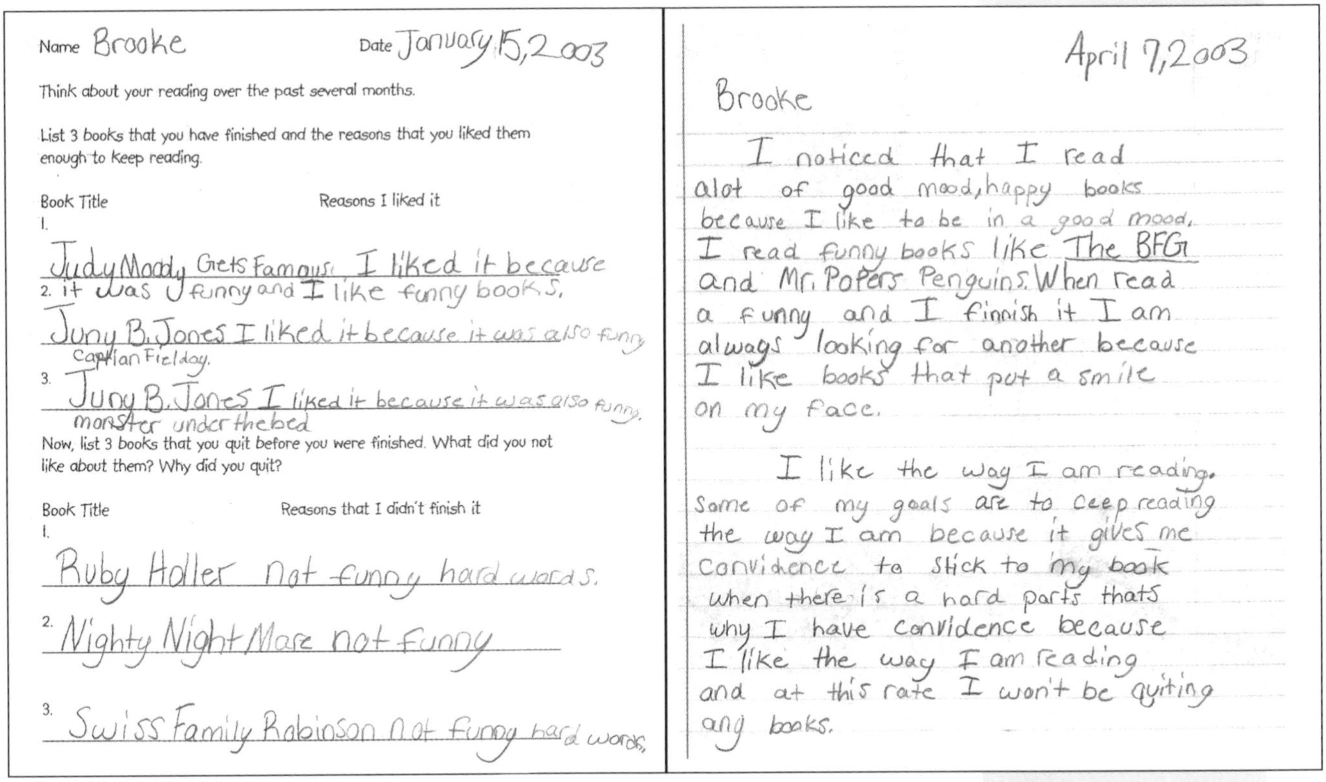

Name Brooke   Date January 15, 2003

Think about your reading over the past several months.

List 3 books that you have finished and the reasons that you liked them
enough to keep reading.

Book Title   Reasons I liked it
1.
Judy Moody Gets Famous. I liked it because
2. it was funny and I like funny books.
Juny B. Jones I liked it because it was also funny
    Captian Fielday.
3.
Juny B. Jones I liked it because it was also funny.
    monster under the bed
Now, list 3 books that you quit before you were finished. What did you not
like about them? Why did you quit?

Book Title   Reasons that I didn't finish it
1.
Ruby Holler not funny hard words.

2.
Nighty Night Mare not funny

3.
Swiss Family Robinson not funny hard words.

April 7, 2003

Brooke

I noticed that I read
alot of good mood, happy books
because I like to be in a good mood.
I read funny books like The BFG
and Mr. Popers Penguins. When read
a funny and I finnish it I am
always looking for another because
I like books that put a smile
on my face.

I like the way I am reading.
Some of my goals are to ceep reading
the way I am because it gives me
convidence to stick to my book
when there is a hard parts thats
why I have convidence because
I like the way I am reading
and at this rate I won't be quiting
any books.

Figure 7.3
In January, Franki met with Brooke
and helped her think about her book
choices. Brooke was then able to find
more books that were good enough
to finish.

We always have a few students who continue to struggle with book choice. Often these students seem excited about a book as they begin to read it but abandon it a few days later. When this happens, we have an individual conference to ask the student to reflect on his or her book choice. These students are usually eager to find a book that engages them, but they have trouble sticking with a book until the end. When we have conferences like these, we ask students to recall the names of three books they have finished over the last several months and to think about what made each book worth finishing. Then we ask them to recall three books they've abandoned and the reasons that the books weren't worth finishing. Often this helps them discover which types of books work for them and with future book choices. (The form we use for this is in the appendix; Figure 7.3 shows one student's completed form.)

Book Bins to Support Book Choice and Engagement

Some years, our students keep individual book bins in which they keep books they are currently reading and a book or two that they plan to read next. We have found that book bins serve many purposes. They are a tangible way for our middle grades readers to make plans as readers. We want our students to

Students each have an individual book bin that houses books for independent reading time as well as annotation tools. The bins are housed in several places in the classroom.

know that readers make plans. Thinking ahead as readers is important, so having a spot to put a book they will read in the near future is important.

We have also found that having a book bin builds stamina. Because readers know they can keep a book for later, they are more apt to finish a book they started because the "next read" is safely in the bin.

Our students know that their job is to keep their book bins up-to-date and that they need to have enough books in the bin to engage them during the entire reading workshop time.

Reading Logs as a Tool for Book Choice

During a recent workshop we were leading, a teacher came up and said she was shocked that Franki had shared a student reading log in one of our slides. "I thought we weren't supposed to do logs any more," she said, sounding confused. "I keep hearing that they are a bad idea." It seems that the "in" thing these days is to get rid of reading logs in reading workshops. We are not sure how this conversation began or how it has evolved, but we've caught wind of it several times recently.

This teacher's stress over what she was "supposed to do" worried us. Too often we read one article or hear one expert and throw out a practice that has worked for us. We must confess that we did just that when it came to reading logs a few years ago. We heard the buzz and quickly decided to start the school year without a routine in place for students to log their reading. Looking back, it is clear that it was definitely not the right decision. Without logs, students had no way to anchor routines of reflection and goal setting.

Are Reading Logs Authentic?

We think classroom reading logs have gotten a bad rap because they've turned into something inauthentic. Keeping them can be a meaningless activity designed to "prove" that our students have read something. We have never liked the idea of reading logs as a way for students to be "accountable." We don't think keeping reading logs for accountability is useful. We've found that sometimes students read but forget to mark it down. Other times, students include reading that they didn't do. The reading log has the potential to become a source of stress for children and families when it's used for accountability.

We thought about this years ago when a colleague mentioned how inauthentic reading logs were, and how they seemed to be something we used only in schools. We wondered about this and did some research. Reading logs can be used in authentic ways. Many readers keep track of their reading lives in some way. Each of us used to have a notebook in which we logged finished books. A friend of ours keeps a notebook with favorite lines from each book she reads. Many of us use digital tools such as Shelfari and Goodreads to log our lives as readers. And we discovered that logs are important to people outside the reading community. Runners, bird-watchers, and dieters all use logs to reflect and to help them reach new goals.

Logs are authentic when they matter to readers—when they use them to reflect on their reading life and to set new goals. Logs are essential for reflection in Franki's classroom, and they are critical tools for growth. We recently had the opportunity to hear Donalyn Miller speak at the All Write Summer Institute in Warsaw, Indiana. She talked about the role of reading records and the importance of student ownership of them. She tells her students, "I can help you better if you keep records of what you read." Not only are logs a tool for students, but they also become a great tool for teachers when conferring with a child about his or her reading. How can our students reflect on their lives as readers and know how important that is if they never have the chance to keep a log and use it in a way that helps them grow?

So, instead of throwing out a practice that has worked for so long, instead of getting rid of reading logs, we continue to ask ourselves these important questions to keep the logs purposeful and authentic:

- What reading behaviors do I want my students to be able to reflect on?
- Is the log simple enough that it doesn't take time away from what really matters—reading?
- Will the log support future book choice and goal setting?
- How will I make time in the classroom for reflections and celebrations around the log?

Our most basic logs ask students to jot down the title of the book, the pages read, the time spent reading, and the date every time they read. That is enough information to begin to look back at reading tastes, book choices, reading habits, and stamina. We have done paper versions but currently use a Google Form. Colleagues use Biblionasium and Bookopolis for their students. We want to help our students see a reading log as a quick tool readers use to reflect, celebrate, and set goals. We have found that some type of reading log is a valuable tool that allows students to look back before looking ahead at their reading choices.

Strategy Lesson

Using Online Sources to Find Good Books

■ **Why We Teach It:** As our students grow as readers, their tastes often change. Avid readers often spend a great deal of time online, shopping for good books. Although this lesson can be introduced in a whole-group setting, we often use it again when we are meeting with children who are struggling with book choice. It helps them learn to find books on their own.

■ **How We Teach It:** We usually teach this lesson with the student sitting at the computer or a group of students sitting at individual computers. If we teach it to the whole class, we often project the computer image onto a larger screen so that everyone can see it. We ask students to think about books that they have recently enjoyed or authors whose books they have read. Then we show them a variety of ways to search for other books in that genre or other books by that author. Here are some of our favorite websites to use in a lesson like this:

KidsReads (www.kidsreads.com)
Dogo News Book Reviews (www.dogobooks.com)
Spaghetti Book Club (www.spaghettibookclub.org)
Mr. Schu's Blog, Watch.Read.Connect (http://mrschureads.blogspot.com)

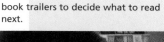
Students often visit websites or watch book trailers to decide what to read next.

■ **Follow-Up:** After we have visited each website with the students, we bookmark the sites or add them to our class website so that students can return to them easily. Students are then encouraged to explore the websites on their own. They often need an entire reading workshop session to explore a site so they can see what it has to offer and remember how to use it. This is also a great time to let students know that many authors have a New Books section on their web pages, so students can go to author websites to see what has been recently published. (We've sometimes created Symbaloo pages of favorite authors that easily link to authors kids know.)

■ ■ ■

Adult Readers Share Their Reading Lives

In *Beyond Leveled Books* (2008), we talked about the need to extend the reading community for our students. One of our favorite traditions is to invite adult readers into the classroom to talk to our students about their lives as readers. We know it is important for children to talk to other readers if we want them to become lifelong readers. Inviting adult readers into the classroom, however, gives students much more than the chance to learn about other readers. Powerful conversations have resulted from the children's parents and staff members coming in to talk about their reading.

The adults come to the classroom with a stack of books and describe their reading lives to the children. They talk about the books they enjoy and the books they can't wait to read. They tell our students about the behaviors and attitudes that define them as readers. Some of our best teaching comes from these conversations. Over the past few years, we have started to take notes when parents come in to talk to our students. We have found that we can build on what the parents say throughout the year. For example, Emily's mother talked about how important book reviews were in helping her choose books. We continued this line of thinking with students. Throughout the year, when we talked about book reviews, we would often start by saying, "Remember when Emily's mom came in and told us about the ways she uses book reviews?"

Jordan's mother collects books when she goes on trips. Whenever she goes to a foreign city, she finds a bookstore and buys a book about that city. She has hundreds of books about the cities she has visited. This idea started two conversations. One was about reading for information, because Jordan's mother liked to learn about the places she visited. It also started a conversation about book collections. After hearing about Jordan's mother's collection of books about different cities, we talked about one of our friends, who collects different versions of the story of Little Red Riding Hood. She has several books in English as well as several in other languages. We also told students about our friend Patty, who started a collection for each of her children of books with their names in the title. When our students extend these conversations, they might discover that their mother has all the Nancy Drew books or that their aunt collects cookbooks from around the world.

Several mothers mentioned having read *Little House on the Prairie*, Nancy Drew books, *Charlotte's Web*, and *Stuart Little*. The children were amazed that these books, popular today, were "soooo old"! This prompted a conversation about books that have become classics. We asked, "What makes a book or a series so good that it is still good fifty years later? Will the Harry Potter series become a classic?"

Book Collections That We Have Learned About

Travel books
Little Red Riding Hood stories
Fairy tales from a specific country or area
Cookbooks
Nancy Drew books
Books about an interesting topic
Favorite books from childhood
Books about an interesting person
Books about cats

We also have staff members come in and talk. Recently, Mr. Hoover, Franki's assistant principal, shared his reading life. He shared all the ways that he reads the news and said he often starts his day by reading the news on his phone. He also gets the daily newspaper on his Nook and gets a paper copy of the newspaper on Sundays.

Many people said that they did not have libraries or bookstores nearby when they were growing up. Some parents talked about the bookmobile in their community. Karýnn's mother lived outside the United States; the only books she had access to were books written in Spanish, so she learned to read in Spanish. This started conversations about access to books, where we get the books we read, and why we read.

Most adult readers mentioned favorite authors. If we invite parents into the classroom early in the year, it is easy to tie this conversation into using the classroom library. We can also connect these conversations to the author baskets students use throughout the year.

The children often ask adults to name their favorite book, and not one of our visitors has ever been able to name just one. Most mentioned a few. This sparked a great conversation throughout the year about loving different books in different ways.

Several of the adult readers who came to our classroom have something they read every day. Some read the daily newspaper, the Bible, or work-related information from the Internet. This started great conversations about reading habits. Jordan's father talked to us about how he carries books with him everywhere he goes. He also told us that he hates to shop, so whenever he goes to the mall with his wife, he brings a book. This started a conversation about the places where people read. We asked our students, "Where are some places you take books? Where are surprising places where you've seen people reading?"

We keep track of the conversations that adults start with our students in the classroom. It is easy to forget what the guests talked about if we don't take notes during their visits. These visits are perfect opportunities for us to help our students learn reading behaviors, by connecting what adult readers do and what we want our students do. We try to highlight those pieces of the conversations that are worth continuing throughout the year.

Listening to the adults' descriptions of their reading lives for behaviors and strategies that will help our students gives us a wonderful opportunity to encourage our students to think about their own reading. As more and more adults come into the classroom, students begin to make connections and have lots of questions for the readers. Each question adds new insights into what it means to be a reader.

One year, the students became interested in opinions on movies based on books. They asked every reader who came in whether they read the book first or watched the movie first. We learned that most adult readers enjoy the book more and often won't see the movie until after they've read the book.

Many conversations are started when parents and other adults talk to our students about their reading habits.

Our principal, Mrs. Schwanke, helped us think even more with her answer. She said, "Movies help me think about books in a different way."

Sometimes we take these threads and focus on them for whole-class or even whole-school exploration. For example, one year the students and teachers at Indian Run Elementary took pictures of different places where they read. They wrote captions for the pictures and hung them on a display in a busy hallway at school. Another year, students and teachers were asked to take a photo of themselves reading over the summer and to write about their summer reading. Another year, teachers reflected on their reading from childhood and wrote about it below pictures of themselves as young children. These are three easy and enjoyable ways to extend the reading community to the entire school. When we place displays like this in busy school hallways, we always notice students, parents, and teachers stopping to read and talk about their own reading with others. Great conversations about reading have started because of these displays.

Conferring Around Book Choice

We rely on individual conferences for much of our work around book choice. We know we can start from where students are and invite them to stretch to new kinds of readings when we listen to what they have to say about their reading. Reading conferences around book choice take on many forms, but they are often the time we need to "ladder" students to new books. Often a child asks for a conference so that he or she can get some book recommendations. Other times a student is ready for a new kind of reading but needs a bit of support. We see our role in these conferences as supporting student choice while helping them meet new goals as readers.

In a conference with Franki, Maggie mentioned that she was worried about reading books with no pictures, although she really wanted to. She relied on the pictures to help her understand what she was reading. Franki asked if she understood the book that was being read aloud in class. Maggie said yes but that having to read the words and visualize was a little too hard. Franki met with Maggie a few days later with a stack of books that she might like—books with fewer pictures than those she was used to. From the stack, Maggie chose *Leroy Ninker Saddles Up*, a book from a series Franki had read aloud and with which Maggie was familiar. Franki and Maggie set up conferences every few days, and Maggie committed to reading ten pages a day until she finished the book. In this instance, Maggie needed a bit of support in meeting a personal goal, and after that first book, she knew she could read books like that independently.

Often books are recommended by friends.

Beth, another student, asked Franki for a conference because she was reading the last book in the Heidi Heckelbeck series. She had loved this series and was hoping Franki could suggest some similar books and series. Franki and Beth visited the series section of the classroom library, where Franki pointed out series with characters who were familiar to Beth. Of the six or seven baskets Franki shared, Beth seemed most interested in two of them and put a book from each in her book bin. Later Beth requested other books from the public library on the board that Franki had set up.

Max enjoyed nonfiction and could spend days poring over a single book. But as Franki observed, he wasn't always reading the book. She scheduled a conference, and Max shared that he liked to read only quick facts, and chose bits and pieces of the nonfiction books he read. He rarely read a whole page or an entire book. Even on websites such as Big Universe and Wonderopolis, Max read bits and pieces of nonfiction. Although skimming and scanning is an important nonfiction skill, Franki wanted Max to be more engaged in his nonfiction reading and suggested that he read whole books. At first Max explained that he didn't have the desire to read a whole book, that he was worried he wouldn't be able to do it. Once Franki realized he lacked confidence, she chose a stack of books to share with him that were written to be read from front to back. After that conference, Max read and enjoyed several books from the Smart Kids series. He admitted to Franki that he was surprised that he could do it and that "there weren't as many words" as he'd thought. Franki then shared books with lots of text on a page, and Max seemed confident about trying them. Not only was he reading more, but he was also excited about all that he was learning now that he was reading more of the book.

When students learn about a book they might want to read in a conference or when talking to peers, they can add it to the request sheet and Franki requests it from the public library.

Many of our conversations about books and book choice begin in the classroom. They occur all day and in informal ways, but they are always an integral part of the classroom community. As our readers develop new skills and interests, it is important to continue these conversations throughout the year. Extending these talks beyond the classroom by having students interact with other readers outside the classroom enriches the experience and will help our students develop confidence in their ability to choose books for years to come.

Next-Read Stack: Conferring for Independence

http://sten.pub/sltr4

In this clip, Franki confers with a third grader who is having difficulty finding books for independent reading.

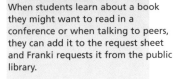

Getting More from Wonderopolis

http://sten.pub/sltr5

In this clip, Franki teaches a mini-lesson using the popular website Wonderopolis.

Chapter 8

Text Complexity: Scaffolding for Reading Fiction

e have both worked in grades 3–6 for most of our careers. Early on, we became fascinated by how much changed for readers in grades 3–6. Even though we didn't name it as text complexity then, we were looking at all the ways text became more complex and what that meant for readers as they moved beyond the beginning stages of reading instruction. We found that without instruction and scaffolding for more complex texts, it was easy for readers to get stuck in this transitional stage.

The Common Core State Standards approach text complexity as a three-part model for determining how easy or difficult a particular text is to read. According to the CCSS, text complexity consists of three equally important parts:

Qualitative dimensions of text complexity
Quantitative dimensions of text complexity
Reader and task considerations

We believe that in grades 3–6, it is our responsibility to support students in growing across these three dimensions and helping them become independent at making sense of texts at deeper levels.

Over the years, through our professional reading, our work with students and our own personal reading, we've come to learn the ways that texts become more complex in grades 3–6. In this chapter, we focus primarily on fiction text and the ways in which our readers must change and grow to access more complex texts.

In grades 3–6 readers often learn to

- read across an entire, longer story;
- visualize more of the story because there are fewer illustrations;
- struggle through meaning and become comfortable with the struggle;

- use text evidence to understand the author's meaning;
- be patient with longer introductions to stories;
- infer events in a plot;
- understand beyond what is written on the page;
- keep track of multiple characters;
- know when there is a change in setting and keep track of multiple settings;
- read and understand stretches of dialogue;
- recognize internal and external conflicts;
- follow characters' changes over time;
- know characters beyond surface-level character traits;
- understand metaphor and symbolism and its role in a story;
- understand the big message and theme of a book;
- understand settings that are unfamiliar;
- recognize and understand new text structures such as flashbacks and elapsed time; and
- understand various perspectives.

Read-aloud is an important part of our work in scaffolding students and moving them from what they are reading independently to more complex books. But our read-aloud time usually is anchored around chapter books. Students need more than that as they begin to learn to navigate more complex texts. Mini-lessons, small-group instruction, and individual conferences are equally important.

We have learned that we can't teach every skill readers will need to understand every piece of text they encounter. Instead we want our students to have a variety of experiences that help them think deeply about a text, to question it and to dig in deeper when things don't make sense. We want them to learn the power of reading when they go beyond the surface level of understanding. We agree with what Dorothy Barnhouse and Vicki Vinton say in their book *What Readers Really Do*: "We need to teach each student the *way* readers think as they read, not *what* to think, helping them to experience texts as readers, rather than putting specific thoughts about texts into their heads" (2012, 7). It is important for our students to independently navigate a book with a clear understanding that they have created along the way. We try to keep this in mind as students move from simple to more complex books in grades 3–6.

Scaffolding with Picture Books

The goal of reading ladders is to slowly move students from where they are to where we would like them to be.

—Teri Lesesne

We love Teri Lesesne's idea of reading ladders, because they help us be thoughtful about the books we choose to share with our students. Slowly moving students from where they are to where we would like them to be is always on our minds when we plan. We "ladder" books when we think about mini-lesson work, when we book talk titles to students, when we meet with students in small groups, and when we confer with students. We want our mini-lessons to be accessible to all students in our classroom. We know that all students are not at the same point as readers, but we want our mini-lessons to help move all of them forward as readers. For this to happen, we rely on picture books and wordless picture books for much of our mini-lesson work.

We believe that our role in supporting students with effective scaffolds as they move to more complex text is essential. We must know our students, know the standards, and know the resources available to us to best support our students. Terry Thompson describes scaffolding as "a series of actionable steps, decisions, and interactions that support the learner in growing toward increasing degrees of independence. It differentiates itself from other ways learning might occur, because students are actively involved in a rich, interactive experience that invites them to construct new learning with a teacher who supports them every step of the way, offering just enough assistance while allowing them to take on greater stages of independence the instant they're ready" (2015, 5).

Because we agree with Terry Thompson when he says we must "start with what the learner can actually do without support," we plan lesson cycles with wordless books and picture books to help our middle grades readers learn all that is possible in stories.

When we think about how to best scaffold our readers, we try to break down the standards in a way that helps them think more deeply about the text. We build a menu of resources for mini-lessons so we can build strategies over time. We have discovered that certain books invite certain kinds of discussions, so we always read with an eye toward the lens of the reader. Below are some cycles of lessons we use to break down bigger ideas for our readers. These cycles can be done as whole-class lessons, with small groups of readers, or in individual conferences.

Planning Lesson Cycles That Help Readers Grow

We sometimes build cycles around a series of wordless picture books. Starting conversations with wordless picture books levels the playing field in our classrooms. No matter what the reading level of the students is, each one can participate fully in the idea of the mini-lesson. In this series, we use two wordless picture books by Bill Thompson to introduce readers to the ways that readers think while they read. In grades 3–6, we want our students to know the power of thinking while they read. We also want them to recognize the connections they make as readers and focus on those that help them understand more complex texts.

Readers Have Expectations When They Know the Author or Series	Book	Lesson Focus	Language We Might Use with Students to Start the Conversation
Day 1	*Chalk* by Bill Thomson	Readers think while they read.	Stopping at each page, we ask readers, "What are you thinking? What in the book made you think that?"
Day 2	*Fossil* by Bill Thomson	Readers connect with other books to deep understanding.	"How can your thinking about *Chalk* help you understand *Fossil*?"

Scaffolding Deeper Thinking by Rereading the Same Book Over Several Days

Rereading is a key strategy that readers need to have so that they can read more complex texts. Often our readers are reluctant to reread, so we design lessons to illustrate the power of rereading. In this series of lessons, we use a wordless picture book over several days and track what we notice and the questions we have.

Scaffolding an Idea Across Several Books: Problem and Solution

We have found that it is powerful to think about an idea across several books. We try to break down ideas (such as problem and solution in this next cycle) in a way that makes them clear to readers. We look for books that illustrate

Students work with partners during a rereading lesson cycle using *The Farmer and the Clown* by Marla Frazee.

The Power of Rereading to Understand More Deeply	Book	Lesson Focus	Language We Might Use with Students to Start the Conversation
Day 1	*The Farmer and the Clown* by Marla Frazee	Readers think during reading.	"Jot down what you notice yourself thinking during this first read."
Day 2	*The Farmer and the Clown* by Marla Frazee	Readers notice things as they reread.	"What are some things you noticed and wondered this time that you didn't notice or wonder on the first read?"
Day 3	*The Farmer and the Clown* by Marla Frazee	Readers try to answer the questions they have as they focus on rereading.	"What questions do you have that you hope to answer during this next read?"

the idea we want to point out as we cycle through the lessons. Students become sophisticated at thinking about the strategy, literary element, or structure of the cycle.

Understanding Problem and Solution Across a Story	Book	Lesson Focus	Language We Might Use with Students to Start the Conversation
Day 1	*Where's Walrus?* by Stephen Savage or *A Ball for Daisy* by Chris Raschka	Stories have problems and solutions that last throughout the book.	"What is the problem and how is it solved? How do the problem and solution tie the story together? What makes you think that?"
Day 2	*Lilly's Purple Plastic Purse* by Kevin Henkes	It is often the main character in the story who has a problem.	"What do we learn about Lilly by the way she handles the problem? What makes you think that?"
Day 3	*Each Kindness* by Jacqueline Woodson	Sometimes the problem in the story is an internal one—something that the character is dealing with on the inside.	"What is the problem that people can see? What is the character's internal problem? What makes you think that?"
Day 4	*A Bad Case of Stripes* by David Shannon	The author often hopes that readers learn the lesson that the character in a story learns.	"What is the character's problem? What does the character learn? What makes you think that?"

Scaffolding More Complex Ways to Think About Characters

In this cycle, we introduce readers to various ways we learn about characters in stories. Each lesson has a different focus under this big umbrella. We begin with a simple picture book and a simple idea about a character. We move slowly to more complex ideas about characters.

Think About Characters in More Complex Ways	Book	Lesson Focus	Language We Might Use with Students to Start the Conversation
Day 1	*Hank Finds an Egg* by Rebecca Dudley	Readers learn about a character through the character's actions.	"What do we know about Hank in the story? Did your ideas about Hank change as the story went on? Why?"
Day 2	*South* by Patrick McDonnell	Readers often learn about characters through their relationships with others.	"What do we know about each character? How do they treat each other? What does that tell us?"
Day 3	*Bluebird* by Bob Staake	Characters change over the course of a story because of the events that occur.	"How did the character change across the book? What events caused the changes? Why do you think that?"
Day 4	*Here I Am* by Patti Kim	Readers try to understand a character's perspective to better understand the story.	"How is the character's perspective the same or different from your own?"

Getting to Know a Character Over Time

We may not think about series books as being complex because they often feel formulaic, with a lot that readers can count on from one book to another. But series books are important to readers in grades 3–6 for this very reason. Series books support comprehension because readers can build on one book without having to relearn characters, plot sequence, setting, and other features. To help readers think more deeply when reading series books, we can help them build understanding over time and books. In this cycle, we help readers see that knowing a character over several books helps them better predict and understand that character's behaviors. We have also used picture

Getting to Know a Character Across Books	Book	Lesson Focus	Language We Might Use with Students to Start the Conversation
Day 1	*Olive and the Bad Mood* by Tor Freeman	Readers become familiar with a character as they read.	"What do you know about Olive from the story? How do you know?"
Day 2	*Olive and the Big Secret* by Tor Freeman	As readers read more books in the series, they add to what they know about a character.	"What new things did we learn about Olive as a character? What did we already know that was confirmed in this new story?"
Day 3	*Olive and the Embarrassing Gift* by Tor Freeman	Readers can predict a character's actions based on what they already know about the character.	"Before we read this story, what can you predict about Olive based on what we know about her from other books?"

Theme	Book	How Complexity of Text Increases
Day 1	*Sidewalk Flowers* by JonArno Lawson and Sydney Smith	Wordless book with accessible theme
Day 2	*Otis and the Scarecrow* by Loren Long	Picture book with accessible theme
Day 3	*To the Sea* by Cale Atkinson	Picture book with accessible theme
Day 4	*Those Shoes* by Maribeth Boelts	Picture book with more complex theme
Day 5	*City Dog, Country Frog* by Mo Willems	Common themes of friendship and loss
Day 6	*Each Kindness* by Jacqueline Woodson	Character's learning is clue to theme of book
Day 7	*How to Heal a Broken Wing* by Bob Graham	The story is symbolic of a more universal theme about healing.
Day 8	*Sam and Dave Dig a Hole* by Mac Barnett	This book's theme is difficult to determine without many rereads.

Wordless (or Almost Wordless) Picture Books

Journey by Aaron Becker
Quest by Aaron Becker
A Circle of Friends by Giora Carmi
Unspoken by Henry Cole
The Lion and the Bird by Marianne Dubuc
The Farmer and the Clown by Marla Frazee
Red Sled by Lita Judge
Here I Am by Patti Kim
Moo by David LaRochelle
Wave by Suzy Lee
The Red Book by Barbara Lehman
The Flower Man by Mark Ludy
AH HA! by Jeff Mack
South by Patrick McDonnell
Hippo! No, Rhino! by Jeff Newman
Look . . . Look Again by John O'Brien
The Boy and the Airplane by Mark Pett
The Girl and the Bicycle by Mark Pett
The Lion & The Mouse by Jerry Pinkney
A Ball for Daisy by Chris Raschka
Daisy Gets Lost by Chris Raschka
Where's Walrus? by Stephen Savage
The Stray Dog by Marc Simont
Bluebird by Bob Staake
Ball by Mary Sullivan
Chalk by Bill Thomson
Fossil by Bill Thomson
Mr. Wuffles! by David Wiesner
Tuesday by David Wiesner

Graphic Novels We've Used to Scaffold Readers

Giants Beware! by Jorge Aguirre and Rafael Rosado
Dragons Beware! by Jorge Aguirre and Rafael Rosado
El Deafo by Cece Bell
Zita the Spacegirl (series) by Ben Hatke
Sunny Side Up by Jennifer Holm and Matt Holm
Roller Girl by Victoria Jamieson
The Gingerbread Man Loose in the School (part of a series) by Laura Murray
Sidekicks by Dan Santat
Sleepless Knight by James Sturm, Alexis Frederick-Frost, and Andrew Arnold
Sisters by Raina Telgemeier
Smile by Raina Telgemeier
Drama by Raina Telgemeier
Guinea Pig, Pet Shop Private Eye (series) by Colleen AF Venable

books such as the Otis books by Loren Long, the Binky Adventures by Ashley Spires, and Little Elliot books by Mike Curato for this cycle of lessons or for students who need more time and practice with the idea.

Theme is often a difficult concept for readers, and as books become more complex, recognizing the theme of a book becomes more difficult. When planning instruction, we try to find a menu of books and sequence them in a way that builds on readers' understanding of theme and the way story works. We believe that each of these books and lessons becomes a little more complex as readers work toward determining the author's message. Students can use what they learn from one book and lesson to build on the next. This may or may not work as planned, but having a menu of books to use that build reader expectations across days is helpful to scaffold this work with readers.

Scaffolding with Graphic Novels

We have discovered that graphic novels provide another scaffold for our readers. Many books in graphic novel form have a great deal of depth. The combination of visual support and text clues helps readers grow. Students are often able to read more complex texts without having to give up the support of pictures. Sharing graphic novels using the document camera or by projecting the Kindle app gives students access to the visuals and text and the ways that they work together. Toon Book Reader is an online resource that has several graphic novels available digitally (www.professorgarfield.org/toon_book_reader/).

Short Texts to Support Reading Deeply

We find that collections of short texts are often key to helping our students read more deeply. By reading a short piece or story, we can have discussions around an entire complex text without spending weeks reading it. Short pieces are powerful ways to introduce our students to literary elements as well as reading strategies. These are some of our favorite short texts:

Marshfield Dreams by Ralph Fletcher

Looking Back: A Book of Memories by Lois Lowry

Every Living Thing by Cynthia Rylant

Knucklehead by Jon Scieszka

Knots in My Yo-Yo String by Jerry Spinelli

Pixar Shorts (www.pixar.com/short_films/home)(Many are appropriate and accessible for grades 3–6.)

Using Online Resources to Think More Deeply About Stories

We can also find a variety of resources to help our students understand stories more deeply.

Sunny Side Up is a graphic novel by Jennifer Holm and Matthew Holm that tells the story of a girl who spends the summer with her grandfather. But there is much more to the story than that, and there are several layers for readers to discover and understand. Colby Sharp and Travis Jonkers created a series of podcasts about the making of this book (Series 1 of The Yarn at http://100scopenotes.com/the-yarn/) that give readers various insights into the story behind it and help them understand the book at deeper levels. Much of text complexity is about learning to dig deeper and to think about layers of meaning in stories. Resources like The Yarn allow readers to do just that.

We can also take advantage of learning from authors through Skype visits. When we had a Skype conversation with Erin Soderberg, we learned a bit more about the characters in The Quirks series and how they developed, which helped us understand them at a deeper level. Kate Messner has a list of Authors Who Skype on her blog (www.katemessner.com/authors-who-skype-with-classes-book-clubs-for-free/).

Technology often allows students to understand a text at a deeper level. Having the opportunity to Skype with Erin Soderberg, author of The Quirks, gave students new insights into the characters in the series.

We've found that it's often worthwhile to revisit a book trailer *after* reading a book. After reading *Greetings from Nowhere* by Barbara O'Connor, watching the book trailer (https://www.youtube.com/watch?v=VKj4y_-U2UE) moved a class of third and fourth graders to rethink the ways that each character changed because of the others.

Blogs give us new insights into things we've read. Hearing other readers' thoughts about a book is a way to expand our own thinking.

Using Sticky Notes for Understanding

Years ago, when we began strategy instruction with our students, we often encouraged them to use sticky notes for different purposes. We approach our teaching a bit differently now. We use the information we get from students to begin several lessons that will help them learn strategies for understanding. In many think-aloud lessons, we use highlighters and sticky notes to help them work through text.

Students will also begin to use sticky notes for many reasons in their own reading. Brooke used them in a chapter that didn't make sense to her, marking places that didn't seem to fit in with the rest of the story. Sam used them in the mystery he was reading to mark clues that he thought might help him solve the case. Kelly marked places in the text that she thought might help her understand what the title of the book meant. And Kelsey wrote words and phrases on her sticky notes to help her keep track of the important events in the story she was reading.

We use these students' work as examples for the rest of the class. These early conversations help all of our students see the many possibilities for highlighting and flagging text with markers and sticky notes. At the beginning of the year, students may go a bit overboard with sticky notes, but we always help them identify the more useful examples of when the sticky notes helped them understand the text more deeply.

We use sticky notes to keep track of characters.

How Readers Use Sticky Notes and Other Annotation Tools

Readers can use sticky notes to
  mark clues to solve a mystery,
  keep track of new characters,
  highlight descriptions and attitudes of characters,
  note the amusing parts,
  mark changes in setting,
  keep track of how much they read (goal setting),
  mark places in the text to talk about,
  mark evidence to support their thoughts and predictions,
  mark something that is important, and
  mark places in the text that they don't understand.

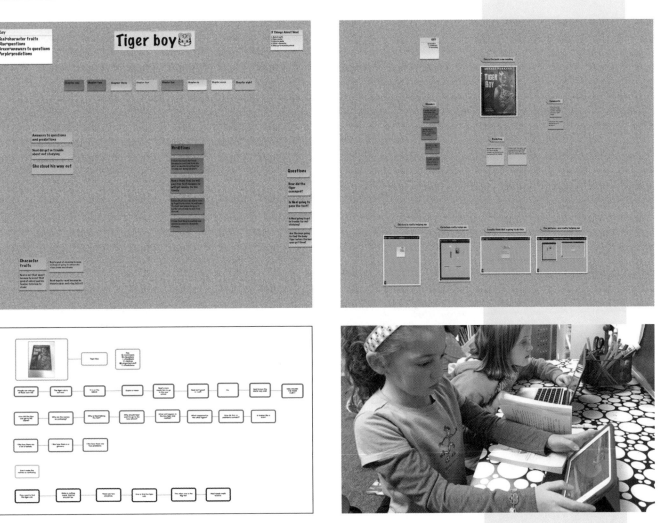

Students use a variety of tools for writing while reading. These are examples of Corkulous and Popplet, used for tracking and organizing thinking during a read-aloud.

Many students have found that using sticky notes for different reasons supports their understanding. They may design elaborate, color-coded patterns of notes, with each color used for a different purpose. If we limit children to a single strategy, they will not learn that many strategies can help them understand the text better. One year in third grade, a classroom conversation showed us that students saw two main reasons for using sticky notes: to help them understand the text and to help them respond to the text. They understood that both were important.

Transitioning Learning to Independent Reading

Read-aloud time (described in depth in Chapter 6) provides a perfect opportunity to scaffold students to longer books and to use annotation tools to understand more complex texts. We are very flexible with our expectations for read-aloud, because we want students to play with tools, talk about annotation techniques, and see the possibilities. For some kids, following the plot and stopping to talk is enough to help them grow as readers. For others, writing simple things helps. And others are ready for deeper thinking using various annotation tools. Much of our work in grades 3–6 lies in helping kids transfer skills we learned in read-aloud to independent reading; read-aloud often becomes a bridge for that.

We never require our students to transfer the skills we learn in mini-lessons to read-aloud time, but students who are ready for a different kind of thinking often do so on their own.

In a recent read-aloud of *Shelter Pet Squad: Jelly Bean* by Cynthia Lord, students chose various ways to annotate their thinking. Some had copies of the book and jotted thinking on sticky notes. Others used iPad apps such as Corkulous or Popplet. Some used laptops and annotated by sketching on Pixie. Others used their reading notebooks to keep track of their thinking in writing.

We focus on the kinds of thinking each tool supports, and in this way students are exposed to many ways to dig in when reading more complex texts. They learn that thinking specifically about how a character changes throughout the book gives them insights they may not have had without keeping track of their thinking. They learn that keeping track of their questions helps them focus on the big issues in the story that they are wondering about. This exploration with tools and annotation strategies is an important step in helping our students learn to read more complex texts.

The Power of Conferring

No matter what changes we make to our teaching, we know that conferring is one of the most powerful components of our reading workshops. Over the years, we have learned to do more listening than talking, and we've learned to help students grow in the ways they approach texts. As Dorothy Barnhouse and Vicki Vinton remind us in *What Readers Really Do*, "What we don't do, however, is use our experience to direct or guide students toward our own understanding of any given text. This is critical for several reasons— especially if you're a teacher, as we are, who aims for and values student independence" (2012, 6).

We approach our conferences ready to listen first. Our first responsibility is to understand the child's thinking—to realize how he or she is making sense of text. And then our job is to build on that and help that child read a bit more deeply. Sometimes that means we merely ask a genuine question that pushes them to read a bit differently. Sometimes readers are stuck and need a tool or strategy to help them.

We learn the most when we confer with students, but we stay true to all we know about scaffolding readers and making sure they are the ones mak-

Students often write their goal in their notebook after an individual conference. Then they keep it near them as a reminder during independent reading time.

ing sense of the text. Most times our conferences focus on students' individual goals, and sometimes we help them by creating tools together that might support them during independent reading time. When Mridhini was so excited about discovering new books that she couldn't stick with the book she was reading, Franki helped her develop a reflective tool to monitor herself and then met with her again to continue working toward the goal of finishing books. When Mac was reading a new series and trying to learn as much as he could about the characters, he talked to Franki about how to keep track of them in the first book and created a page in his notebook to do that. When getting stuck on new words was getting in the way of Joey's reading, Franki and Joey created a bookmark to remind him of strategies he could use during independent reading. Our reading conferences are designed to help students think more deeply about the complexities in text and give them the tools they need to work toward their goals independently.

Sometimes a tool such as a bookmark scaffolds a child during independent reading time.

Strategy Lesson

Using Context Clues to Understand Unfamiliar Words

We repeat this lesson several times over the course of the year with a variety of genres.

- **Why We Teach It:** Often our students come across words that they don't understand. Sometimes the words are defined in the text or there are clues in the text that can help the reader. This lesson repeated over time helps our students begin to make inferences about words so they can understand the text.

- **Possible Anchor Book:** A great resource for this lesson is A Series of Unfortunate Events by Lemony Snicket, who defines many unfamiliar words for the reader.

- **How We Teach It:** We look for articles in newspapers and on websites that have several words that may be unfamiliar to our students. We are also on the lookout for articles containing words that are defined in the context of the text. We give our students a copy of the article and project a copy onto the screen. We model our own thinking in the first few paragraphs of the text. We also model how we read ahead to look for clues and use photos and other features to help us. Then we let the children work independently or with a friend to continue through the article on their own. We give them 1-by-3-inch sticky notes and ask them to mark any unfamiliar words they may find with a sticky note. Then we ask them to find evidence in the text to help them infer the meaning of each marked word and to highlight that evidence. On the sticky note, students can write a possible definition for the word.

■ ■ ■

Strategy Lesson

Monitoring Successful Reading Strategies

We repeat this lesson several times over the course of the year as our students become more sophisticated in their reading.

- **Why We Teach It:** We want our students to monitor their own understanding of a text. As we begin to teach them various strategies, we expect them to use those strategies in their independent reading. However, we want them to use the ones that best help them handle particular problems.

- ■ **Possible Anchor Text:** Articles in a newspaper or a student news magazine. We prefer to use an article from our student news magazine so that students can mark and highlight if necessary.

- ■ **How We Teach It:** After we have worked with students on how to recognize when text is difficult for them, and after we've demonstrated a variety of strategies for getting "unstuck" in their reading, we ask them to begin monitoring their own strategies. We give each student four or five arrow-shaped sticky notes. We ask them to keep these with them while they are reading and to use them to mark places where they get stuck in their reading. Then, when they use strategies to get unstuck, we ask them to write a word or two telling what they did that helped them. After this independent work, we gather the students together to discuss their experience. We ask them to look at their arrows and see if they were usually able to understand the text after they tried a strategy. Then we ask them to see if there was one strategy that seemed to help them most often.

■ ■ ■

Encountering Unfamiliar Features

As the year progresses, different features of difficult text emerge in our conversations. One of the reasons we need to help children become strategic readers is that we can't teach them about every feature that they may encounter in their reading. Some elements are unique to particular books.

Listening is key during individual conferences.

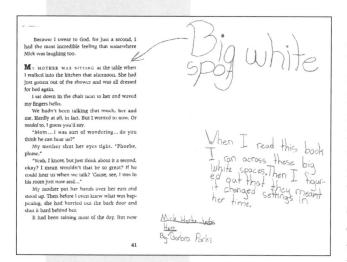

Figure 8.1
Glen added this discovery to our "Why did the author do that?" board.

Wall space provides opportunities for student discussion. It also provides scaffolds for their thinking while they read independently.

For example, Kelly approached us one day with a copy of the book she was reading. It was one of the books in A Series of Unfortunate Events by Lemony Snicket. Kelly was sure that there had been a mistake made in the printing, because two pages at the beginning of Chapter 5 looked almost identical. We took a look and realized that the author's subject was the phenomenon of déjà vu and that he was deliberately repeating text to give his readers the feeling of déjà vu. We asked Kelly to go back and read the two pages again and see if she could figure out "why the author did that." Kelly came back a few minutes later, excited to have figured out just how purposeful this author had been in his decision to put this feature in the book.

Kelly shared her discovery with the class, and they decided to start a wall display titled "Why did the author do that?"—an invitation for students to look for text features that confused them at first and then share them with the rest of the class. Over the next several weeks, a variety of examples appeared. Glen added a page from *Mick Harte Was Here* by Barbara Park. (See Figure 8.1.) Throughout this book, the author leaves white space between some paragraphs. Glen eventually realized that the spaces indicated a change in setting. Other students added their discoveries to the wall. Displays like this are very helpful for students as they learn how to make sense of complex text. By having samples of text hanging on the walls, students are encouraged to chat about the unique features they have noticed in their own reading. They are also more motivated to figure out puzzling features on their own.

Reading Notebooks Discussion

http://sten.pub/sltr6

Franki discusses reading notebooks with her students.

Chapter 9

Text Complexity: Scaffolding for Reading Nonfiction

We have always tried to give our students experiences with nonfiction text. When talk of the Common Core State Standards first began and we learned that there would be more of an emphasis on nonfiction reading, even at the elementary level, we started to reflect on the ways in which it was already a part of our classrooms. We felt pretty confident about the amount of nonfiction in our classroom libraries. And we had always tried to keep up with the best in children's nonfiction. But most of the mini-lessons in both writing and reading focused on fiction, unless the class was in the midst of a nonfiction unit of study. For example, if Franki was teaching a writing lesson on crafting good language, it never occurred to her to choose a nonfiction book for the lesson.

What was missing from Franki's nonfiction teaching? It seemed that she had become caught up in the traditional thinking of nonfiction as reading for information and finding topics of interest. But she realized that if she wanted her students to become readers of nonfiction, she would have to change her approach.

A New Stance on Nonfiction Reading

In the first edition of this book, most of the nonfiction we wrote about was limited to the idea of difficult text. We didn't think as much about nonfiction as part of a balanced reading life. We didn't think about reading nonfiction with depth. But with a new commitment to this genre, we've realized we have to change our stance on nonfiction. We can no longer think of nonfiction as a separate type of reading or as a one-time unit of study.

We've realized that we need to think in bigger ways about nonfiction reading in our classrooms and change our entire stance on teaching it. We need to see nonfiction reading as something that matters every day, not just during content time and not just during a unit of study on nonfiction. We've had to reflect on our teaching to recognize our own biases toward fiction and the reasons we didn't incorporate more nonfiction into mini-lessons, small-group work, conferring, and read-aloud time. These are some of the questions we've been asking ourselves as we change our practice when it comes to nonfiction reading.

Questions We Ask Ourselves About Our Stance on Nonfiction

- Do I know many nonfiction authors who write for readers this age?
- Do I include texts in my teaching that go beyond a traditional book or article?
- How often do I read fiction versus nonfiction aloud to students?
- Do I tend to rely on fiction books for comprehension and writing craft mini-lessons? Is that necessary, or are there nonfiction books that can meet the need?
- How often do I use nonfiction texts in small-group work or conferring?
- How often do my students choose nonfiction for independent reading time?
- When shopping for new books at the bookstore and library, do I pay attention to nonfiction choices?
- Do I focus only on nonfiction text that connects to content units that are part of the curriculum?
- Do I give book talks about nonfiction books when sharing titles with students for independent reading?
- Do I give students individual pieces of nonfiction to read?
- How do my students define nonfiction? What do they see as the purpose of nonfiction reading?
- Do I choose nonfiction that merely shares information, or do I choose pieces that explore ideas and invite readers to think about an issue?

When we think about text complexity with nonfiction reading, we think about it in ways that are a bit different from the ways we think about fiction. We realized that many of the types of information our students gravitated toward was fact-based, with little for the reader to bring to the text. We discovered that one of the main types of informational books marketed in large bookstores is very basic. "All About" books or books with topics such as "300 Facts About Animals" tend to be the types we see in bookstores. The message this gives kids is that reading nonfiction is just a passive activity in which they learn cool "facts."

In *Reading Nonfiction*, Kylene Beers and Robert Probst say, "When we tell students that nonfiction means true, we inadvertently have excused them from the task of deciding if the text is accurate, if the author's biases have skewed information, if new information now contradicts 'old' information in that text or in our own thinking. By telling students that *nonfiction* means *true*, we've implied that their job, when reading nonfiction, is simply to learn and absorb the information in the text, not to question it" (2015, 16). They go on to define nonfiction in this way: "Nonfiction is that body of work in which the author purports to tell us about the real world, a real experience, a real person, an idea or a belief" (21).

The way that nonfiction is marketed to children does not match our own beliefs or hopes for them as nonfiction readers. The format of the kind of books we mention above reminds us of joke books. You can turn to any page and read a quick joke, laugh for a minute, and move on. We want our young readers to read information that compels them to think, to talk, and to problem solve. We want them to find texts that give them things to wonder about. We want them to dig into complex texts and work through challenges and struggles as they make sense of important issues in their world. If we want this for our students, we need to give them the best nonfiction reading experiences we can.

Our First Step: Being a Reader of Nonfiction for Children

We are both big readers, but we have recently realized that we haven't made an effort to get to know children's nonfiction in the same way that we've come to know children's fiction. Much of that is our fault, but we've also discovered that it takes a bit more effort to find high-quality nonfiction.

If we want our kids to be thoughtful readers of nonfiction, we have to rethink much of what we've relied upon. We have to go beyond studying text features to help students question text, reflect on information, and build new ideas based on their reading. We also have to expand our definition of "texts," especially when it comes to information. Our students not only get information from reading traditional books, but read hyperlinked texts, watch informational videos, listen to podcasts, learn how to do things on YouTube, and hear various perspectives by listening to online interviews. For our students to be active consumers of nonfiction, we can't hold on to our limited definition of text, and we need to read as many nonfiction formats as possible so we have the right resources at our fingertips.

We've also found that building on what we know about fiction reading helps us support students as they read nonfiction. We want them to choose authors and topics they love. We want them to know favorite authors and favorite series. We want them to have expectations as readers and a stance that allows them to question and have new ideas. We want them to use strategies for understanding beyond the surface level of the text when they read nonfiction.

Nonfiction Authors We Can Rely On

When we realized that it was important for our students to know nonfiction authors as well as they knew fiction authors, we knew we would need to know more favorite authors ourselves. As we mentioned in Chapter 2, we discovered we knew the names of just a few nonfiction authors. We would need to read more high-quality nonfiction for children.

When we dug a bit deeper, we learned there was a reason it was harder to know nonfiction authors: many authors of nonfiction are not illustrators. As a result, many nonfiction authors use a variety of illustrators or photographers for their work. So, unlike fiction authors, whose work is often published to look recognizable, nonfiction authors' books are all unique.

We also thought about the reasons it would be important for our students to know nonfiction authors in the same ways they knew fiction authors. One was that it would help students develop a reader identity, and part of that identity means knowing your preferences as a reader. But we knew there was more to it than that. Having favorite nonfiction authors means having authors whose work you trust. In our own nonfiction reading, our favorite authors are those whose work we trust, whose research we can count on, who help us think about issues we are interested in. Not only do we like the style of our favorite nonfiction writers, but we trust the information they share.

Online Sources for Nonfiction

Online Source	Link
Wonderopolis	www.wonderopolis.org
Steve Harpster YouTube Channel	https://www.youtube.com/user/tgif38
Friends with Fins	www.friendswithfins.com
Ruth Ayres Writing Mini-Lessons	https://www.youtube.com/channel/UCJPPLNhnoElX7i71NEW5Vnw
TED Talks for and by Kids	http://blog.ted.com/9-talks-by-impressive-kids/
The Hive Society Podcasts	http://hivesociety.weebly.com/the-radio
DogoNews	www.dogonews.com
Sports Illustrated for Kids	www.sikids.com
Zooborns	www.zooborns.com

Nonfiction Author Baskets

Author	Website
Gene Baretta	www.genebarretta.com
Chris Barton	www.chrisbarton.info
Nic Bishop	www.nicbishop.com
Loree Griffin Burns	http://loreeburns.com
Jason Chin	http://jasonchin.net
Nicola Davies	www.nicola-davies.com
Bruce Goldstone	http://brucegoldstone.com
Steve Jenkins	www.stevejenkinsbooks.com
Irene Kelly	www.irenekellybooks.com
Sandra Markle	http://sandra-markle.blogspot.com
Kadir Nelson	www.kadirnelson.com
Doreen Rappaport	http://doreenrappaport.com
Seymour Simon	www.seymoursimon.com
Melissa Stewart	www.melissa-stewart.com

Favorite Nonfiction Series Baskets

An Egg Is Quiet by Dianna Hutts Aston
Discover Science (various authors)
Eye on the Wild by Suzanne Eszterhas
Face to Face with Animals (various authors)
Inside Series (various authors)
National Geographic Readers (various authors)
National Geographic Kids Jump Into Science (various authors)
National Geographic Kids Chapters (various authors)
National Geographic Kids Everything (various authors)
Ordinary People Change the World by Brad Meltzer
Science of Living Things by Bobbie Kalman
Scientists in the Field (various authors)
Smart Kids by Roger Priddy
Take Along Guides (various authors)
Which Animal Is Which? by Melissa Stewart
Who Would Win? by Jerry Pallotta

Anna chooses a book from a picture-book biography basket.

Picture-Book Biographies

Touching the Sky by Louise Borden
The Beatles Were Fab (and They Were Funny) by
    Kathleen Krull and Paul Brewer
*Who Says Women Can't Be Doctors? The Story of
    Elizabeth Blackwell* by Tanya Lee Stone
*Brave Girl: Clara and the Shirtwaist Makers' Strike of
    1909* by Michelle Markel
Nelson Mandela by Kadir Nelson
Bill the Boy Wonder: The Secret Co-Creator of Batman by
    Marc Tyler Nobleman
Growing Up Pedro by Matt Tavares

Nonfiction Book Basket Labels and QR Codes

Recently we added QR codes to many of our book baskets. We wanted our students to have easy access to author websites when browsing nonfiction books. We knew it gave the message that reading led to new questions and often more reading. When you read one book by an author, you might want to learn more about that book or that author, or you might want to explore other books that we may not have in our classroom library.

The QR code on this nonfiction basket makes it easy for students to find the author's website.

When we have favorite authors, we come to a text with certain expectations that help us dig deeper into the information. Knowing something about an author and his or her writing makes it easier to focus on the thinking rather than navigating the format or style the author has chosen. Familiarity with various nonfiction series helps as well. And because many of our students come to our classrooms with favorite fiction authors and series, it's easy to build on those favorites. We now organize much of the nonfiction portion of our classroom library into author and series baskets. This helps our students choose books they can enjoy, develop tastes and preferences as nonfiction readers, and dig deeper into big ideas explored by certain authors.

We also have been committed to finding online nonfiction resources that are accessible for our students. Thinking about our expanded definition of "text," we have found several sites that we share with them.

Learning Strategies for Understanding Complex Text

When we wrote the first edition of this book, we realized that we rarely read nonfiction text that we did not *choose* to read. Because of that, we rarely read nonfiction that was difficult for us. To understand more clearly the challenges our readers face, Karen decided to see what it was like to read a difficult text. She wanted to pay attention to what she did when faced with a challenge in her reading. She subscribed to *Newsweek* magazine, thinking it would probably contain articles that would challenge her in new ways. Although she always considered herself a good reader, Karen knew she read more fiction than nonfiction and had developed many strategies for reading even the most challenging works of fiction. She also had a great deal of background knowledge for the professional nonfiction she read. When she started reading *Newsweek*, Karen realized that she was struggling with nonfiction articles about political and economic issues. Her background knowledge wasn't strong enough to support her as she read. She could breeze through an article in the *Reading Teacher*, but she was unable to get past the first few sentences in an article about the economy in *Newsweek*.

Because Karen is a confident reader, she knew she would be able to get through these articles but would have to work hard to understand them. Over time, she also found that the more articles about the economy she read, the more her background knowledge grew and the easier the articles were to read. After a few months, she understood more clearly what the economic issues were and was able to approach these once-challenging articles with more understanding. She also realized that within a single issue of *Newsweek*, some articles were difficult, whereas others were easy. Karen simply had to know what strategies helped her understand any of the articles she wanted to read.

We notice our use of strategies more often as we navigate online resources. When we encounter an unfamiliar website, it often takes us a bit of time to make sense of the layout. When the news we are interested in is only in the form of a video, we must use skills that are different from those we use with traditional text. When we read a piece with ideas that go against our own beliefs, we are challenged as we compare the different perspective with our own.

We want our students to know that all readers encounter texts that challenge them and topics or genres that they find difficult. We also want them to know that readers are different—that, for example, unlike Karen, some readers find all *Newsweek* articles easy to read because they have the skills and background knowledge, but they might find professional books about teaching reading difficult. We can learn a great deal about ourselves as readers and about what our young readers face by reading difficult texts and paying attention to our own reading strategies, skills, and behaviors.

Reading Is Thinking

We talk all year with our students about reading challenging and complex texts, recognizing when our reading doesn't make sense, and integrating strategies that will clarify meaning. We demonstrate what we do when we struggle with content and genres that are unfamiliar to us.

We often use current issues of *Time for Kids* to teach children ways to approach more complex texts. Our first lessons are often simple. We ask students to find a place in the room to read, either with a friend or on their own. We give them ample time to read the entire magazine. Before they go off to read, we give them each two sticky notes. We ask them to place one sticky note on the article that is the most interesting to them and the other sticky note on the article that is the least interesting. When the students are finished reading, they talk as a class about their choices of most interesting and least interesting articles. Students are always amazed by the diversity in the selections—and they always enjoy reading and discussing the articles in *Time for Kids*.

The following week, we pass out the next issue of *Time for Kids*. Again we give students two sticky notes and ask them to read the entire issue, but this time we ask them to mark the article that is the easiest to understand and the one that is the hardest to understand. When they are finished, the class meets in front of the easel and we list their choices. We continue to use this procedure with students, and it still promotes thoughtful conversations about nonfiction reading. Here is the result of one such session:

Hardest Article	Number of Readers	Easiest Article	Number of Readers
Why Iraq	9	What Makes Geckos Stick	2
The New Gym	7	The New Gym	2
Spotlight	1	Gabon's Wild Plan	5
What Makes Geckos Stick	1	Cartoon of the Week	1
Smashing Sisters	1	9/11	3
		Spotlight	1
		Smashing Sisters	3
		If the Slipper Fits	2

We asked students what they noticed about the list. At first, they couldn't get over the fact that so many articles were listed under each category. They had each assumed that the article they had chosen was the hardest. It was an eye-opener for them to see that reading difficult text was such an individual matter. They were also amazed that most articles on the hardest list also turned up on the easiest list. They said to their classmates, "How did you think that was *easy*?" or "I thought that one was so hard!" Kelsie was surprised that someone found the article "Smashing Sisters" easy to read. The article was about a tennis match, and Kelsie knew nothing about tennis, so she found the piece very difficult. Karýnn was one of the students who found the article easy to read. She told the class that she had watched the match on television, so the article was easy for her to understand. This conversation gave students a sense of the role that background knowledge plays in reading.

After reflecting on their choices, we asked the children to think about what made an article hard or easy to understand. They listed on the board the features that they believed made the text easy or hard:

Hard	**Easy**
Not interested	Interested in topic
Names are hard to say	Know a lot about the topic
Lots of unknown words	Pictures to help
Long	Familiar/small words
Too much information	Enjoy topic/want to read it
Don't know anything/much	Short
at all about the topic	Agree with the author's opinion
Want to learn about the topic	

The article that seemed difficult to most students in the class was "Why Iraq." With the exception of Sam, those students who didn't think it was the single hardest article admitted that it was pretty difficult. When asked what made it difficult to read, they agreed that it was

> long,
> filled with words they didn't know,
> filled with big words,
> "boring!" and about a subject they didn't know much about. (Many students asked if Iraq was a person. Some wondered if Iraq was Afghanistan.)

Although that is an example from long ago, when we were writing the first edition of this book, we have had similar conversations over the years, and the patterns remain the same: Different readers find different text easy or difficult. Different readers find different text boring or interesting. No matter what the topic of our discussion, these same messages about all readers

A small group meets to discuss an article in *Time for Kids*.   A student reflects on what makes some reading difficult.

being challenged with text at some point in their reading life becomes clear to students. When they become comfortable with understanding this idea, they can be aware of strategies that might help them when they get stuck.

We often use the article students find most difficult to begin to model thinking aloud with them. We project the article so they can see the text and understand our reading and thinking. After we read the article, students list all the things they have learned from it. Even though they may not understand everything in the article, they usually understand enough to start building knowledge.

In 2003, one class listed the ideas they understood about the article:

Kuwait is by Iraq.
Saddam Hussein is leader/president.
Saddam Hussein has broken U.N. rules repeatedly.
They have dangerous weapons.
They supported terrorists.
He mistreats people.
Iraq is hiding weapons.
In 1958 the royal family was forced from power.
Iraq used to be Mesopotamia.
Iraq is a huge threat to world peace.
President Bush wants to stop them/put pressure on them/destroy their
          weapons.

The next step was to plan weekly lessons on *Time for Kids* articles about Iraq, because it was likely that the topic would be addressed in many issues over the next several months. By using articles on the same topic, students learn how to read difficult text and build background knowledge at the same time. As time went by, students added to the list of things they understood after reading each article. The articles became easier for students to read over time as they became more familiar with the issues. The articles and the students' list were posted on the board for several weeks so that the students could actually see how their understanding was growing.

Even after just a few articles on a topic, students begin to identify ways to work through difficult text:

- Think about our own thinking.
- Write things down in the margins.
- Go back and reread.
- Look for answers to things we don't understand.
- Put thinking together with friends.
- Use box of information and map—flip your eyes back and forth on the page.
- Read the whole sentence or paragraph to figure out what a word means.

Now, with so many online resources, finding several articles on a topic or issue over time is easier. The goals are still the same for our readers, but we have found that we are better able to find a variety of texts for lessons like these.

The task of dealing with challenging and complex text varies throughout the year. Students are asked to use highlighters, sticky notes, two-column charts, and other strategies to identify reading that is easy and reading that is difficult for them and then to think about what strategies they used to help them understand.

Now, years later, we have found that even though we have many more nonfiction resources at our fingertips, our students still struggle with topics that are uninteresting to them. They are still quick to realize how important background knowledge is. And they still come to understand that they have strategies to help them work through challenging text.

Because so many of Franki's fourth graders one year were sports fans and read about sports regularly, she decided to show them how reading about sports was difficult for her. She took an article from the *Columbus Dispatch*, the local newspaper, about the Columbus Blue Jackets hockey team and projected it for students. Franki read it aloud with her students sitting around her. She looked up as she read to think aloud so her students could understand her strategies for thinking as she read. She wanted them to see the strategies

---

Teaching with News Magazines and Informational Websites

We enjoy subscriptions to classroom magazines such as *Time for Kids, National Geographic Explorer,* and *Scholastic News*. These magazines provide great resources for teaching reading strategies for nonfiction. With each new issue, we consider the following questions when we plan lessons:

Which articles will spark interesting conversations?
Which articles might be easy or difficult for the majority of students?
Which articles will be the most and least interesting for most students?
Are there nonfiction text features in any of the articles that can be used for a mini-lesson or for small-group instruction?
Is there an article that has pictures, maps, graphs, or captions that are needed to better understand the text?
Is there an article with difficult vocabulary or an article with definitions embedded in the text?
Is there an article dealing with a topic about which many students have little background knowledge?
Is there an article with information that is connected to a previous article students have read?
Is there an article about a topic that will most likely be addressed again in future issues?
Is there an article that would support student work in finding important information and/or summarizing information?

We want students to use text features to help them understand their reading. Often, knowing how these features work is the first step.

she used when she got stuck in her reading. She asked her students to write down what they noticed in the Strategies section of their reading notebooks so they could talk about it later. (See Figure 9.1.) Many students were amazed at how much thinking she did as she read. Many of them wanted to jump in and explain the sports-specific terms. Franki had to make the point over and over again that she wanted to make sense of the article on her own.

Figure 9.1
Trent and Julie kept track of Franki's reading in different ways.

NOT that easy of an artical
She is reading the word carefully and if there is something she isn't sure of she has a prediction. She's trying to find out her questions. She's finding out things and rereads to get more clues on what is going on. If there's something she doesn't really know what it means but she has thoughts on what might happen. If she doesn't remember something she goes back and reads it over. Circaling things she doesn't know At the end she practically knew the whole thing.

She is circeling the things that she doesn't know what it means

She is stoping to think about the artickle

She is guessing

She is paying atenshion

She is going back to read again

She is making a line for the things she doesn't understand

She is looking back

She is telling us what she is thinking

She does the easy stuff first

After Franki finished reading the article, the class identified only two pieces of information that she could not make sense of without discussing it with someone who understood hockey. The students realized that although Franki pronounced many of the players' names incorrectly, she could still understand what she was reading. After watching Franki struggle through this sports article, especially one that many of the children in the class found easy, the students felt more comfortable talking about the struggles they were having in their own reading.

When we talk about our reading, we try to make our lessons comfortable and informal. Sitting on the floor with the children feels more informal and encourages natural conversations around text. We want students to be part of our reading and to really understand how we make sense of texts.

We must also model connecting several pieces of reading on the same topic, idea, or issue. There are many different ways to get information, and we want our students to have the thinking skills to make sense of any format or challenge they come upon. Whether they are reading a biography in graphic-novel form or watching an informational video, our students need to

What Does a Person's/Character's Actions Tell Us About Him or Her?	Book	Lesson Focus	Language We Might Use with Students to Start the Conversation
Day 1	*Emmanuel's Dream: The True Story of Emmanuel Ofosu Yeboah* by Laurie Ann Thompson	How a person deals with struggles and challenges often helps us understand the person more deeply.	"What was this person's biggest challenge? How did he overcome it?"
Day 2	*Bill the Boy Wonder: The Secret Co-Creator of Batman* by Marc Tyler Nobelman	Decisions that people make often tell us a great deal about them.	"What decisions about the writing did Bill make that affected his life positively and negatively?"
Day 3	*Drum Dream Girl: How One Girl's Courage Changed Music* by Margarita Engle	The subtitle often gives us insight into the author's message about a character/story.	"What does the subtitle tell us? How did this story show courage?"
Day 4	*The Day-Glo Brothers: The True Story of Bob and Joe Switzer's Bright Ideas and Brand-New Colors* by Chris Barton	A person's relationship with others often tells us about the character.	"What can we learn about the brothers through their relationship with each other?"
Day 5	*Fly High!: The Story of Bessie Coleman* by Louise Borden and Mary Kay Kroeger	Often writers focus on an important character trait throughout a story.	"What trait is a thread in this story? Why would the author choose to focus on this trait?"

be able to navigate the format with the knowledge that they have the skills to make sense of it.

We have discovered that picture-book biographies are perfect for students in grades 3–6. They are engaging and interesting, and they invite readers to think deeply about a person in history. Picture-book biographies are incredible resources because they don't often tell the entire life of a person. Rather they focus on one thing that is fascinating to the author. Often the thread in the story is a key characteristic such as perseverance. We use picture-book biographies to think more deeply about what a person or character's actions tell us about him or her.

Main Idea Versus Interesting Facts

One challenge our students often have is moving beyond isolated facts to get big ideas from their informational reading. To help our readers see the ways that facts go together in a text, we look for books that have interesting facts but also a clear umbrella topic.

How Do the Interesting Facts Fit Together to Teach Us Something Bigger?	Book	Lesson Focus	Language We Might Use with Students to Start the Conversation
Day 1	*Timeless Thomas: How Thomas Edison Changed Our Lives* by Gene Baretta	The organization of an informational text helps us understand big ideas.	"How do the organization of this book and these facts help us understand the author's bigger message?"
Day 2	*Water Is Water: A Book About the Water Cycle* by Miranda Paul	The title often helps us understand the big idea.	"How does the title help tie the information of the book together for readers?"
Day 3	*Feathers: Not Just for Flying* by Melissa Stewart	Authors give us information beyond the initial facts.	"The author gives us two layers of information. Why do you think she did that?"
Day 4	*How Did That Get in My Lunchbox? The Story of Food* by Chris Butterworth	Looking for patterns across information helps us understand the big idea.	"What does each two-page spread have in common?"
Day 5	*Over and Under the Snow* by Kate Messner	Language in an informational text helps us understand big ideas.	"How does the repeated language of the book help us understand what the author is trying to teach us?"

Students have time to talk about the main ideas and issues in news magazines.

Textbooks and Other Assigned Reading

Reading informational pieces that are assignments poses different challenges for readers. Knowing that many upper elementary students have little or no experience reading textbooks and that they will probably need those skills when they leave elementary school, we used to conduct a series of reading lessons with a textbook. Using a text that all students have in common helps build an anchor for reading any difficult text. (More recently, since we have moved away from using textbooks, we make copies of a nonfiction text to share with students.) Then we adapt Cris Tovani's idea from *I Read It, but I Don't Get It* (2000) and give each of the students a green highlighter and a yellow highlighter. We tell them to use the green one when they learn something new and the yellow one when they're confused or don't completely understand what they're reading. After giving the students enough time to read and highlight the chapter, we ask them to look over their highlighted pages and be ready to talk about what made reading the textbook difficult.

A class of fourth graders listed the reasons why they found textbooks difficult to read. Textbooks

- have bigger words;
- have lots of topics on a page;
- have important information;
- are not a story;
- are nonfiction;
- make it hard to get a picture in your head as you read;
- have graphs/photos/maps and more things to look at and understand;

- don't tell you about just one thing (one page might be about the Civil War, the next about Native Americans);
- have big pages, more pages, and smaller words than other books;
- have units that are bigger than chapters in most books;
- are about topics we don't understand;
- are boring, so we get sluggish; our minds wander and we can't get into it; we know it will be slow going the whole time, with no exciting parts;
- aren't books we want to read;
- have tests, which makes them no fun to read because you have to memorize what is in them; and
- are all serious, with no funny jokes.

Even though these students had very little experience with textbooks, they seemed to connect textbooks with memorization and testing. They identified some common difficulties in reading nonfiction generally, but we noticed that many of them had highlighted several places in the chapter that said, "See map below" or "See graph." The students did not know what to do when they were directed somewhere else on the page. We realized that some of the features of textbooks would be very easy to teach, whereas others would be more difficult.

The following day, we asked students to go back to the chapter, find three to five important ideas, and write those on sticky notes. Our goals were to help them begin to think about how to identify important information and to help us learn more about the way our students read nonfiction. The chapter they had read was on maps and globes. It introduced terms such as "longitude" and "latitude" and defined different types of maps. When the students discussed the ideas they thought were important, many marked a map of the United States that appeared in the chapter because "you have to memorize all of the states" and a map of Ohio because "you have to know where the cities are." However, both maps were placed in the chapter as examples of political maps. It appeared that the students were not reading the headings and captions beside the maps, for if they had, they might have realized the true reason the maps were in the chapter.

We realized that one of the students' problems with textbooks was that they were ignoring many of the headings, bold words, and captions that are important parts of these books. The next day, we had the class create a chart on the board listing all the headings and bold words in the chapter. Once the students saw all these words and phrases together, they realized that the main theme of the chapter was map reading. Another problem they had was the subheadings within the chapter, many of which were in the form of questions. The students assumed that they were supposed to answer them. These misconceptions confused them as they read, but they were able to recognize their mistakes when they saw what they'd written on the board.

After the lesson, we had students go back to their sticky notes and decide whether the ideas they had written really represented the important information from the chapter. Many of them realized that not reading the captions, headings, and bold words had made it difficult to understand the text. Many admitted that they'd breezed right over those features so they could "get it over with" faster.

We've always worked with students to help them understand the format and features of textbooks. We used to start by asking them to look through a textbook to see what they noticed. We came to realize that although children can often identify the features in a textbook that can help a reader, they don't necessarily use them while they read. Once we realized that, we were able to adjust our teaching to help our students not only identify features of textbooks but also use those features to make sense of the text.

As textbooks become less and less relevant and other sources of information become more important, we have come to use lessons like this when helping students navigate any challenging informational text. Whether it is a website with information with hyperlinks or a magazine article, our students come upon the same challenges that they do when they are reading textbooks. Helping them see the particular struggles this type of reading causes as well as the power they have as readers to make sense of it is important, whether they are reading textbooks or other assigned readings.

Visual Features

One of the biggest challenges that upper elementary readers face is pulling together all the pieces of information in nonfiction texts. This is becoming more and more important as visuals have become more common. A single piece of nonfiction text may include charts, graphs, maps, and more. Although our students have learned to read these items in isolation, they often have a hard time figuring out how a graph, for example, might help them understand the text. We try to give our students time to learn how to read and understand how these pieces of nonfiction text work together.

We like to use infographics to help our students make sense of text and visual information that works together. There are several sources for infographics online. Our favorites are KidsDiscover.com Infographics and Reading Rockets's Infographic Pinterest page (https://www.pinterest.com/readingrockets/infographics/). We have our students break into pairs for ten or fifteen minutes to explore several infographics that we share on paper or electronically. Then we ask them to share two interesting things that they learned. The next day we ask them to go back to the infographics that they found most difficult or confusing and think about how to make sense of them. Then we ask them to come up with a list of ideas for reading infographics. We ask, "What do readers do to read and understand infographics?" One class came up with this list:

- Read the title.
- Pay attention to words that are bigger.
- Look at the clues about which part to read first.
- Check the key and/or the color code.
- Go back and forth with your eyes while you're reading.
- Read the words that are there.
- Think about how the information goes together.

Even though many students can read graphs, they rarely think of graph reading as a reading skill, because it is often addressed in math. We want students to see that graph reading is a kind of *reading*. By continually going back to the question "What do you do when you read difficult text?" we can help students add to the strategies, skills, and behaviors they are learning without changing focus each week or month. These conversations are ongoing throughout the year and lead students to deeper understanding.

Strategy Lesson

How Do Text Features Support the Reader?

■ **Why We Teach It:** Often students ignore many of the text features included in news articles to support readers. The children read the text from beginning to end without ever looking at the features that could help them make better sense of the information.

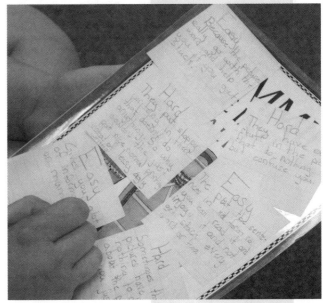

Glen finds features that make this book easy and difficult.

■ **How We Teach It:** For these lessons, we try to find two articles on the same topic. We often use a current issue of *Time for Kids* as well as a local news source and find a piece from each. Then we photocopy both articles onto a large sheet of paper so that students can see both of them at the same time. We give a copy to each child and ask them to read and discuss with a partner which article is easier to understand and why. Most articles in *Time for Kids* have several text features that aren't found in the newspaper articles. The headlines in the magazine articles are often more helpful. Photos, maps, and captions also support the reader. After several lessons like this, students begin to see how important it is to use such features.

■ ■ ■

Strategy Lesson

Building Background Knowledge

- **Why We Teach It:** We know that background knowledge is essential for understanding text, but as students move up the grades, they will be required to read about topics for which they have little or no background knowledge. We often do a lesson like this early in a research project or in a whole-class study of a content topic, though it can be taught at any time.

- **How We Teach It:** We ask students to collect three to five books on the same topic (a topic of their choice) over a period of several days. We then show them a stack of our own. We hold up each book and talk about the features that we think would make the book hard for us to understand as well as the features that we think would support us. We then ask the students to look through each of their books to discover the features that might make the book difficult or easy for them. We have them jot these features on sticky notes and place them on the front of the book. After small-group discussions about the features, we ask the students which books they plan to read first and why. Having spent a great deal of time with the books at this point, children often choose the book they think will be the easiest for them. We then discuss with them the importance of building background knowledge and how reading easy texts can give them the background knowledge they need to understand more difficult texts on a given topic.

- **Follow-Up:** As the students read their books over the course of several days or weeks, we bring the class back together to discuss what they are reading. We focus our talk on the importance of building background knowledge on your own before moving on to more difficult reading.

■ ■ ■

Readers have certain expectations that they bring to nonfiction texts. This is most obvious when reading nonfiction books that are part of a series or written by the same author. When readers read several books in a series, or several books by a particular author, they come to expect similar style, features, visuals, and so on in future reading. This sets our nonfiction readers up to think before they read and to recognize the expectations they have as they read.

Cycle of Mini-Lessons

Expectations as a Reader

- **Why We Teach It:** We want students to know that we know certain things as readers that give us expectations for future reading. Because of our experiences as readers, we have certain expectations that support future reading.

- **How We Teach It:** This cycle of exploration lessons usually takes a few days. We begin with six to eight baskets of nonfiction series or author books from the nonfiction section of our classroom library. We put kids in groups of three or four and rotate various baskets to each group for exploration. During the exploration, we ask kids to browse and or read books from the basket, looking for similarities. Then we come together as a group and chart the features we could expect in each of the baskets. We discuss the idea that once you know a series or author, you come to the next book with expectations as a reader that help you understand.

- **Follow-Up:** We have used this cycle to kick off nonfiction reading early in the school year. This serves two purposes: the goal of the mini-lesson as well as giving students time to get their hands on several nonfiction books. We often refer to the chart we create after this cycle as we read books aloud, think about other authors, and so on. This is also a natural way to discuss common nonfiction text features without isolating them in a features-only unit of study. Once this conversation becomes natural, we can extend the same idea to expectations when we read an article on a certain website, expectations when we read a visual such as a graph, and more.

■ ■ ■

Mini-Lesson

Making Decisions When Reading Online

- **Why We Teach It:** Our nonfiction readers are faced with many decisions. Even when books were the only source of nonfiction our students read, students could decide when to read a book from cover to cover and when to skip around to sections of interest. Now, with so many online resources, readers have to make many decisions as readers. Some, such as clicking on a hyperlink for more information, can deepen understanding, whereas other decisions, such as checking out an advertisement on a web page, can take the reader away from the ideas.

■ **How We Teach It:** We often teach this lesson or series lesson first as a shared experience. We love to use articles from Wonderopolis, because the site is filled with many options for readers. We often do the first article as a think-aloud and talk through our own decisions as we read through an article projected onto the Smartboard or screen. As we go through the article, we articulate when and why we decide to click on or skip a link. ("I know what this highlighted word means, so I don't need to click on it for more information.") We then reflect on the decisions we made and how each decision helped us understand the text more deeply.

Students use a variety of tools for annotating digital resources too.

■ **Follow-Up:** We follow this first think-aloud with some more collaborative decision making as we move to a shared experience for the class. Projecting a new article from the same site onto the board, we talk through the decisions we will need to make and decide as a class what to do. Then we go back and reflect on them. Finally, we give kids time to attend to their own decision making (possibly annotating it as they go) by giving them time to read a post of their choice on the Wonderopolis website.

■ ■ ■

Mini-Lesson

Learning from Informational Videos

■ **Why We Teach It:** As we expand our definition of text, it is important that students have access to a variety of media and use that media for learning. We have noticed over the years that our students love video but often see it as a form of entertainment. We want them to have access to information in many forms, and video provides a great deal of information in today's world.

■ **How We Teach It:** We like to use short videos such as those found on the Friends with Fins site (friendswithfins.com). This site is filled with short videos about the ocean, with a variety of topics and formats. We start the lessons by watching a video with little direction. We then rewatch the video and ask kids to watch with an eye toward learning. What new things do they learn when they watch it a second time?

■ **Follow-Up:** Rewatching a video is similar to rereading a book in that the viewer often learns more in the second viewing. We might do this with a few videos, adding some type of note taking as students become comfortable watching to learn. Conversations about the differences between videos for entertainment and videos for learning are embedded in all of these lessons.

■ ■ ■

Mini-Lesson

Information Embedded in Fiction

- **Why We Teach It:** Often information is embedded in fiction text. As more formats are available and more authors create hybrid texts, we want our students to be comfortable with many ways to learn information through reading.

- **How We Teach It:** For these lessons, we like to use books by Louise Borden, who has written a variety of fiction, nonfiction, and historical fiction. Her historical fiction includes a great deal of research that ensures accuracy in the stories and details. We often begin the cycle of lessons with books such as *A. Lincoln and Me*, a fiction story with embedded information that makes the separation of fiction and information obvious to readers. We then share books such as *Paperboy* by Mary Kay Kroeger and Louise Borden and *Sleds on Boston Common* by Louise Borden to discuss ways authors embed historical information into a fiction narrative.

- **Follow-Up:** We can follow up by comparing a historical account of an event with a historical fiction book on the same topic. Showing kids the ways that authors use fiction to share information in this way helps them see the difference in craft and the ways in which embedding information in a narrative helps readers understand in a different way.

■ ■ ■

Mini-Lesson

Mini–Book Study on *Look Up!*

- **Why We Teach It:** We want our students to have the experience of studying a book over several days. Visiting and revisiting a book that they may not choose on their own often changes students' perceptions of nonfiction. We love to find books with a variety of interesting text features to help students see that informational books are often surprising and clever. The book *Look Up! Bird-Watching in Your Own Backyard* by Annette LeBlanc Cate is a book that surprises readers and embeds a variety of features in different ways.

- **How We Teach It:** We usually spend about three or four days on this book study. We try to get multiple copies from our local library so that kids can work in partnerships for the duration of the study. On the first day we preview the book together, having conversations about what we might expect based on the cover, back cover, and inside flap. Then kids go off to explore the book in whatever way they want to. Each day, we come back together to share things students have discovered and any thinking that has changed.

- **Follow-Up:** This usually sets the stage for exploring informational text over time. For students who have merely spent time skimming and scanning nonfiction in the past, this gives them a way to dig deeper. We often follow this by visiting other types of informational pieces over several days and having similar conversations. Studying informational videos, news articles, and podcasts helps kids dig deeper as nonfiction readers.

■ ■ ■

Making the Most of News Magazines

http://sten.pub/sltr7

Franki shares strategies for using *Time for Kids* in the classroom.

Chapter 10

The Role of Close Reading in Grades 3–6

Thus, close reading is an intensive analysis of a text in order to come to terms with what it says, how it says it, and what it means.

—Timothy Shanahan

What do you make of the following?

When danger dares to cross my path, I stretch my majestic twelve-foot height, thrash my fearsome four-inch claws, and roar a sharp-toothed growl backed by every ounce of my one thousand pounds. But I don't do it often. Mama Bear doesn't like it when I raise my voice. She likes my teeth better when I smile . . . which makes me smile a lot. The other thing Mama isn't fond of is my big belly, and aw, she's right. A few hundred extra pounds does call for a large dose of discipline, diet, and exercise. I just don't care much for exercise. In fact, on the morning of "the Incident" I'd fixed some high-fiber oatmeal and set it on the table, hoping to get out of our morning walk. Mama sweetly thanked me . . . then insisted we hit the road and enjoy breakfast when we came back. How could I argue? She and my boy were willing to join me in my battle of the bulge, and along the way Mama generously ignored my checking the beehives for honeycomb, looking under logs for moth larvae, and grabbing treats from picnic garbage cans. Our walk went fine, but when we returned home, we found our front door ajar. (Starbright Foundation 2001, 41)

When you start to read this story, you may be confused about just who is telling it. Once you think you have identified the narrator, you can go back over what you've read to find phrases that validate your thinking. But upper elementary readers are still learning how to make inferences and predictions using evidence from the text to validate their thinking.

It is hard to teach children who want to be "right" that their thoughts, inferences, and predictions while reading often change as they discover more in the text. Children want to read the ending that they hope will happen. Despite the evidence in the text, young readers tend to hold on to their initial ideas, and comprehension often suffers as a result. As stories become more complex, initial thoughts, inferences, and predictions are less likely to be accurate. Skilled readers use what they read to support or negate their previous ideas. We want our students to be able to value such changes in thinking. We ask, "What in the book makes you think that?" to encourage them to think more deeply about what they are reading and thinking. We want our students to notice where their thinking changes and when their thoughts and predictions are incorrect. We design experiences for children to surprise them in their reading, and we teach them to watch for evidence that validates their initial reactions to the text. If we encourage and celebrate changes in thinking over time, reading improves.

We know that success on many of the standardized tests that are administered to children across the nation depends on inferential reasoning supported by evidence in the text. We believe that close reading is much more important to a developing reader than the ability to perform well on a standardized test. We want much more for our students. We believe that close reading is rigorous but joyful work as students are empowered by their more sophisticated thinking. Our goal is to help our students develop all the skills and strategies they need to make sense of texts and to become readers and thinkers in a complex world.

Supporting Thinking with Evidence in the Text

To help students begin to use evidence in their reading, we often use the book *The Stranger* by Chris Van Allsburg. The reader must put together the clues that the author weaves through the text to figure out who the title character might be. Children often need to reread the book several times, because they miss many of the author's clues during the first or second reading. When we teach this lesson, we often start by reading the book aloud to students. After the first read, most students are frustrated to find that Van Allsburg does not specifically identify the stranger. (One year, students even asked if there was a website that would tell them the answer!)

We might read this book three or four times to the same group of students, giving them a chance to find as many clues as they can. Then we ask them who they think the stranger is, based on the evidence in the text. When we ask them to validate their thinking with evidence from the text, students can no longer just come up with an unsubstantiated idea or thought. They need to learn to rethink their original assumptions based on knowledge they have gained from the text. We scaffold this learning with two-column forms to track thinking. (See Figure 10.1; the form is provided in the appendix.)

These conversations are often the first step in building students' reading stamina. They begin to see a new purpose for reading, and they understand that as books become more complex, reading becomes a more sophisticated process. Their job becomes a bit more challenging, but also more rewarding. They begin to see that a single reading may not be enough to fully understand a text. They begin to realize the power of rereading and rethinking.

We know that we need to do more than simply teach comprehension strategies in order for students to apply them independently. We realized early on that students aren't often aware of what works for them or when they need to stop reading to clarify meaning. They are familiar with various comprehension strategies and can discuss them with us. They can tell us they are making a connection or making an inference, but they don't always know how and when to use that strategy when reading difficult texts on their own.

We've all had students who make predictions and respond to questions without taking into account what they have learned so far from the text. One year, Meg suggested that a character had been robbed and knocked down when in fact the story clearly implied that the character had had a heart attack. When we asked Meg to explain why she thought this, she said, "I just think that it happened. It could have happened." Even though Meg had nothing to substantiate her inference, she believed that readers could make their own decisions about what happens in a story. Of course, misinformation like this can change the entire message of the text.

We want to encourage our students to go back into the text to validate their thinking. We want them to realize that there are signals to be found in

---

Different Possibilities for Headings in Two-Column Notes

- What do you know about the character? How do you know that?
- How did your thinking change? What part of the text changed your thinking?
- What do you think will happen? What in the text makes you think that?
- What connections do you have? How do the connections help you understand the text better?
- Which part of the text was difficult to understand? What did you do to help yourself?

Who is the stranger?	What in the book makes you think that?
Father Time	I think that because the trees didnt change color when he was with them but the trees next to their home turned colors. Then I also think that because befor the frost os the winds he said see you next fall.

Figure 10.1
Kelly's two-column chart

the text that can shape their thinking as they read, and we want them to know that they can review the text and change their thinking. Going back into the text to support thinking is something we focus on all year. We know that when students can justify their thinking through use of the text, their skills at inferring, predicting, and synthesizing are sharpened.

Strategy Lesson

Understanding Alternative Perspectives

■ **Why We Teach It:** Students in the upper elementary grades often encounter texts that show differing viewpoints. We want our students to be able to weigh the evidence in the texts that they read to form their own opinions that they can support.

■ **Possible Anchor Book:** A great book for a lesson like this is *Should There Be Zoos?* by Tony Stead, a compilation of eight essays written by fourth-grade students, each presenting an argument either for or against zoos.

■ **How We Teach It:** The idea here is to provide opportunities for students to see many perspectives on a single issue and to consider their own opinions, in this case, on zoos. After reading the text, students can move into book-talk groups or write about their own opinions about zoos while supporting those opinions with information presented in the book.

■ ■ ■

We keep our eye out for poetry and other short texts to help students begin to learn how critical it is to use evidence from text in their thinking. A favorite book of poetry is *When Riddles Come Rumbling: Poems to Ponder* by Rebecca Kai Dotlich. This book is filled with poems that give readers clues about the object described in the poem. For one lesson, for example, we chose a poem about a roller coaster. We copied the poem on the left half of a sheet of paper and left the right half blank so that students could record their thinking. Students struggled with the meaning of the poem, but they had fun with it.

We noticed that many students used just one word or phrase on which to base their decision about the poem, without checking to see if the entire poem fit their interpretation. For example, when one student read the word "twirl" in the poem, she decided that the subject was a washing machine, even though the rest of the poem didn't support that idea. During a later lesson, another student shared her response with the class. She was able to show

I think it's a gumbal machine because I have evanins, I is a gumbal

You put a coin in the gumbar machine

With just one coin ①
t
u
m ← Gumbars tumble out.
b
l
e
out
from a round glass world   The gumbal sits on the glass
through a silver   srere.
s
p   Gumbals go though
o   the silver
u   Pocket
t.

Figure 10.2
Kevin found evidence in many places to support his thinking.

that all of the evidence in the text supported her thinking. She explained how she thought through each line to see if her prediction was accurate. After that demonstration, we gave students another poem to read so they could try their hand at using the evidence in the entire text to support their thinking. (See Figure 10.2.)

When reading *The Table Where Rich People Sit* by Byrd Baylor, students naturally fall into a conversation about what it means to be rich. The text presents two perspectives of what it means to be rich. We use this book to help students see another way to use evidence from the text to support their ideas, and we have them use that evidence to write a response. We give them a two-column sheet (see the form in the appendix); students decide whether the evidence they find should go in the "Yes" column (meaning "yes, the people in the book were rich") or in the "No" column ("no, they were not rich"). (See Figure 10.3.) This activity leads to interesting conversations. For example, Tessa asked Peter how he had decided that the family was rich, because his "Yes" column did not seem to have the most evidence. This led to a thoughtful conversation about the strength of the evidence. The children tried to determine if it was more important to have *more* evidence or *stronger* evidence to support their thinking.

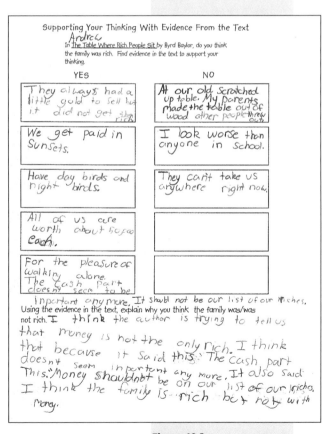

Supporting Your Thinking With Evidence From the Text
Andrew
In <u>The Table Where Rich People Sit</u> by Byrd Baylor, do you think the family was rich. Find evidence in the text to support your thinking.

YES	NO
They always had a little gold to sell but it did not get them rich	At our old scratched up table. My parents made the table out of wood other people threw out
We get paid in Sunsets.	I look worse than anyone in school.
Have day birds and night birds.	They can't take us anywhere right now.
All of us are worth about 50,000 cash.	
For the pleasure of walking alone. The cash part doesn't seem to be	

important any more. It shubl not be our list of our riches. Using the evidence in the text, explain why you think the family was/was not rich. I think the author is trying to tell us that money is not the only rich. I think that because it said this. The cash part doesn't seem important any more. It also said This. Money shouldnot be on our list of our riches. I think the family is rich but not with money.

Figure 10.3
Andrew collected evidence while listening to *The Table Where Rich People Sit.*

Choosing Close Reading

Close reading is when a reader independently stops at moments in a text (or media or life) to reread and observe the choices an author has made. He or she reflects on those observations to reach for new understandings that can color the way the rest of the book is read (or song heard or life lived) and thought about.

—Chris Lehman and Kate Roberts

It is when our students take control of their own reading and decide on their own to read with a certain lens that we see the power of close reading. We know that it is important for our students to see what is possible, so we guide them to try things in mini-lessons, in small-group work, and through read-aloud conversations. But it is when students come up with their own purpose for close reading that we are confident the skills they are building in grades 3–6 will support them in all of their lifelong reading.

Supporting Close Reading in Individual Reading Conferences

Often we learn of a student's close reading strategies during individual conferences. We spend a great deal of our time in reading conferences listening to students' thinking.

We have found that goal setting is an important part of reading conferences with students. We ask, "What is your goal for the next several days of reading? What are you wondering as a reader? Is there a tool that can help you figure this out?" We have worked hard to focus our conference time on supporting readers in their decisions about how to read the text they are currently reading. Every book does not need a close read, and it is up to the child to decide whether a certain lens is needed and how best to go about it.

For students, reading with a focused lens becomes the anchor for our talk. In a recent conference with third grader Kayla, she talked about how she was struggling to remember who was who in her first Babysitters' Club graphic novel by Ann M. Martin and Raina Telgemeier. She wanted to try keeping track of things she learned about each character on two colors of sticky notes (one for Kristy and one for Stacey). When she had finished the first book, Kayla compiled the sticky notes onto a large piece of construction paper and we met again. Her notes helped her know each character well, and by the time of this conference, she could talk at length about each one.

Elizabeth often chose to use a dry erase board to jot down her thinking as she read and reread favorite picture books. When Franki asked her about it, she said it helped her to jot down the things she wanted to think about as

Olivia uses the dry erase table to collect new thinking during a reread of a favorite book. She then takes a picture of it so that she can go back and make sense of it.

she read. She didn't feel like she needed to keep the thinking (which is why she chose the dry erase board as a temporary spot to record it), but the act of planning her thinking and her lens helped her read more closely.

Gabe became a fan of mythology in fourth grade and was fascinated by the similarities and differences in some of the versions of the stories. He created his own chart comparing the similarities and differences he found in some of his favorite myths.

Koki decided to spend days closely reading the website Wonderopolis. He wanted to become an expert at navigating the site even though he had not had many experiences reading online, so he spent days of his reading workshop time exploring it. But he wasn't just freely exploring. He wanted to become an expert at how the site worked so he could teach others some tips about navigating and finding information, so he read it with that lens. One lesson we learned from Koki is that close reading is never just about a single text. He said, "I'm reading nonfiction articles online. First I wasn't good at it. Now I'm good at it because I explored a new website. It's called Wonderopolis. Wonderopolis is a website that collects wonders that people wonder and post an article that has a conclusion at the end." In grades 3–6, we have to remember that we are teaching readers, and we hope the skills they learn when reading closely help them understand texts they will read in the future.

Ava reads to discover whether cats or dogs make better pets. She keeps an ongoing list of her findings over several days.

Ava decided to read all of the dog books in our book basket to find any facts that were new to her. Then she decided to determine whether dogs or cats made better pets. She began a list that grew to over 100 reasons. Going into this self-designed project, Ava considered herself an expert on dogs. The power of her reading and thinking came when two other students in the class approached Ava to compare their research, because they too had been reading a great deal about dogs. They wanted to see if they would find discrepancies in the facts and things that they had to dig into because sources gave conflicting information.

Jack became a huge fan of Sandra Markle's nonfiction. Once he read several books from her Animal Predators and Animal Scavengers series, he was thrilled to discover that she wrote other books. He started to read her books to find similarities between them. At first he thought she was a writer who was passionate about animals. He expanded this idea when he discovered her book about chocolate and read to find connections between topics.

When we focus our conferences with students on the thinking work they are doing, they become aware of this thinking and in turn, grow as readers. Thinking, talking, and writing around a text becomes a joyful part of learning rather than merely compliance.

Strategy Lesson

Using Evidence in the Text to Support an Inference

- **Why We Teach It:** Inferring from the text is a critical skill as readers become more sophisticated. Students need to use the clues that the author leaves to make sense of what they read.

- **Possible Anchor Book:** *Mirror Mirror: A Book of Reverso Poems* by Marilyn Singer. These poems, focused on favorite fairy tales, share poems from two perspectives. The perspectives of the fairy tale characters are humorous and cleverly written.

- **How We Teach It:** We share one of the poems with our students. We ask them to infer the identity of the narrator. They look for evidence in the text to defend their thinking. They can use the evidence they have found to write a response or to talk to others in a group to determine whether their inference is correct. (Figure 10.4 shows the same lesson with another book.)

- **Follow-Up:** Some of the poems are obvious and require minimal inferring. Others are quite tricky. After working through an easier poem, you might try your students on the more difficult ones. Singer has two other books in this series of Reverso poems that are also fun reads.

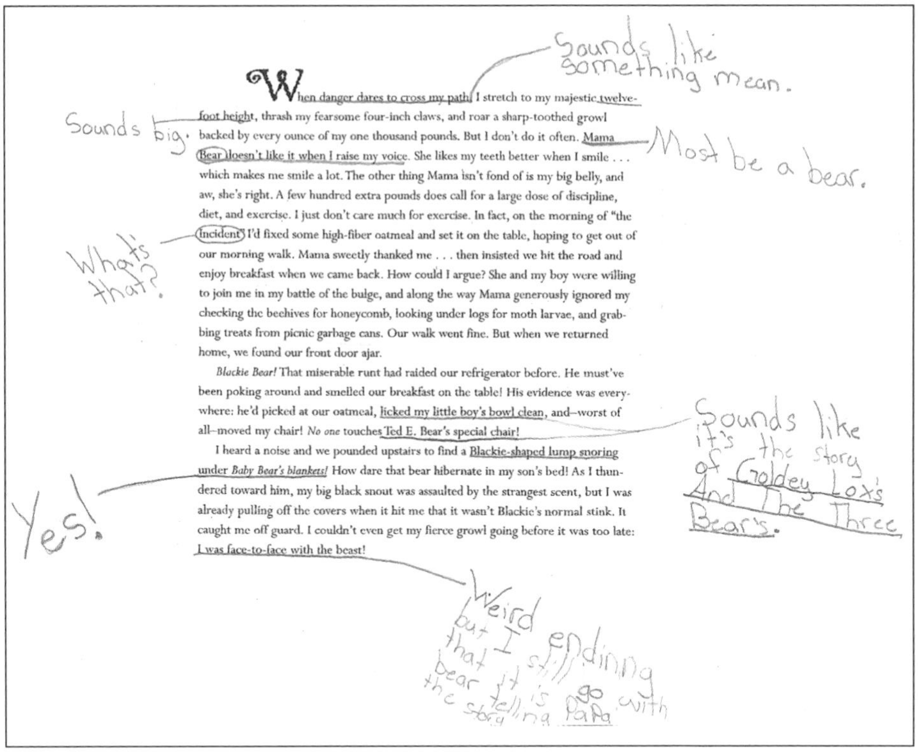

When danger dares to cross my path, I stretch to my majestic twelve-foot height, thrash my fearsome four-inch claws, and roar a sharp-toothed growl backed by every ounce of my one thousand pounds. But I don't do it often. Mama Bear doesn't like it when I raise my voice. She likes my teeth better when I smile . . . which makes me smile a lot. The other thing Mama isn't fond of is my big belly, and aw, she's right. A few hundred extra pounds does call for a large dose of discipline, diet, and exercise. I just don't care much for exercise. In fact, on the morning of "the incident" I'd fixed some high-fiber oatmeal and set it on the table, hoping to get out of our morning walk. Mama sweetly thanked me . . . then insisted we hit the road and enjoy breakfast when we came back. How could I argue? She and my boy were willing to join me in my battle of the bulge, and along the way Mama generously ignored my checking the beehives for honeycomb, looking under logs for moth larvae, and grabbing treats from picnic garbage cans. Our walk went fine. But when we returned home, we found our front door ajar.

Blackie Bear! That miserable runt had raided our refrigerator before. He must've been poking around and smelled our breakfast on the table! His evidence was everywhere: he'd picked at our oatmeal, licked my little boy's bowl clean, and–worst of all–moved my chair! *No one* touches Ted E. Bear's special chair!

I heard a noise and we pounded upstairs to find a Blackie-shaped lump snoring under *Baby Bear's blankets!* How dare that bear hibernate in my son's bed! As I thundered toward him, my big black snout was assaulted by the strangest scent, but I was already pulling off the covers when it hit me that it wasn't Blackie's normal stink. It caught me off guard. I couldn't even get my fierce growl going before it was too late: I was face-to-face with the beast!

Figure 10.4
Glen marked evidence in the text to determine the identity of the narrator in this excerpt from *Once Upon a Fairy Tale*.

Strategy Lesson

Using Evidence in the Text to Support Your Thinking

- **Why We Teach It:** Students benefit from learning how to find evidence from the text to support their thinking in many ways. This lesson allows them to use evidence from the text to support their personal response.

- **Possible Anchor Book:** The picture book *Old Henry* by Joan W. Blos tells the story of a man who doesn't do things the way everyone else does. For that reason he decides to leave the home he loves.

- **How We Teach It:** We share the book with students as a read-aloud. During the first read, students listen to the story and talk about whether they agree with the choices the neighbors and Henry made throughout the story. We ask, "Which choices do you agree with and which do you disagree with?" We then reread the book, asking them to be on the lookout for words and phrases that make them think differently about their first opinions as well as words or phrases that support their opinion. After their reading, we ask students to write a response about whether they thought the neighbors were

Figure 10.5
Peter decided he would never want to be a "Master Sniffer" after reading the description in *Odd Jobs*.

A master sniffer is someone who smells armpits for a living. They smell the armpits to test how well deoderants work. You might wonder how they get people to work for them. Well, they put an ad in the newspaper asking for people with a "sensitive nose," but the ad does not tell what the job is. Then, when people call about the ad, they tell the caller, and they almost always refuse. However, some want to stay and try it out. The "odor judges" put them through a test where they sniff bottles instead of armpits. Usually, they don't pass.

I would never ever ever EVER want to be an armpit sniffer no matter what the pay! I mean, you are smelling REAL peoples armpits! It says in the article that you have to have a "willingness." I think you must have more than that! though it is true that somebody has to do it, I don't want to be that somebody!

right in their actions. (Figure 10.5 shows a student response from a similar lesson using the book *Odd Jobs: The Wackiest Jobs You've Never Heard Of* by Ellen Weiss. Although that book is out of print, it is well worth trying to get your hands on a copy!)

■ **Follow-Up:** As a whole class, chart all of the phrases that students marked. As you do so, sort the phrases into two columns: phrases that made them think they agreed with the neighbors and phrases that made them think they disagreed with them.

■ ■ ■

■ ■ ■

Because finding evidence in the text is a topic of conversation throughout the year, it comes up during read-aloud discussions. During a reading of *Wringer* by Jerry Spinelli, for example, students were beginning to find evidence that the main character's mother did not like the town's tradition of Pigeon Day. You can use student-initiated conversations as a way into a lesson on how they can make more informed decisions while reading. Students were accustomed to working with sticky notes, but because it was important

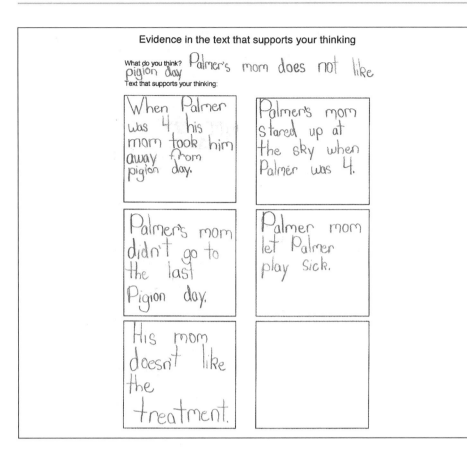

Figure 10.6
Sam collected evidence from *Wringer* to prove that Palmer's mother did not like Pigeon Day.

that they keep track of their thinking over time, we created a sheet that resembled six sticky notes on a page. We gave students this sheet of "invisible" sticky notes to collect evidence that supported or went against their prediction. They used this strategy throughout the reading of *Wringer* as they collected ideas that helped them think through the text. (See Figure 10.6; a form that may be used for this activity is provided in the appendix.)

Students can also use evidence in the text to help them determine the meaning of unfamiliar words. They can learn to look for the clues the author places in the text to identify what a word might mean.

Strategy Lesson

Problem-Solving the Meaning of Unknown Words

■ **Why We Teach It:** As students encounter more difficult texts, especially content-related texts, they will continue to come across words that are unfamiliar to them. Students at this stage should be able to decode the unknown word as well as determine its meaning to comprehend the text.

■ **Possible Anchor Book:** *Baloney (Henry P.)* by Jon Scieszka is a picture book about an alien, Henry P. Baloney, who is in trouble for being late to school. On the inside flap of the book, we learn that the book is about not only using your imagination to get out of tight spots, but "that weird feeling you get when you are learning to read and every other word looks like it comes from outer space." Henry's very special language in the text uses words (in bold) that are conspicuously unfamiliar to readers. This is a great book to use with students, because it is obvious that we wouldn't expect them to have previously seen the boldface words. At first glance, each word seems like a nonsense word. But at the end of the book is a "decoder" page. There, readers discover that each word is from a different language on earth and each one means something very familiar.

■ **How We Teach It:** This lesson can be taught as a read-aloud with a small group, or each child can have a copy of the text for shared reading. While reading the book, we stop at each unknown word. We ask children how they would say the word. We tell them that often readers can say a word correctly without knowing what it means. We remind students that understanding is what reading is all about. Then we ask them if they can use the context of the sentence and the pictures to make a prediction about what the word means. After each prediction, we ask them to explain their thinking and encourage them to tell how they used the context and pictures to predict the meaning. We continue with this conversation through the entire book. They use sticky notes to record their predictions. (See Figure 10.7; a form that may be used is provided in the appendix.)

Figure 10.7
Chris inferred the meanings of unknown words during a mini-lesson.

Baloney by Jon Scieszka		
Unknown word	What do you think it means?	What makes you think that?
Zimulis	I think a Zimulis is a Pencil	Because of the Picture
Deski	Desk	Because of the flat surface
Torakku	A garbage truck	Because thats what I would do if I had a truck
Szkola	School	
Razzo	Ship	Because thats what I would say if I was on a [illegible]
Pordo	Portal	launchpad
Buttuna	Button	Because it sais it brought him Some where els
Astrosus	A Person	Because he couldn't Jam anything els
Piksas	A joke	Because of the Picture. Because jokes are funny

■ **Follow-Up:** Make a chart of the strategies the children used when they came to a word they didn't understand. Use the glossary in the book to check the meaning of the unknown words. Go back into the text to look at the context and the pictures again to look for clues that readers may have missed the first time through.

Encourage children to write the words they don't understand in their independent reading on sticky notes. On each sticky note or on a form, they can write the unknown word, their prediction for what the word means, and the basis for their thinking.

■ ■ ■

Strategy Lesson

Using the Context of a Sentence or Paragraph to Determine the Meaning of an Unknown Word

- **Why We Teach It:** Often, words are defined within the context of the text a child is reading. But too often, children don't realize this and don't pick up on the information. Using the context to help determine meaning will help them see that there are clues in the text to help us as we read.

- **Possible Anchor Book:** *Pirate Diary: The Journal of Jake Carpenter* by Richard Platt features a diary format as nine-year-old Jake Carpenter recounts his daily adventures on a pirate ship. The glossary and index in this book are unique. Page numbers that are underlined in the index show where words that pirates would have used are explained in the text. This makes it a great resource for this type of lesson.

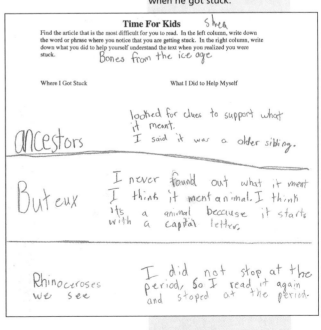

Figure 10.8
Shea kept track of strategies he used when he got stuck.

- **How We Teach It:** Because the book is in the form of a diary, daily excerpts can be used independently as single-page lessons. Using the glossary, we choose an excerpt that has one or more difficult words that are defined in the text. We ask children to read the text independently and share what they think is the meaning of the unknown word. Then we have them highlight the words in the rest of the text that helped them determine the meaning. Children can do this several times with different excerpts from the book or with issues of a news magazine. (See Figure 10.8; a form for this activity, using *Time for Kids*, may be found in the appendix.)

- **Follow-Up:** After doing this activity several times, we have children chart the types of signals in the text that helped them realize that the word was already defined for them.

■ ■ ■

Changing Your Thinking During Reading

Other Picture Books That Encourage Going Back into the Text

Sam and Dave Dig a Hole by Mac Barnett
The Table Where Rich People Sit by Byrd Baylor
Voices in the Park by Anthony Browne
Two White Rabbits by Jairo Buitrago
Last Stop on Market Street by Matt De La Peña
Baseball, Snakes, and Summer Squash by Donald Graves
Beyond the Pond by Joseph Kuefler
Strictly No Elephants by Lisa Mantchev
Ring! Yo? by Christopher Raschka
The Most Magnificent Thing by Ashley Spires
Lenny and Lucy by Philip Stead
And the Dish Ran Away with the Spoon by Janet Stevens
The Stranger by Chris Van Allsburg
Each Kindness by Jacqueline Woodson
The Other Side by Jacqueline Woodson

Figure 10.9
Ben changed his thinking several times while reading "Clothesline" by Ralph Fletcher.

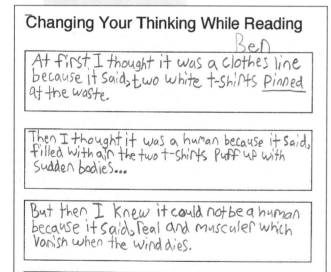

Changing Your Thinking While Reading

Ben

At first I thought it was a clothes line because it said, two white t-shirts pinned at the waste.

Then I thought it was a human because it said, filled with air the two t-shirts puff up with sudden bodies...

But then I knew it could not be a human because it said, real and musculer which vanish when the wind dies.

But then I didn't know if it was the clothes line because it's not the main thing the clothes are the main thing.

Then I knew it couldn't be a clothes line because it said, the wind lifts the towel until it lies horizontally.

Readers often change their thinking as they read. They pick up a new piece of information from the author that sometimes forces them to rethink their predictions and inferences. Children do not always realize that readers do this, and they may not always be aware when they are revising their own thinking. We help them recognize these revisions by using short texts and a form we created that helps them track the changes in their thinking as they read and write. Originally, we had students track their thinking on sticky notes, but they often fell off the page and got out of order, which made it difficult for students to see how their thinking had changed. So we created a form that works like sticky notes—only they don't fall off! We use these "invisible" sticky notes only after students have had a lot of experience with regular sticky notes.

We often start by asking students to track the changes in their thinking with a short text. We like to use poetry because the language is often figurative, so children's initial predictions are likely to change as they reread and gain understanding. For example, we may give students a copy of Ralph Fletcher's poem "Clothesline," from his book *Ordinary Things*. We delete the title before we hand it out and ask students to use the form to track the changes in their thinking as they read and reread. (See Figure 10.9.)

Upper elementary readers have the potential to become sophisticated readers of many texts. We plan experiences to help our students learn to notice signals in the text that can clarify their understanding, and we encourage them to go deeper into the text to extend their thinking. Once they realize that authors leave clues for the reader, children begin to read in different ways.

Epilogue

Tests are . . .
A big jumble of words
Printed on paper
one hour
Two hours
Three hours later
We are trying to make
ourselves think straighter.
But all we can do
Is sit and stumble
Head over heals
In our minds.
All we think about
Is running out of time,
Like every second
costs us a dime.

~Emily, grade 4

Emily reminds us of the stress our children face with the high-stakes testing that is all too common in the upper elementary grades. As teachers, we know that learning and reading are much more than testing. The authors of *A Teacher's Guide to Standardized Reading Tests* (Calkins, Montgomery, and Santman 1998) write, "In the current educational climate, we cannot afford to ignore assessment demands that seem alien to our educational philosophy and practice. But neither should we passively acquiesce, become apathetic and let these demands take over our teaching" (6). The writers urge us on: "This is an emergency because we all know that learning and reading are enhanced by teachers who know their students and their curriculum well and who use their knowledge of children to diversify instruction to meet their students' needs" (6).

We aim to create learning communities that surround our students with a treasure trove of books and conversations about reading. We value what children show us about their reading lives and plan thoughtful and purposeful learning. We engage our students in reading experiences that will help them build independence and develop the sophisticated thinking and reading skills they will need as they grow as readers. We focus our teaching on the most critical threads of learning throughout the school year. Most important, we listen to what our students tell us about their reading lives.

We began this book with a thought about reading that Courtney shared with us early in the school year:

"I've known how to read for almost four years now."

Courtney reminded us that learning to read includes all that we accomplish along the way. But it is also the result of challenges that encourage us to learn new skills and strategies as we become more sophisticated readers.

One January, we asked fourth graders to think about the books that had helped them as readers. We wanted them to think about those books that had had the greatest effect on their lives as readers.

Courtney was a Harry Potter fan and had decided early in the year that there wasn't much worth reading before the next Harry Potter book was published the following summer. After talking to her mother about Nancy Drew mysteries, Courtney decided to read all of the Nancy Drew books while she waited for the Harry Potter book to arrive. When we asked Courtney to think about the books that were most important to her, it wasn't surprising that many on her list were from the Nancy Drew series. Courtney wrote about the books that helped her become a better reader and why she felt they had affected her changing life as a reader.

The Mystery of the Glowing Eye by Carolyn Keene

This Nancy Drew book helped me because it helped me know what kind of Nancy Drew book I should read next, or what to look for to make sure my book was not boring when I read it. I thought it was boring because Nancy found nothing but puzzles and there was no action.

The Secret of Red Gate Farm by Carolyn Keene

This Nancy Drew book helped me because it was my favorite. It also taught me what to look for before I read a Nancy Drew to make sure it was the right kind of story for me.

The Crooked Banister by Carolyn Keene
This Nancy Drew book helped me because it was the first Nancy Drew book I ever read. If I had never read this book, I would never be reading the Nancy Drew series and I really like Nancy Drew.

The Secret of Shadow Ranch by Carolyn Keene
This Nancy Drew book helped me because it was the only Nancy Drew book I had a lot of difficulty with. It taught me what to do when I get stuck on something. Nancy Drews are very hard to read. Especially when Nancy is trapped. It also took me a very long time to read this book.

Wringer by Jerry Spinelli
This book by Jerry Spinelli helped me because it taught me how much thinking you have to do in books. Ever since we read that book, my reading hasn't been the same!

Courtney understood that learning to read was a journey that happens over time. She recognized that each book she read and each conversation she had with other readers could affect her reading life. Courtney was becoming a confident, reflective reader. From her reading so many Nancy Drew books, we might have worried that Courtney wasn't getting enough variety and therefore was not growing as a reader. But when we paid close attention to what Courtney said, we realized that she knew each book had helped her reading in a very different way. We were interested to see that one of the class read-alouds, *Wringer*, also made her list. It reminded us of how important teaching time was to Courtney. Not only was Courtney growing as a reader, but she was also able to reflect on her reading in sophisticated ways.

Later that spring, Courtney looked over her reading log and set a new goal for herself:

I need to work on my variety. My goal is to have a variety. My old goal was to read all the Nancy Drew books, but I got tired of them and decided to read all kinds of different books. But so far I have only read Andrew Clements, Harry Potter, Nancy Drew, myths, and Junie B. Jones. I want to have a variety because I don't want to read the same kind of book over and over and then get tired of it like Nancy Drew.

Although the Nancy Drew books played a very important part in Courtney's year as a reader, she also had a variety of reading experiences during read-aloud time, mini-lessons, small-group work, and content work. And that spring, Courtney told us that she was ready to move on. She understood how she was changing as a reader and set a new goal for herself. We're sure that Courtney will grow as a reader for a very long time to come.

As adult readers, we know that we learn from every book we read. Our lives as readers are shaped by our reading experiences, and we are continually learning how to read and expand our lives as readers. Courtney and the other young readers in our classrooms have been reading for some time. They have much to celebrate about their lives as readers. But as teachers we need to keep in mind that they still have more to learn. The children who enter our upper elementary classrooms have new journeys to travel because they are still learning to read.

It has been some time since we wrote the first edition of *Still Learning to Read*. Learning landscapes have changed, and new perspectives have affected our lives as learners, teachers, and literacy leaders. Schools and classrooms are bombarded with an urgency to have our students perform well on standardized tests. Across the country, children are being tested and teachers are being measured by student performance. Now more than ever we need to focus on what is right for our students.

In that same time, authors have given us rich and superbly written texts for our students to read. The digital world has created new learning opportunities for our students. Children have learned to engage with texts in many new ways. As teachers and leaders, we have continued to learn, to expand our teaching strategies, and to design the most desirable learning environments for our students to grow and learn.

We stand strong on our beliefs. We plan authentic experiences so our students can understand what it is to be lifelong readers. We celebrate a joyful reading life with them. Please join us on this journey. We are *all* still learning to read.

Appendix:
Some Useful Forms

Reading Log

_____'s **Reading Log**

Author	Title of Book	Date Began Date Finished	Pages

Family Interview

Name _____ **Date** _____

Interview your family members. Ask them what they remember about your reading when you were young. Who read to you? What books did you love to hear over and over? What was the first book that you ever read? Ask them to tell you anything they remember about your life as a reader.

Reflecting on Reading

Name _____ **Date** _____

How would you describe yourself as a reader?

What are you currently reading?

What kinds of things do you like to read?

What kinds of things do you not like to read?

What are you going to read next?

How do you choose the books you read?

What do you do when you get stuck?

What do you do when you start to read each day?

How do you keep track of the characters in the books you are reading?

What kind of reading is easy for you?

What kind of reading is hard for you?

Student Data Chart

Name	Interview	Observation	DRA	Survey	Tests	Goals

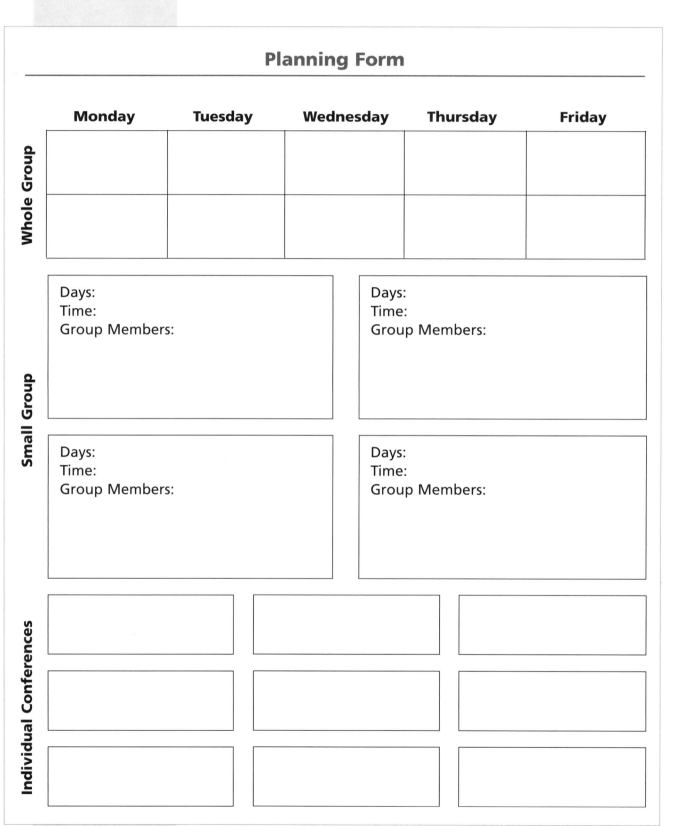

Planning Form

	Monday	Tuesday	Wednesday	Thursday	Friday
Whole Group					

Small Group

Days:
Time:
Group Members:

Days:
Time:
Group Members:

Days:
Time:
Group Members:

Days:
Time:
Group Members:

Individual Conferences

From *Still Learning to Read: Teaching Students in Grades 3–6, Second Edition* by Franki Sibberson and Karen Szymusiak. Copyright © 2016. Stenhouse Publishers.

Sticking with Books

Name _____ **Date** _____

Think about your reading over the past several months.

List 3 books that you have finished and the reasons that you liked them enough to keep reading.

Book Title   Reasons I liked it

1.

2.

3.

Now, list 3 books that you quit before you were finished. What did you not like about them? Why did you quit?

Book Title   Reasons that I didn't finish it

1.

2.

3.

Two-Column Form for *The Stranger*

Who is the stranger?	What in the book makes you think that?

Supporting Your Thinking with Evidence from the Text

In *The Table Where Rich People Sit* by Byrd Baylor, do you think the family was rich? Find evidence in the text to support your thinking.

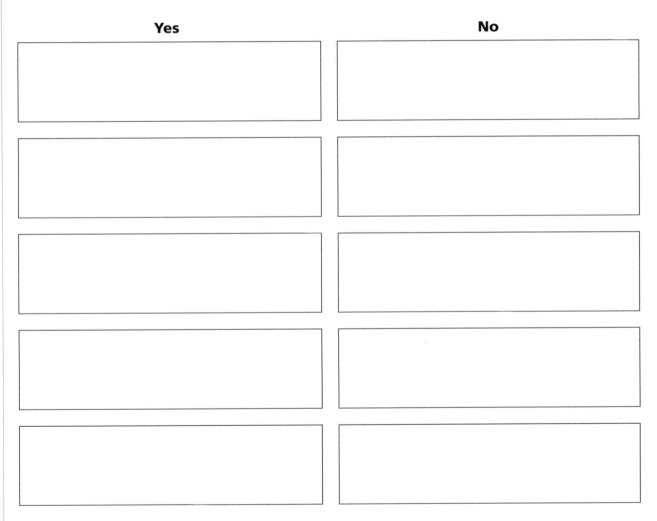

Yes	No

Using the evidence in the text, explain why you think the family was/was not rich.

Evidence in the Text That Supports Your Thinking

What do you think?

Text that supports your thinking:

Form for Unknown Words in *Baloney*

Baloney by Jon Scieszka

Unknown word	What do you think it means?	What makes you think that?
Zimulis		
Deski		
Torakku		
Szkola		
Razzo		
Pordo		
Buttuna		
Astrosus		
Piksas		
Giadrams		
Cucalations		
Kuningas		
Blassa		
Sighing flosser		
Fracasse		
Uyarak		
Zerplatzen		
Speelplaats		
Aamu		

Getting Stuck—*Time for Kids*

Find the article that is the most difficult for you to read. In the left column, write down the word or phrase where you notice that you are getting stuck. In the right column, write down what you did to help yourself understand the text when you realized you were stuck.

Where I got stuck   **What I did to help myself**

Changing Your Thinking While Reading

References

Professional Resources

Allington, Richard. 2000. *What Really Matters for Struggling Readers: Designing Research-Based Programs.* New York: Longman.

———. 2002. "What I've Learned About Effective Reading Instruction." *Phi Delta Kappan* (June): 740-747.

Allington, Richard, and Rachael E. Gabriel. 2012. "Every Child, Every Day." *Educational Leadership* 69 (6): 10-15.

Barber, Janette. 2001. "On Being a Harry Potter Fan." *Rosie Magazine* (August): 42–43.

Barnhouse, Dorothy, and Vicki Vinton. 2012. *What Readers Really Do.* Portsmouth, NH: Heinemann.

Beers, Kylene, and Robert E. Probst. 2013. *Notice and Note: Strategies for Close Reading.* Portsmouth, NH: Heinemann.

———. 2015. *Reading Nonfiction: Notice and Note Stances, Signposts and Strategies.* Portsmouth, NH: Heinemann.

Calkins, Lucy. 2000. *The Art of Teaching Reading.* New York: Longman.

Calkins, Lucy, Kate Montgomery, and Donna Santman. 1998. *A Teacher's Guide to Standardized Reading Tests: Knowledge Is Power.* Portsmouth, NH: Heinemann.

Feigelson, Dan. 2014. *Reading Projects Reimagined.* Portsmouth, NH: Heinemann.

Fountas, Irene, and Gay Su Pinnell. 2001. *Guiding Readers and Writers (Grades 3–6): Teaching Comprehension, Genre, and Content Literacy.* Portsmouth, NH: Heinemann.

———. 2012-2013. "Guided Reading: The Romance and the Reality." *Reading Teacher* 66 (4): 268-284.

Fox, Mem. 2001. *Reading Magic: Why Reading Aloud to Our Children Will Change Their Lives Forever.* New York: Harcourt.

Hahn, Mary Lee. 2002. *Reconsidering Read-Aloud*. Portland, ME: Stenhouse.

Harvey, Stephanie. 2007. *Strategies That Work: Teaching Comprehension for Understanding and Engagement*. Portsmouth, NH: Heinemann.

———. 2013. "Comprehension at the Core." *The Reading Teacher* 66 (6): 432–439.

Harwayne, Shelley. 2002. "Inspiration to Begin." *Instructor* (August): 21.

Johnston, Peter H. 2004. *Choice Words: How Our Language Affects Children's Learning*. Portland, ME: Stenhouse.

———. 2012. *Opening Minds: Using Language to Change Lives*. Portland, ME: Stenhouse.

Keene, Ellin, and Susan Zimmermann. 1997. *Mosaic of Thought: Teaching Comprehension in a Reader's Workshop*. Portsmouth, NH: Heinemann.

Krashen, Steve. 2004. *The Power of Reading: Insights from the Research*. Englewood, CO: Libraries Unlimited.

Landrigan, Clare, and Tammy Mulligan. 2013. *Assessment in Perspective: Focusing on the Readers Behind the Numbers*. Portland, ME: Stenhouse.

Lehman, Chris, and Kate Roberts. 2013. *Falling in Love with Close Reading: Lessons for Analyzing Texts—and Life*. Portsmouth, NH: Heinemann.

Lesesne, Teri. 2010. *Reading Ladders*. Portsmouth, NH: Heinemann.

Martinelli, Marjorie, and Kristine Mraz. 2015. "Getting to the Chart of the Matter." Chartchums (blog). https://chartchums.wordpress.com/2015/10/18/getting-to-the-chart-of-the-matter/.

Mere, Cathy. "DigLit Sunday: Have a Hub." *Reflect and Refine: Building a Learning Community* (blog). http://reflectandrefine.blogspot.com/2015/07/diglit-sunday-have-hub.html.

Miller, Debbie. 2002. *Reading with Meaning: Teaching Comprehension in the Primary Grades*. Portland, ME: Stenhouse.

———. 2008. *Teaching with Intention: Defining Beliefs, Aligning Practice, Taking Action, K–5*. Portland, ME: Stenhouse.

Miller, Donalyn. 2009. *The Book Whisperer: Awakening the Inner Reader in Every Child*. San Francisco: Jossey-Bass.

———. 2013. *Reading in the Wild: The Book Whisperer's Keys to Cultivating Lifelong Reading Habits*. San Francisco: Jossey-Bass.

National Council of Teachers of English. 2013. *"21st Century Literacies?"* www.ncte.org/positions/statements/21stcentdefinition.

National Governors Association Center for Best Practices and Council of Chief State School Officers. 2010. *Common Core State Standards for English Language Arts*. Washington, DC: NGA/CCSSO.

OWP/P Architects, VS Furniture, and Bruce Mau Design. 2010. *The Third Teacher: 79 Ways You Can Use Design to Transform Teaching and Learning*. New York: Abrams.

Pearson, P. David, Laura R. Roehler, Janice A. Dole, and Gerard G. Duffy. 1992. "Developing Expertise in Reading Comprehension." In *What Research Has to Say About Reading Instruction*, ed. J. Samuels and A. Farstrup. Newark, DE: International Reading Association.

Ray, Katie Wood. 2002. *What You Know by Heart: How to Develop Curriculum for Your Writing Workshop*. Portsmouth, NH: Heinemann.

Robb, Laura. 2002. "The Myth: Learn to Read/Read to Learn." *Scholastic Instructor* (May–June): 23–25.

Routman, Regie. 2003. *Reading Essentials: The Specifics You Need to Teach Reading Well*. Portsmouth, NH: Heinemann.

Shanahan, Timothy. "What Is Close Reading?" *Shanahan on Literacy* (blog). www.shanahanonliteracy.com/2012/06/what-is-close-reading.html.

Sibberson, Franki, and Karen Szymusiak. 2003. *Still Learning to Read*. Portland, ME: Stenhouse.

Szymusiak, Karen, and Franki Sibberson. 2008. *Beyond Leveled Books: Supporting Transitional Readers in Grades 2–5*. 2nd ed. Portland, ME: Stenhouse.

Thompson, Terry. 2015. *The Construction Zone: Building Scaffolds for Readers and Writers*. Portland, ME: Stenhouse.

Tovani, Cris. 2000. *I Read It, but I Don't Get It: Comprehension Stategies for Adolescent Readers*. Portland, ME: Stenhouse.

Worthy, Jo, and Misty Sailors. 2001. "That Book Isn't on My Level: Moving Beyond Text Difficulty in Personalizing Reading Choices." *The New Advocate* 14 (3): 229–239.

Literature

Adoff, Arnold. 1990. *Sports Pages*. New York: HarperCollins.

Aguirre, Jorge, and Rafael Rosado. 2012. *Giants Beware!* New York: First Second.

———. 2015. *Dragons Beware!* New York: First Second.

Albom, Mitch. 1997. *Tuesdays with Morrie*. New York: Doubleday.

Alexander, Kwame. 2014. *Crossover*. Boston: HMH Books for Young Children.

Allende, Isabel. 2002. *Portrait in Sepia*. New York: HarperCollins.

Anderson, William. 1998. *Pioneer Girl: The Story of Laura Ingalls Wilder*. New York: HarperCollins.

Applegate, Katherine. 2012. *The One and Only Ivan*. New York: HarperCollins.

Aston, Dianna Hutts. 2014. *An Egg Is Quiet*. San Francisco, CA: Chronicle Books.

Atkinson, Cale. 2015. *To the Sea*. New York: Disney Publishing Hyperion Books for Children.

Avi. 1997. *Poppy*. New York: Camelot.

———. 1999. *Poppy and Rye*. New York: Camelot.

———. 2000. *Ragweed*. New York: HarperCollins.

———. 2001a. *Ereth's Birthday*. New York: HarperCollins.

———. 2001b. *The Secret School*. New York: Harcourt.

Baker, Jeanie. 2002. *Window*. New York. Walker.

Baretta, Gene. 2012. *Timeless Thomas: How Thomas Edison Changed Our Lives*. New York: Henry Holt.

Barnett, Mac. 2014. *Sam and Dave Dig a Hole*. Somerville, MA: Candlewick.

———. 2015. *The Skunk*. New York: Roaring Brook.

Barnett, Mac, and Jory John. 2015. *The Terrible Two*. New York: Henry N. Abrams.

Barton, Chris. 2009. *The Day-Glo Brothers: The True Story of Bob and Joe Switzer's Bright Ideas and Brand-New Colors*. Watertown, MA: Charlesbridge.

Baylor, Byrd. 1998. *The Table Where Rich People Sit*. New York: Aladdin Library.

Beasley, Cassie. 2015. *Circus Mirandus*. New York: Dial Books for Young Readers.

Becker, Aaron. 2013. *Journey*. Somerville, MA: Candlewick.

———. 2014. *Quest*. Somerville, MA: Candlewick.

Bell, Cece. 2014. *El Deafo*. New York: Amulet Books.

———. 2015. *I Yam a Donkey*. New York: Clarion.

Blos, Joan W. 1987. *Old Henry*. New York: Morrow.

Boelts, Maribeth. 2009. *Those Shoes*. Somerville, MA: Candlewick.

Borden, Louise. 2000. *Sleds on Boston Common: A Story from the American Revolution*. New York: Margaret K. McElderry.

———. 2001. *A. Lincoln and Me*. New York: Scholastic Paperbacks.

———. 2003. *Touching the Sky: The Flying Adventures of Wilbur and Orville Wright*. New York: Margaret K. McElderry.

———. 2014. *Baseball Is . . .* New York: Margaret K. McElderry.

Borden, Louise, and Mary Kay Kroeger. 2001. *Fly High! The Story of Bessie Coleman*. New York: Margaret K. McElderry.

Boyd, Lizi. 2013. *Inside Out*. San Francisco, CA: Chronicle Books.

———. 2014. *Flashlight*. San Francisco, CA: Chronicle Books.

Bradley, Kimberly Brubaker. 2015. *The War That Saved My Life*. New York: Dial Books for Young Readers.

Bridges, Ruby. 1999. *Through My Eyes*. New York: Scholastic.

Brisson, Pat. 1999. *The Summer My Father Was Ten*. Honesdale, PA: Boyds Mills.

Brown, Peter. 2013. *Mr. Tiger Goes Wild*. Boston: Little, Brown.

Browne, Anthony. 1998. *Voices in the Park*. New York: DK.

Buitrago, Jairo. 2015. *Two White Rabbits*. Toronto, ON: Groundwood Books.

Burleigh, Robert. 1998. *Home Run: The Story of Babe Ruth*. New York: Silver Whistle.

Burns, Loree Griffin. 2014. *Handle with Care: An Unusual Butterfly Journey*. Brookfield, CT: Millbrook Pr Trade.

Butterworth, Chris. 2013. *How Did That Get in My Lunchbox? The Story of Food*. Somerville, MA: Candlewick.

Card, Orson Scott. 1994. *Ender's Game*. New York: Tor Books.

Carmi, Giora. 2003. *A Circle of Friends*. New York: Star Bright Books.

Cate, Annette LeBlanc. 2013. *Look Up! Bird-Watching in Your Own Backyard*. Somerville, MA: Candlewick.

Christopher, Matt. 1998. *Center Court Sting*. Boston: Little, Brown.

Clements, Rod. 1998. *Grandpa's Teeth*. New York: HarperCollins.

Cline-Ransome, Lesa, and James E. Ransome. 2000. *Satchel Paige*. New York: Simon and Schuster Books for Young Children.

Cole, Henry. 2012. *Unspoken: A Story from the Underground Railroad*. New York: Scholastic.

Coy, John. 2013. *Hoop Genius: How a Desperate Teacher and a Rowdy Gym Class Invented Basketball*. Minneapolis, MN: Carolrhoda Books.

Cranston, Patty. 1998. *Magic on Ice*. Toronto: Kids Can Press.

Creech, Sharon. 2000. *Wanderer*. New York: HarperCollins.

———. 2001. *Love That Dog*. New York: HarperCollins.

Cronin, Doreen. 2000. *Click, Clack, Moo*. New York: Simon and Schuster.

———. 2015. *Chicken Squad: The First Misadventure*. New York: Atheneum Books for Young Readers.

Curtis, Christopher Paul. 1995. *The Watsons Go to Birmingham—1963*. New York: Scholastic.

Dadey, Debbie. 1991. *Santa Doesn't Mop Floors.* New York: Scholastic.

———. 1995. *Pirates Don't Wear Pink Sunglasses.* New York: Little Apple.

Dawson, George, and Richard Glaubman. 2013. *Life Is So Good.* New York: Random House.

Dee, Catherine. 1999. *The Girls' Book of Wisdom.* Boston: Little, Brown.

Deedy, Carman Agra. 1991. *Agatha's Feather Bed: Not Just Another Wild Goose Story.* Atlanta, GA: Peachtree.

De La Peña, Matt. 2015. *Last Stop on Market Street.* New York: G. P. Putnam's Sons Books for Young Readers.

dePaola, Tomie. 1999. *26 Fairmont Avenue.* New York: Penguin Putnam.

Diamant, Anita. 1997. *The Red Tent.* New York: Picador.

DiCamillo, Kate. 2000. *Because of Winn-Dixie.* Cambridge, MA: Candlewick.

———. 2001. *The Tiger Rising.* Somerville, MA: Candlewick.

———. 2009. *The Miraculous Journey of Edward Tulane.* Somerville, MA: Candlewick.

———. 2012. *Bink and Gollie: Best Friends Forever.* Somerville, MA: Candlewick.

———. 2015a. *Flora and Ulysses: The Illuminated Adventures.* Somerville, MA: Candlewick.

———. 2015b. *Leroy Ninker Saddles Up: Tales from Deckawoo Drive.* Somerville, MA: Candlewick.

———. 2015c. *Francine Poulet Meets the Ghost Raccoon: Tales from Deckawoo Drive.* Somerville, MA: Candlewick.

Digh, Patti. 2008. *Life Is a Verb: 37 Days to Wake Up, Be Mindful, and Live Intentionally.* Charleston, SC: Skirt.

Divakaruni, Chitra Banerjee. 2000. *Sister of My Heart: A Novel.* Harpswell, ME: Anchor.

Doerr, Anthony. 2014. *All the Light We Cannot See.* New York: Scribner.

Doh, Jenny. 2013. *Craft a Doodle: 75 Creative Exercises from 18 Artists.* Asheville, NC: Lark Crafts.

Doodler, Todd H. 2010. *Animal Soup: A Mixed-Up Animal Flap Book.* New York: Golden Books.

Dotlich, Rebecca Kai. 2001. *When Riddles Come Rumbling: Poems to Ponder.* Honesdale, PA: Boyds Mills.

Draper, Sharon. 2015. *Stella by Starlight.* New York: Atheneum Books for Young Readers.

Dubuc, Marianne. 2014. *The Lion and the Bird.* Brooklyn, NY: Enchanted Lion Books.

Dudley, Rebecca. 2013. *Hank Finds an Egg.* White Plains, NY: Peter Pauper.

Duhigg, Charles. 2014. *The Power of Habit: Why We Do What We Do in Life and Business.* New York: Random House.

Eagen, Terry, Stan Friedman, and Mike Levine. 1993. *Macmillan Book of Baseball Stories.* New York: Simon and Schuster.

Editors of Sports Illustrated Kids Magazine. 2012. *Sports Illustrated: The Big Book of Why Sports Edition.* New York: Time Home Entertainment.

Elliott, David. 2014. *On the Wing.* Somerville, MA: Candlewick.

Elya, Susan Middleton. 2014. *Little Roja Riding Hood.* New York: G. P. Putnam's Sons.

Engle, Margarita. 2014. *Silver People: Voices from the Panama Canal.* Boston: HMH Books for Young Readers.

———. 2015. *Drum Dream Girl: How One Girl's Courage Changed Music.* Boston: HMH Books for Young Readers.

Escoffier, Michael. 2014. *Take Away the A.* New York: Enchanted Lion Books.

Feiffer, Jules. 1999. *Bark, George.* New York: HarperCollins.

Fleischman, Paul. 1980. *Half a Moon Inn.* New York: HarperCollins.

Fletcher, Ralph. 1995. *Fig Pudding.* New York: Clarion.

———. 1997a. *Ordinary Things: Poems from a Walk in Early Spring.* New York: Atheneum Books for Young Readers.

———. 1997b. *Twilight Comes Twice.* New York: Clarion.

———. 1998. *Flying Solo.* New York: Clarion.

———. 2012. *Marshfield Dreams.* New York: Macmillan.

Flood, Nancy Bo. 2013. *Cowboy Up! Ride the Navajo Rodeo.* Honesdale, PA: Wordsong.

Frazee, Marla. 2006. *Walk On!* Boston: HMH Books for Young Readers.

———. 2014. *The Farmer and the Clown.* New York: Beach Lane Books.

Freeman, Tor. 2012. *Olive and the Big Secret.* Dorking Surrey, UK: Templar.

———. 2013. *Olive and the Bad Mood.* Dorking Surrey, UK: Templar.

———. 2014. *Olive and the Embarrassing Gift.* Dorking Surrey, UK: Templar.

Frost, Helen. 2008. *Diamond Willow.* New York: Farrar, Straus and Giroux.

———. 2015. *Sweep the Sun.* Somerville, PA: Candlewick.

Fusco, Kimberly Newton. 2015. *Beholding Bee.* New York: Yearling.

Gantos, Jack. 1998. *Joey Pigza Swallowed the Key.* New York: HarperCollins.

Gardiner, John Reynolds. 1980. *Stone Fox.* New York: HarperCollins.

Gash, Amy. 2004. *What the Dormouse Said: Lessons for Grown-Ups from Children's Books.* New York: Algonquin Books.

Gaynor, Hazel. 2015. *A Memory of Violets: A Novel of London's Flower Sellers.* New York: William Morrow.

George, Jessica Day. 2011. *Tuesdays at the Castle.* New York: Bloomsbury.

Giff, Patricia Reilly. 2002. *Pictures of Hollis Woods.* New York: Random House.

Graff, Lisa. 2006. *The Thing About Georgie.* New York: Laura Geringer Books.

Graham, Bob. 2008. *How to Heal a Broken Wing.* Somerville, MA: Candlewick.

Graves, Donald. 1996. *Baseball, Snakes, and Summer Squash: Poems About Growing Up.* Honesdale, PA: Wordsong.

Greenfield, Eloise. 1988. *Grandpa's Face.* New York: Philomel Books.

Gulledge, Laura Lee. 2011. *Page by Paige.* New York: Harry N. Abrams.

Gwynne, Fred. 2005. *A Chocolate Moose for Dinner.* New York: Aladdin Paperbacks.

Haddix, Margaret Peterson. 2002. *Because of Anya.* New York: Simon and Schuster.

Hatke, Ben. 2011. *Zita the Spacegirl.* New York: First Second.

Hawkins, Paula. 2015. *The Girl on the Train.* New York: Riverhead Books.

Heard, Georgia. 1997. *Creatures of Earth, Sea, and Sky.* Honesdale, PA: Boyds Mills.

Henkes, Kevin. 1999. *The Birthday Room.* New York: Greenwillow Books.

———. 2006. *Lilly's Purple Plastic Purse.* New York: Greenwillow Books.

Holbrook, Sara. 2002. *Wham! It's a Poetry Jam: Discovering Performance Poetry.* Honesdale, PA: Boyds Mills.

Holm, Jennifer, and Matthew Holm. 2015. *Sunny Side Up.* New York: GRAPHIX.

Holub, Joan. 2012. *Heroes in Training: Zeus and the Thunderbolt of Doom.* New York: Aladdin Paperbacks.

Horvath, Polly. 2001. *Everything on a Waffle.* New York: Farrar, Straus and Giroux.

Howe, James. 1996. *Bunnicula.* New York: Aladdin Books.

James, Simon. 1999. *Ancient Rome.* New York: Scholastic.

Jamieson, Victoria. 2015. *Roller Girl.* New York: Dial Books.

Janeczko, Paul. 2014. *Firefly July: A Year of Very Short Poems.* Somerville, MA: Candlewick.

———. 2015. *The Death of the Hat: A Brief History of Poetry in 50 Objects.* Somerville, MA: Candlewick.

Joyce, Susan. 1998. *Alphabet Riddles.* Columbus, NC: Peel Productions.

Judge, Lita. 2011. *Red Sled.* New York: Atheneum Books for Young Readers.

Kim, Patti. 2014. *Here I Am.* North Mankato, MN: Picture Window Books.

Kingsolver, Barbara. 1998. *The Poisonwood Bible.* New York: HarperFlamingo.

Kinney, Jeff. 2007. *Diary of a Wimpy Kid.* New York: Amulet Books.

Klassen, Jon. 2011. *I Want My Hat Back.* Somerville, MA: Candlewick.

Knudsen, Michelle. 2015. *Marilyn's Monster.* Somerville, MA: Candlewick.

Kroeger, Mary Kay, and Louise Borden. 1996. *Paperboy.* New York: Clarion Books.

Krull, Kathleen, and Paul Brewer. 2013. *The Beatles Were Fab (and They Were Funny).* Boston: Harcourt Children's Books.

Kuefler, Joseph. 2015. *Beyond the Pond.* New York: HarperCollins.

Lagercrantz, Rose. 2014. *My Heart Is Laughing.* Wellington, NZ: Gecko.

Lai, Thanhha. 2011. *Inside Out and Back Again.* New York: Harper.

LaRochelle, David. 2014. *Moo.* New York: Bloomsbury USA Children's Books.

Law, Ingrid. 2010. *Savvy.* New York: Puffin Books.

Lawson, JonArno, and Sydney Smith. 2015. *Sidewalk Flowers.* Toronto, ON: Groundwood Books.

Lean, Sarah. 2012. *A Dog Called Homeless.* New York: Katherine Tegen Books.

Lee, Suzy. 2008. *Wave.* San Francisco, CA: Chronicle Books.

Leedy, Loreen. 2003. *There's a Frog in My Throat.* New York: Holiday House.

Legge, David. 1995. *Bamboozled.* New York: Scholastic.

Lehman, Barbara. 2004. *The Red Book.* Boston: HMH Books for Young Readers.

L'Engle, Madeleine. 1987. *A Wrinkle in Time.* New York: Farrar, Straus and Giroux.

Letts, Billie. 1995. *Where the Heart Is.* New York: Warner Books.

Lewis C. S. 1978. *The Lion, the Witch, and the Wardrobe.* New York: HarperCollins.

Lewis, J. Patrick. 2015. *National Geographic Book of Nature Poetry.* Washington, DC: National Geographic Children's Books.

Lin, Grace. 2011. *Where the Mountain Meets the Moon.* New York: Little, Brown.

Lineker, Gary. 1994. *The Young Soccer Player.* New York: Dorling Kindersley.

Long, Loren. 2014. *Otis and the Scarecrow.* New York: Philomel Books.

Lord, Cynthia. 2006. *Rules.* New York: Scholastic.

———. 2014. *Shelter Pet Squad: Jelly Bean.* New York: Scholastic.

————. 2015. *A Handful of Stars*. New York: Scholastic.

Lowry, Lois. 2000. *Looking Back: A Book of Memories*. New York: Delacorte Press Books for Young Readers.

Ludy, Mark. 2005. *The Flower Man*. Windsor, CO: Green Pastures.

Mack, Jeff. 2013. *AH HA!* San Francisco, CA: Chronicle Books.

MacLachlan, Patricia. 1993. *Baby*. New York: Bantam Doubleday Dell.

————. 2011. *Waiting for Magic*. New York: Atheneum Books for Young Readers.

————. 2013. *White Fur Flying*. New York: Margaret K. McElderry Books.

Mantchev, Lisa. 2015. *Strictly No Elephants*. New York: Simon and Schuster/Paula Wiseman Books.

Markel, Michelle. 2013. *Brave Girl: Clara and the Shirtwaist Makers' Strike of 1909*. New York: Balzer and Bray.

Martin, Ann M. 2014. *Rain Reign*. New York: Felwel and Friends.

Mattick, Lindsay. 2015. *Finding Winnie*. New York: Little, Brown Books for Young Readers.

McCall, Frances, and Patricia Keeler. 2002. *A Huge Hog Is a Big Pig: A Rhyming Word Game*. New York: Greenwillow Books.

McDonald, Megan. 2000. *Judy Moody*. Cambridge, MA: Candlewick.

————. 2001. *Judy Moody Gets Famous*. Cambridge, MA: Candlewick.

————. 2010. *Judy Moody Was in a Mood. Not a Good Mood. A Bad Mood*. Cambridge, MA: Candlewick.

McDonnell, Patrick. 2008. *South*. New York: Little, Brown Books for Young Readers.

McGhee, Alison. 2015. *Firefly Hollow*. New York: Atheneum Books for Young Readers.

McMillan, Bruce. 1982. *Puniddles*. Boston: HMH Books for Young Readers.

Medina, Meg. 2015. *Mango, Abuela, and Me*. Somerville, MA: Candlewick.

Merrill, Jean. 1972. *The Toothpaste Millionaire*. Boston: Houghton Mifflin.

Messner, Kate. 2012. *Capture the Flag*. New York: Scholastic.

————. 2014. *Over and Under the Snow*. San Francisco, CA: Chronicle Books.

————. 2015a. *How to Read a Story*. San Francisco, CA: Chronicle Books.

————. 2015b. *Ranger in Time: Rescue on the Oregon Trail*. New York: Scholastic.

Miles, Miska. 1972. *Annie and the Old One*. Boston: Little, Brown.

Miyares, Daniel. 2015. *Float*. New York: Simon and Schuster Books for Young Readers.

Mochizuki, Ken. 1993. *Baseball Saved Us*. New York: Lee and Low.

Morales, Yuyi. 2014. *Viva Frida*. New York: Roaring Brook.

Moss, Marissa. 1995. *Amelia's Notebook*. New York: Scholastic.

Murray, Laura. 2015. *The Gingerbread Man Loose in the School*. New York: G. P. Putnam's Sons Books for Young Readers.

Naylor, Phyllis Reynolds. 1991. *Shiloh*. New York: Bantam Doubleday Dell.

Nelson, Kadir. 2008. *We Are the Ship: The Story of Negro League Baseball*. New York: Jump at the Sun.

————. 2013. *Nelson Mandela*. New York: Katherine Tegen Books.

Newman, Jeff. 2006. *Hippo! No, Rhino!* New York: Little, Brown and Company Books for Young Readers.

Nobleman, Marc Tyler. 2012. *Bill the Boy Wonder: The Secret Co-Creator of Batman*. Watertown, MA: Charlesbridge.

Nye, Naomi Shihab. 2014. *The Turtle of Oman.* New York: Greenwillow Books.

O'Brien, John. 2012. *Look . . . Look Again.* Honesdale, PA: Boyds Mills.

O'Brien, Robert C. 1971. *Mrs. Frisby and the Rats of NIMH.* New York: Simon and Schuster.

O'Connor, Barbara. 2007. *How to Steal a Dog.* New York: Farrar, Straus and Giroux.

———. 2010. *The Fantastic Secret of Owen Jester.* New York: Farrar, Straus and Giroux.

———. 2015. *Greetings from Nowhere.* New York: Macmillan.

O'Faolain, Nuala. 2002. *My Dream of You.* New York: Riverhead Books.

Ohi, Debbie Ridpath. 2015. *Where Are My Books?* New York: Simon and Schuster Books for Young Readers.

O'Ryan, Ray. 2013. *Galaxy Zack: Hello, Nebulon!* New York: Little Simon.

Palacio, R. J. 2012. *Wonder.* New York: Alfred A. Knopf Books.

Park, Barbara. 1992. *Junie B. Jones and the Stupid Smelly Bus.* New York: Random House.

———. 1995. *Mick Harte Was Here.* New York: Alfred A. Knopf Books.

Paschkis, Julie. 2015. *Flutter and Hum: Animal Poems/Aleteo y Zumbido: Poemas de Animales.* New York: Henry Holt.

Patchett, Ann. 2002. *Bel Canto.* New York: Perennial.

Paul, Miranda. 2015. *Water Is Water: A Book About the Water Cycle.* New York: Roaring Brook.

Perkins, Mitali. 2015. *Tiger Boy.* Watertown, MA: Charlesbridge.

Pett, Mark. 2013. *The Boy and the Airplane.* New York: Simon and Schuster Books for Young Readers.

———. 2014. *The Girl and the Bicycle.* New York: Simon and Schuster Books for Young Readers.

Pinkney, Andrea. 2014. *The Red Pencil.* New York: Little, Brown Books for Young Readers.

Pinkney, Jerry. 2009. *The Lion and the Mouse.* New York: Little, Brown Books for Young Readers.

Platt, Richard. 2014. *Pirate Diary: The Journal of Jake Carpenter.* Somerville, MA: Candlewick.

Priddy, Roger. 2011. *Word Play Fruit Cake: A Fruit-Filled Play on Words.* New York: Macmillan.

Quindlen, Anna. 1998. *How Reading Changed My Life.* New York: Random House.

Raczka, Bob. 2014. *Santa Clauses: Short Poems from the North Pole.* Minneapolis, MN: Carolrhoda.

Rappaport, Doreen, and Lyndall Callan. 2000. *Dirt on Their Skirts: The Story of Young Women Who Won the World Championship.* New York: Penguin Putnam.

Raschka, Chris. 2000. *Ring! Yo?* New York: Dorling Kindersley.

———. 2011. *A Ball for Daisy.* New York: Schwartz and Wade.

———. 2013. *Daisy Gets Lost.* New York: Schwartz and Wade.

Rose, Carolyn Starr. 2015. *Blue Birds.* New York: Puffin Books.

Rosenthal, Amy Krouse. 2013. *I Scream, Ice Cream: A Book of Wordles.* San Francisco, CA: Chronicle Books.

Ruddell, Deborah. 2015. *The Popcorn Astronauts and Other Biteable Rhymes.* New York: Margaret McElderry Books.

Russo, Richard. 2002. *Empire Falls*. New York: Vintage.

Ruth, Greg. 2014. *Coming Home*. New York: Macmillan.

Rylant, Cynthia. 1985. *Every Living Thing*. New York: Bradbury.

———. 2006. *Van Gogh Café*. Boston: HMH Books for Young Readers.

Sachar, Louis. 1996. *Wayside School Gets a Little Stranger*. New York: Camelot.

———. 1998. *Holes*. New York: Farrar, Straus and Giroux.

———. 2003. *Stanley Yelnats' Survival Guide to Camp Green Lake*. New York: Yearling.

Santat, Dan. 2011. *Sidekicks*. New York: Arthur A. Levine Books.

———. 2014. *The Adventures of Beekle: The Unimaginary Friend*. New York: Little, Brown Books for Young Readers.

Sarcona-Roach, Julia. 2015. *The Bear Ate Your Sandwich*. New York: Knopf Books for Young Readers.

Savage, Stephen. 2011. *Where's Walrus?* New York: Scholastic.

Say, Allen. 1995. *Stranger in the Mirror*. Boston: HMH Books for Young Readers.

———. 1996. *Emma's Rug*. Boston: Houghton Mifflin.

Schneider, Josh. 2015. *The Meanest Birthday Girl*. Boston: HMH Books for Young Readers.

Scieszka, Jon. 1989. *The True Story of the Three Little Pigs!* New York: Penguin Putnam.

———. 1998. *The Time Warp Trio: Knights at the Kitchen Table*. New York: Puffin Books.

———. 2005. *Baloney (Henry P.)*. New York: Puffin Books.

———. 2008. *Knucklehead: Tall Tales and Almost True Stories of Growing Up Scieszka*. New York: Viking Books for Young Readers.

Selznick, Brian. 2007. *The Invention of Hugo Cabret*. New York: Scholastic.

———. 2011. *Wonderstruck*. New York: Scholastic.

———. 2015. *The Marvels*. New York: Scholastic.

Senisi, Ellen B. 1999. *Reading Grows*. Morton Grove, IL: Albert Whitman.

Shannon, David. 2004. *A Bad Case of Stripes*. New York: Scholastic.

Shurtliff, Liesl. 2014. *Rump: The True Story of Rumpelstiltskin*. New York: Yearling Books.

———. 2015. *Jack*. New York: Alfred A. Knopf.

Shwartz, Ronald. 1999. *For the Love of Books*. New York: Putnam Adult.

Sidman, Joyce. 2014. *Winter Bees and Other Poems of the Cold*. New York: Houghton Mifflin Harcourt.

Siegel, Siena Cherson, and Mark Siegel. 2006. *To Dance: A Ballerina's Graphic Novel*. New York: Atheneum Books for Young Readers.

Simont, Marc. 2003. *The Stray Dog*. New York: HarperCollins.

Singer, Marilyn. 2010. *Mirror Mirror: A Book of Reverso Poems*. New York: Dutton Books for Young Readers.

———. 2013. *Follow Follow: A Book of Reverso Poems*. New York: Dial/Penguin.

Soderberg, Erin. 2014. *The Quirks: Welcome to Normal*. London, UK: Bloomsbury USA Children's.

Sonnichsen, A. L. 2016. *Red Butterfly*. New York: Simon and Schuster Books for Young Readers.

Spinelli, Jerry. 1997. *Wringer*. New York: HarperCollins.

———. 1998. *Knots in My Yo-Yo String.* New York: Ember.

Spires, Ashley. 2014. *The Most Magnificent Thing.* Toronto, ON: Kids Can Press.

Staake, Bob. 2013. *Bluebird.* New York: Schwartz and Wade.

Starbright Foundation. 2001. *Once Upon a Fairy Tale: Four Favorite Stories.* New York: Penguin Putnam.

Stead, Philip. 2015. *Lenny and Lucy.* New York: Roaring Brook.

Stead, Tony. 2002. *Should There Be Zoos?* New York: Mondo.

Stegner, Wallace. 1987. *Crossing to Safety.* New York: Penguin Books.

Sternberg, Julie. 2014. *Like Carrot Juice on a Cupcake.* New York: Amulet Books.

Stevens, Janet. 2002. *And the Dish Ran Away with the Spoon.* New York: Scholastic.

Stewart, Melissa. 2014. *Feathers: Not Just for Flying.* Watertown, MA: Charlesbridge.

Stewart, Sarah. 1995. *The Library.* New York: Farrar, Straus and Giroux.

Stine, R. L. n.d. Scholastic Interview. Scholastic.com.

Stone, Tanya Lee. 2013. *Who Says Women Can't Be Doctors? The Story of Elizabeth Blackwell.* New York: Christy Ottaviano Books/Henry Holt.

Stoop, Naoko. 2014. *Red Knit Cap Girl and the Reading Tree.* New York: Little, Brown.

Sturm, James, Alexis Frederick-Frost, and Andrew Arnold. 2015. *Sleepless Knight.* New York: First Second.

Sullivan, George. 2000. *Lewis and Clark.* New York: Scholastic.

Sullivan, Mary. 2015. *Ball.* Boston: HMH Books for Young Readers.

Sweet, Melisa. 2011. *Balloons Over Broadway.* Boston: Houghton Mifflin Books for Children.

Tang, Greg. 2001. *Grapes of Math: Mind Stretching Math Riddles.* New York: Scholastic.

Tavares, Matt. 2015. *Growing Up Pedro.* Somerville, MA: Candlewick.

Taylor, Mildred. 1990. *Mississippi Bridge.* New York: Bantam Doubleday Dell.

Telgemeier, Raina. 2010. *Smile.* New York: GRAPHIX.

———. 2012. *Drama.* New York: GRAPHIX.

———. 2014. *Sisters.* New York: GRAPHIX.

Terban, Marvin. 2008a. *The Dove Dove: Funny Homograph Riddles.* Boston: HMH Books for Young Readers.

———. 2008b. *Too Hot to Hoot. Funny Palindrome Riddles.* Boston: HMH Books for Young Readers.

Testa, Maria. 2002. *Becoming Joe DiMaggio.* Cambridge, MA: Candlewick.

Thompson, Laurie Ann. 2015. *Emmanuel's Dream: The True Story of Emmanuel Ofosu Yeboah.* New York: Schwartz and Wade.

Thomson, Bill. 2010. *Chalk.* Allentown, PA: Two Lions.

———. 2013. *Fossil.* Allentown, PA: Two Lions.

Time for Kids. 2011. *Big Book of How.* New York: Time for Kids Books.

Tolstoy, Leo. 2004. *Anna Karenina.* New York: Penguin Classics.

Urban, Linda. 2011. *Hound Dog True.* Boston: Harcourt Children's Books.

———. 2015. *Milo Speck: Accidental Agent.* Boston: HMH Books for Young Readers.

Van Allsburg, Chris. 1991. *The Wretched Stone.* Boston: Houghton Mifflin.

———. 1986. *The Stranger*. Boston: HMH Books for Young Readers.

VanDerwater, Amy Ludwig. 2013. *Forest Has a Song: Poems*. New York: Clarion.

Viorst, Judith. 2012. *Lulu and the Brontosaurus*. New York: Atheneum Books for Young Readers.

Walton, Rick. 2002. *Brain Waves Puzzle Book*. Middleton, WI: Pleasant Company.

Weiss, Ellen. 2000. *Odd Jobs: The Wackiest Jobs You've Never Heard Of*. New York: Aladdin.

Wheeler, Lisa. 2013. *The Pet Project: Cute and Cuddly Vicious Verse*. New York: Atheneum Books for Young Readers.

White, E. B. 1952. *Charlotte's Web*. New York: HarperCollins.

Wiesner, David. 2011. *Tuesday*. Boston: HMH Books for Young Readers.

———. 2013. *Mr. Wuffles!* San Francisco, CA: Clarion.

Willems, Mo. 2003. *Don't Let the Pigeon Drive the Bus!* New York: Hyperion.

———. 2010. *City Dog, Country Frog*. New York: Disney Publishing Hyperion Books for Children.

Williams-Garcia, Rita. 2011. *One Crazy Summmer*. New York: Amistad.

Winthrop, Elizabeth. 1986. *Castle in the Attic*. New York: Holiday House.

Wood, Don. 2012. *Into the Volcano*. New York: Blue Sky.

Woodson, Jacqueline. 2001. *The Other Side*. New York: Penguin Putnam.

———. 2012. *Each Kindness*. New York: Nancy Paulsen Books.

———. 2013. *This Is the Rope: A Story from the Great Migration*. New York: Nancy Paulsen Books.

———. 2014. *Brown Girl Dreaming*. New York: Nancy Paulsen Books.

Worth, Valerie. 2013. *Pug and Other Animal Poems*. New York: Margaret Ferguson.

Wulffson, Don L. 1997. *The Kid Who Invented the Popsicle: and Other Surprising Stories About Inventions*. New York: Cobblehill Books/Dutton.

Yolen, Jane, and Rebecca Kai Dotlich. 2013. *Grumbles from the Forest: Fairy Tale Voices with a Twist*. Honesdale, PA: Wordsong.

Yomtov, Nel, and Tim Foley. 2011. *The Bambino: The Story of Babe Ruth's Legendary 1927 Season*. Mankato, MN: Capstone.

Children's Series Books

Aguirre, Jorge. The Chronicles of Claudette.

Angleberger, Tom. Origami Yoda Files.

Applegate, Katherine. Roscoe Riley.

Aston, Dianna Hutts. An Egg Is Quiet.

Avi. Poppy.

Barshaw, Ruth McNally. Ellie McDoodle.

Blume, Judy. Fudge.

Branford, Anna. Violet Mackerel.

Buckley, Michael. The Sisters Grimm.

Coven, Wanda. Heidi Heckelbeck.

Curato, Mike. Little Elliot.

Danziger, Paula. Amber Brown.

DiCamillo, Kate. Mercy Watson.
———. Tales from Deckawoo Drive.
Discover Science (various authors)
DiTerlizzi, Tony, and Holly Black. The Spiderwick Chronicles.
DuPrau, Jeanne. Books of Ember.
Eszterhas, Suzanne. Eye on the Wild.
Face to Face with Animals (various authors)
Giarrusso, Chris. G-Man.
Griffiths, Andy. The Treehouse Books.
Grimes, Nikki. Dyamonde Daniel.
Hatke, Ben. Zita the Spacegirl.
Holm, Jennifer, and Matthew Holm. Babymouse.
———. Squish.
———. Comics Squad.
Holub, Joan. Heroes in Training.
Howe, James. Pinky and Rex.
———. Bunnicula.
Ignatow, Amy. Popularity Papers.
Inside Series (various authors)
Jules, Jacqueline. Zapato Power.
Kalman, Bobbie. Science of Living Things.
Keller, Laurie. Arnie the Doughnut.
Kinney, Jeff. Diary of a Wimpy Kid.
Kline, Suzy. Horrible Harry.
Korman, Gordon. Swindle.
Krosczka, Jarret. Lunch Lady.
Krulik, Nancy. Magic Bone.
Levine, Gail Carson. The Princess Tales.
Lewis, C. S. Chronicles of Narnia.
Lin, Grace. Pacy Lin.
Long, Loren. Otis.
Lord, Cynthia. Shelter Pet Squad.
Lowry, Lois. Anastasia.
Markle, Sandra. Animal Predators.
———. Animal Scavengers.
McDonald, Megan. Judy Moody.
———. Stink.
Martin, Ann M., and Raina Telgemeier. Babysitters Club Graphix.
Meltzer, Brad. Ordinary People Change the World.
Messner, Kate. Marty McGuire.
———. Ranger in Time.
———. Capture the Flag.
Mlynowski, Sarah. Whatever After.
Murray, Laura. The Gingerbread Man.
National Geographic Kids Chapters (various authors)
National Geographic Kids Everything (various authors)
National Geographic Kids Jump into Science (various authors)

National Geographic Kids Weird but True (various authors)
National Geographic Readers (various authors)
Naylor, Phyllis Reynolds. Shiloh.
O'Ryan, Ray. Galaxy Zack.
Pallotta, Jerry. Who Would Win?
Patterson, James. Maximum Ride.
Pearson, Ridley. Kingdom Keepers.
Pennypacker, Sara. Clementine.
Pierce, Lincoln. Big Nate.
Pilkey, Dav, and Dan Satnat. Ricky Ricotta.
Preller, James. Scary Tales.
Priddy, Roger. Smart Kids.
Riddell, Chris. Ottoline.
Riordin, Rick. Olympians.
———. Percy Jackson.
Rowling, J. K. Harry Potter.
Russell, Rachel Renee. Dork Diaries.
Scientists in the Field (various authors)
Scieszka, Jon. Spaceheadz.
———. Time Warp Trio.
Selfors, Suzanne. The Imaginary Veterinary.
Snicket, Lemony. A Series of Unfortunate Events.
Simpson, Dana. Phoebe and the Unicorn.
Skye, Obert. The Creature from My Closet.
Soderberg, Erin. The Quirks.
Soo, Kean. Jellaby.
Spires, Ashley. The Binky Adventures.
Sternberg, Julie. Like Carrot Juice.
Stevenson, Noelle. Lumberjanes.
Stewart, Melissa. Which Animal Is Which?
Take Along Guides (various authors)
Tarshis, Lauren. I Survived.
Thompson, Jill. Magic Trixie.
Thomson, Melissa. Keena Ford.
Venable, Colleen AF. Guinea Pig, Pet Shop Private Eye.
Vernon, Ursula. Dragonbreath.
———. Hamster Princess.
Viorst, Judith. Lulu.
Warner, Sally. Elray Jakes.

Index

Page numbers followed by *f* indicate figures.